African Literatures in the 20th Century

A Guide

Based on the ENCYCLOPEDIA OF WORLD
LITERATURE IN THE 20TH CENTURY,
Revised Edition, Leonard S. Klein, General Editor

The Ungar Publishing Company · New York

1987
Copyright © 1986 by The Ungar Publishing Company.

Based on *Encyclopedia of World Literature in the 20th Century*, Revised Edition, copyright © 1981, 1982, 1983, 1984 by Frederick Ungar Publishing Co., Inc.

Printed in the United States of America

Library of Congress Cataloging-in-Publication Data
Main entry under title:

African literatures in the 20th century.

"Based on the Encyclopedia of world literature in the 20th century, Revised edition, Leonard S. Klein, general editor."
Includes bibliographies and index.
1. African literature—History and criticism—Addresses, essays, lectures. I. Encyclopedia of world literature in the 20th century. Rev. ed. II. Title: African literatures in the twentieth century.
PL8010.A43   1986   809'.889'6   85-24579
ISBN 0-8044-6362-X (pbk.)

All rights reserved. No part of this book may be reproduced, stored in a retrieval system, or transmitted, in any form or by any means, electronic, mechanical, photocopying, recording, or otherwise, without the written permission of The Ungar Publishing Company.

Contents

Preface	vii
Abbreviations for Periodicals	ix
ALGERIAN LITERATURE	1
Mohammed Dib	7
Mouloud Feraoun	9
Kateb Yacine	10
Mouloud Mammeri	12
ANGOLAN LITERATURE	15
José Luandino Vieira	19
BENINIAN LITERATURE	21
BOTSWANA LITERATURE	24
CAMEROONIAN LITERATURE	26
Mongo Beti	28
Ferdinand Oyono	30
CAPE VERDEAN LITERATURE	33
CONGOLESE LITERATURE	36
EGYPTIAN LITERATURE	38
Tawfīq al-Hakīm	47
Tāhā Husayn	49
Yūsuf Idrīs	51
Najīb Mahfūz	54
ETHIOPIAN LITERATURE	57
GAMBIAN LITERATURE	62
Lenrie Peters	63
GHANAIAN LITERATURE	65
Ayi Kwei Armah	68
Kofi Awoonor	70
GUINEA-BISSAU LITERATURE	73
GUINEAN LITERATURE	75
Camara Laye	77

CONTENTS

IVORY COAST LITERATURE	80
Bernard Binlin Dadié	82
KENYAN LITERATURE	85
Ngugi wa Thiong'o	88
LESOTHO LITERATURE	91
Thomas Mofolo	92
LIBERIAN LITERATURE	95
MALAGASY LITERATURE	97
MALAWIAN LITERATURE	102
MALI LITERATURE	105
MAURITIAN LITERATURE	107
MOROCCAN LITERATURE	109
MOZAMBICAN LITERATURE	113
NEGRITUDE	117
NIGERIAN LITERATURE	119
Chinua Achebe	126
John Pepper Clark	129
Cyprian Ekwensi	131
Gabriel Okara	133
Christopher Okigbo	134
Wole Soyinka	136
Amos Tutuola	139
RÉUNION LITERATURE	142
SÃO TOMÉ AND PRÍNCIPE LITERATURE	144
SENEGALESE LITERATURE	146
Birago Diop	152
Ousmane Sembène	153
Léopold Sédar Senghor	156
SIERRA LEONEAN LITERATURE	159
SOMALI LITERATURE	161
Nuruddin Farah	164
SOUTH AFRICAN LITERATURE	166
Peter Abrahams	186
Dennis Brutus	188
Roy Campbell	189
Athol Fugard	191
Nadine Gordimer	194
Alex La Guma	196
Sarah Gertrude Millin	197
Ezekiel (Es'kia) Mphahlele	199

Alan Paton	201
William Plomer	203
Olive Schreiner	206
Pauline Smith	208
SUDANESE LITERATURE	210
TANZANIAN LITERATURE	214
Shaaban Robert	219
TOGOLESE LITERATURE	221
UGANDAN LITERATURE	223
Okot p'Bitek	226
UPPER VOLTA LITERATURE	230
ZAIRIAN LITERATURE	232
ZAMBIAN LITERATURE	235
ZIMBABWEAN LITERATURE	238
Index to Author Articles	245

Preface

This guide is based on the five-volume *Encyclopedia of World Literature in the 20th Century*, revised edition, published by Ungar 1981–84. With the exception of a few minor revisions and corrections, the articles herein are reproduced exactly as they appeared in the original work, and no attempt has been made to update them. The purpose of the present volume, rather, is to provide a handy compilation of articles about the literatures of the African continent plus the Malagasy Republic, Mauritius, and Réunion that contain information available nowhere else in such a compact format.

Coverage encompasses the Arab countries of northern Africa, including Egypt, and both black and white writers of sub-Saharan Africa; writing in English, French, Portuguese, Afrikaans, Arabic, Creole languages, and the indigenous languages of the continent is discussed.

Articles are arranged alphabetically by country, and where applicable, national surveys are followed by articles about major writers of that country. In addition, an article on Negritude is included. An index to author articles is provided at the back of the book.

All pertinent articles that appeared in the original Encyclopedia are reprinted here. When survey articles for certain countries are lacking (e.g., Central African Republic, Chad, Gabon, Libya, Mauritania, Niger, Rwanda), the reason is that written literature there is not sufficiently developed to have warranted discussion.

The reader should note that countries are listed under their current names. Thus, Dahomean literature will be found under Beninian literature, Rhodesian under Zimbabwean, and so forth.

RITA STEIN
Editorial Supervisor
EDITH FRIEDLANDER
Project Coordinator

Abbreviations for Periodicals

AAS	Asian and African Studies
AfricaL	Africa (London)
AfricaR	Africa Report
AfrLJ	Africana Journal
AfrLS	African Language Studies
ALT	African Literature Today
ARD	African Research and Documentation
ArielE	Ariel: A Review of International English Literature
BA	Books Abroad
BAALE	Bulletin of the Association for African Literature in English
BO	Black Orpheus
CALC	Cahiers algériens de littérature comparée
CE	College English
CEAfr	Cahiers d'études africaines
Crit	Critique: Studies in Modern Fiction
ECr	L'esprit créateur
EF	Études françaises
EinA	English in Africa
ESA	English Studies in Africa
FE	France-Eurafrique
FR	French Review
IC	Islamic Culture
JArabL	Journal of Arabic Literature
JARCE	Journal of the American Research Center in Egypt
JASO	Journal of the Anthropological Society of Oxford
JCH	Journal of Contemporary History
JCL	Journal of Commonwealth Literature
JNALA	Journal of the New African Literature and the Arts
LAAW	Lotus: Afro-Asian Writings
LHY	Literary Half-Yearly
London	London Magazine
MEF	Middle East Forum
MES	Middle Eastern Studies
MW	The Muslim World
NewA	New African
NL	Les nouvelles littéraires
NYTBR	The New York Times Book Review
O&C	Œuvres & critiques
PA	Présence africaine

PAJ	Pan-African Journal
PFr	Présence francophone
PMLA	Publications of the Modern Language Association of America
RAL	Research in African Literatures
RNL	Review of National Literatures
ROMM	Revue de l'Occident musulman et de la Méditerranée
RUO	Revue de l'Université d'Ottawa
SBL	Studies in Black Literature
SoRA	Southern Review (Adelaide, Australia)
StTCL	Studies in Twentieth Century Literature
TheatreQ	Theatre Quarterly
TLS	[London] Times Literary Supplement
UES	Unisa English Studies
WAJML	West African Journal of Modern Languages
WLT	World Literature Today
WLWE	World Literature Written in English
YFS	Yale French Studies

ALGERIAN LITERATURE

Algerian literature is now defined to include only the works of native Algerians in Arabic and French, and not those by French writers born in Algeria, such as Albert Camus. While a few literary schools, composed mainly of French writers who considered themselves Algerians, did flourish during the first half of the 20th c., a native literature in French did not begin to develop until around 1950.

In Arabic

But the Algerian literary renascence manifested itself in Arabic from 1925, the date of the beginning of a national magazine, *Al-Shihab,* which in turn led to the founding of the Association of the Muslim 'Ulama of Algeria in 1931, whose activities revolved around the slogan "Algeria is my country, Islam is my religion, and Arabic is my mother tongue."

The Short Story

The most outstanding short-story writer of the pre-World War II period was Muhammad al-'Abīd al-Jilālī (1890?–1967). He criticized abuses of the French colonial system, as well as the evils of his own society. Al-Jilālī's attacks were at times so virulent that he used a pseudonym, "Rashīd." His didacticism, however, is relieved by his wit and irony.

Many short stories were written after World War II. The early postwar period was dominated by Ahmad Ridā Hūhū (1911–1956), who expressed indignation at injustices suffered by women, the corruption of the bourgeoisie, hypocrisy among intellectuals, and the unfavorable political conditions in Algeria. The tone of Algerian short fiction became gradually more revolutionary with changes in the political situation, particularly after the Sétif massacres in 1945.

Literary production came almost to a standstill during the period of armed revolution, beginning in 1954; but after independence came in 1962 it was resumed. The new writers wanted to give a complete picture of the war, although the choice of dramatic moments was almost impossible, since everything seemed crucial and moving. Many of the stories turned out to be mere documentaries. In the introductions to a number of collections the authors point with pride to the realism of their works: in *Nufūs thā'ira* (1962; rebellious souls), 'Abdallāh Ralkībī (b. 1932) declared that the reader could smell the gunpowder while reading his stories. Zuhūr Wanīsī (b. 1937) adopted a similar attitude in her collection *Al-Rasīf al-nā'im* (1967; the quiet sidewalk).

Long after independence the war of liberation continued to provide literary material. Yet some writers succeeded in shedding their emotional involvement and produced moving works on the war based mainly on human situations. "Nawwāh" (n.d.; Nawwāh), by al-Tāhir Wattār (b. 1936), is about a woman who runs away to hide during an air raid on her village, forgetting her child, who perishes. Other writers studied the large social changes wrought by the war, particularly in the life of the women who participated in the armed struggle, often astounding men by their courage and devotion.

Gradually, the story began showing greater interest in the present and the future of the country, and started dealing with personal themes. This change was headed by Wattār, who seems particularly concerned with the emotional life of young Arab men, stifled by old-fashioned norms and traditions, particularly in his collection *Dukhān min qalbi* (n.d.; smoke from my heart). Yet, he soon began concentrating his efforts on the presentation and defense of his socialist ideology, which after this volume infuses most of his works. Wattār, an idealist totally devoted to his cause, refuses to accept any halfway solutions, a position best portrayed in his collection *Al-Shuhadā' 'ā'idūn hādhā al-usbū'* (1974; the martyrs are coming back this week).

Poetry

Although poetry continued almost uninterruptedly during the French occupation, its real renascence took place only in 1925, since the *Shihāb* group included Muhammad al-'Īd Āl Khalifa (1904–1979). Yet despite the new life he infused in modern Algerian poetry, al-'Īd was at first a classical poet, guided by a rather traditional mentality much influenced by the style and spirit of the Koran. After independence, his attitude changed, together with that of society: he even wrote poems praising the role of women in the struggle for liberation. Other poets of al-'Īd's generation retained the forms of classical Arabic poetry while taking political themes and world affairs as their subject matter.

Many collections published after independence contain poems written during the war years by poets who were living outside Algeria during that period. These often reveal the poets' guilt about writing on love and other personal subjects while their country was suffering. Abū al-Qāsim Khammār (b. 1931), who was residing in Syria, in his collection *Awrāq* (1967; leaves), considers the very fact of indulging in the delicate art of poetry a dilettante's occupation, incompatible with the situation in Algeria.

A new, guilt-free treatment of personal themes is seen in the work of Sālih Kharfī (b. 1932), particularly in *Anti Laylāya* (1974; you are my chosen one), which shows a mastery of expression and form, although the tone is somewhat too impassioned.

The younger poets of the 1970s look to the future, reject the emotional attachment to the past, and assess the present with a critical eye. They have adopted free verse and an uninhibited mode of expression, well symbolized by the title *Infijārāt* (1977; explosions), a collection by Ahmad Hamdī (b. 194?). With no embarrassment, Ahlām Mostaghānmī (b. 1953) called her second collection *Al-Kitāba fī lahzat 'ārī* (1976; writing in a moment of nakedness); whether discussing her love life or political problems, her poems are totally frank.

The Novel

Unlike the short story, the novel in Arabic made a late appearance in Algeria; most critics consider 'Abd al-Hamīd ibn Hadūga's (b. 1929) *Rīh al-janūb* (1971; the southern wind) the first real Algerian novel. This and his second novel, *Nihāyat al-ams* (1975; the end of yesterday) plunge the reader into the unvarnished reality of postindependence Algeria. In his novels, as in his short stories, al-Tāhir Wattār, by contrast, offers positive solutions to Algeria's problems within the framework of his socialist ideology.

In French

Algerian literature written in French followed a path similar to that of the Arabic works in the years preceding and immediately following independence, in that writers appointed themselves defenders of their people's rights and their country's freedom. Their aim was to show the difference between the true Algerians and the *colons,* the French settlers who had usurped Algerian land and nationality.

The Novel

The first writings in this intellectual pilgrimage concentrated on contrasting the poverty of the Algerians with the scandalous wealth of the European community. Mouloud Feraoun (q.v.) presents a poignant picture of the situation in his novel *Le fils du pauvre* (1950; the poor man's son); Mohammed Dib (q.v.), too, paints a moving portrait of the poor in different sectors of Algerian society in his trilogy *Algérie* (Algeria): the city in *La grande maison* (1952; the big house), the country in *L'incendie* (1954; the fire), and the world of the workers in *Le métier à tisser* (1957; the loom). Rachid Boudjedra (b. 1941) presents an extreme case of alienation of the Algerian in France in his novel *Topographie idéale pour une aggression caractérisée* (1975; an ideal topography for a specific aggression), where the hero knows only the dialect of his small isolated village. Culture shock, the contradictions between Muslim traditions and European customs, is the subject of Feraoun's *Les chemins qui montent* (1957; the climbing roads), in which the hero, Amer, oscillates between two worlds and is unable to adapt to any. A slightly different situation is described by Mouloud Mammeri (q.v.) in *Le sommeil du juste* (1955; *The Sleep of the Just,* 1958), whose hero, Arezki, experiences discrimination and the clash between two civilizations while fighting in the ranks of the French army during World War II.

The importance of the Algerian cultural heritage, so different from the French, informs such works as Mammeri's *La colline oubliée* (1952; the forgotten hill), and Assia Djebar's (b. 1936) *Les enfants du nouveau monde* (1962; the children of the new world) and *Les impatients* (1958; the impatient ones).

Many novels centered on the political problems of the country. The most original of these was Kateb Yacine's (q.v.) *Nedjma* (1956; *Nedjma,* 1961). Nedjma is a woman the author loved, but she is also the symbol of the homeland.

In the first years of independence, a number of important novels about the war appeared. The most outstanding of these, because of its innovative approach, was Dib's *Qui se souvient de la mer* (1962; he who remembers the sea), in which the war is portrayed in apocalyptic terms. Mammeri used a different approach in *L'opium et le bâton* (1965; opium and the stick), which stresses the human angle, with the express intention of proving the brotherhood of men, in spite of religious, racial, and political differences.

But soon the mood changed, and writers began expressing their disappointments with the revolution, deploring its failure. The defenders turned critics, vehemently denouncing the abuses of the new leaders, the corruption of the bourgeoisie, the reactionaries, some religious traditions, and the exploiters. The most violent attacks came from Mourad Bourboune (b. 1938), and Rachid Boudjedra. Bourboune unleashed his anger in the novel *Le muezzin* (1968; the muezzin), in which the hero, a former imam, wants to start the real revolution. Boudjedra aimed his attacks in *La répudiation* (1969, the repudiation) at the Muslim religion, which he holds responsible for the injustices committed against women. Dib focused on the former fighters for liberation—those who feel cheated because they were forgotten in the race for positions and favors that took place after independence, and those who were unable to adapt to a life of peace, as in *La danse du roi* (1968; the dance of the king).

The 1970s saw a diminishing interest in social and political problems and a tendency to analyze the psychology of the individual in specific situations. Mohammed Dib, in *Habel* (1977; Habel), shows the disarray of the intellectuals in exile in France. Nabil Farès (b. 1941) in *Le champ des oliviers* (1972; the field of olive trees) and *Mémoire de l'absent* (1974; memory of the absent), tries to search for identity in the faraway past of his people.

Poetry

A similar search had been undertaken by the poet Jean Amrouche (1906–1962) in his collection *Étoile secrète* (1937; secret star); he hoped to find peace in the lost paradise of his ancestors. Little poetry in French was written in the preindependence period, although Ait Djafer (b. 1929) wrote a very moving poem *Complaintes des mendiants arabes de la Casbah et de la petite Yasmina tuée par son père* (1953; *Wail for the Arab Beggars of the Casbah,* 1973), showing the abysmal poverty and the injustices the Algerian people endured.

Poetry in French reached a high point during the years of the war of independence. Both Malek Haddad (1927–1978) and Jean Sénac (1926–1973) expressed support for the fighters. In *Le malheur en danger* (1956; wretchedness is in danger) Haddad feels ashamed at being alive while other Algerians have been killed and mourns his dead friends. Sénac, on the other hand, celebrates patriotic feelings in *Soleil sous les armes* (1957; sun under arms), as did other poets of the period, notably Bachir

Hadj Ali (b. 1920), in his collection *Chants pour le onze décembre* (1961; songs for December 11), and Anna Gréki (1931–1966), much of whose poetry was written in prison.

Around the mid-1960s a new generation of poets appeared; their main preoccupation is "to be." They do not hesitate to use bold language to express a violently critical attitude toward society.

Drama

Plays are rather rare in Algerian literature, despite the enthusiasm of the public for theatrical performances. Kateb Yacine's drama can be described as revolutionary. A different spirit animates Mouloud Mammeri's *Le banquet* (1973; the banquet), in which, by dealing with the massacre of the Aztecs, the author subtly alludes to the situation of the Berber in Algeria.

The Short Story

The short story in French gained importance only after independence. The first postindependence stories revolved around the war of liberation and were more realistic than their Arabic counterparts. Kateb Yacine used the short story as a weapon for attacks against religious authority. Emigration was an important subject, as was psychological analysis, as in the work of Hacen Farouk Zehar (b. 1939). Yasmin Amar (pseud. of Leila Hacene, b. 194?) introduced a refreshing note in two stories that describe the experience of a young Algerian woman in Europe.

Algerian literature written in French has a distinctly Arab character: themes are derived from Algerian folklore and tradition, Arabic expressions abound, and a specifically Algerian spirit is pervasive.

BIBLIOGRAPHY: Von Grunebaum, D., *French African Literature: Some Cultural Implications* (1964); Memmi, A., Introduction to *Anthologie des écrivains maghrébins d'expression française* (1964), pp. 11–19; Gordon, C. D., *The Passing of French Algeria* (1966); Lévi-Valensi, J., and Bencheikh, J.-E., *Diwan algérien* (1967); Mérad, A., *Le réformisme Musulman en Algérie, de 1925 à 1940* (1967); Ortzen, I., ed., *North African Writing* (1970); Déjeux, J., *Littérature maghrébine de langue française* (1973)

AIDA A. BAMYA

DIB, Mohammed
Algerian novelist and poet (writing in French), b. 21 July 1920, Tlemcen

D. went to school in Tlemcen, and later in Oujda, Morocco. He never attended the traditional Koranic school, but he was raised as a Muslim. An introspective youth, he began to write poems and stories when he was about fifteen. From 1939 to 1959, D. held various jobs. In 1959 he settled in France, where he still resides.

D. was a member of the group of writers known as the "Generation of '54" (the year of the outbreak of the Algerian revolution), sometimes called the "Generation of '52" for the year of publication of D.'s *La grande maison* (the big house) and Mouloud Mammeri's (q.v.) *La colline oubliée,* the first widely read novels in the modern wave of Algerian literature in French.

D.'s novels may be divided roughly into three categories: (1) the naturalism and social commentary of the early trilogy, *La grande maison, L'incendie* (1954; the fire), and *Le métier à tisser* (1957; the loom); (2) the deliberate experimentation with a variety of styles inspired by cubism (q.v.), science fiction, the techniques familiar to readers of Virginia Woolf, Faulkner, and Kafka, psychoanalysis, and surrealism, as well as the exploration of a Jungian world in which dichotomies of male-female impulses or good and evil compete for preeminence in the individual and in the couple, notably in *Qui se souvient de la mer* (1962; he who remembers the sea), *Cours sur la rive sauvage* (1964; run on the wild shore), *La danse du roi* (1968; the dance of the king), and *Habel* (1977; Habel); and (3) the candid scrutiny of clashes between life styles or sociopolitical convictions in war-torn and postbellum Algeria, as in *Un été africain* (1959; an African summer), *Dieu en Barbarie* (1970; God in Barbary), and *Le maître de chasse* (1973; the hunt master).

All of D.'s novels, as well as his short stories, possess many good qualities, but particularly successful are the narratives that fully convey D.'s keen insight into man's responses to the psychological pressures of human relationships and immediate external events, his sensitive use of discontinuity in time and space, and his vast poetic powers.

D.'s best novels to date are *Qui se souvient de la mer* and *Le maître de chasse.* The former is a tour de force in which a crumbling city, possibly representing colonial values, yields to a nether world where ancient values might once again take root. Frequent references to a mythic sea and variations on the theme of the concept of the soul reflect an imagination conversant with the writings of C. G. Jung.

Le maître de chasse is a powerful ideological diptych contrasting the Algerian technocracy and the vision of a mystic who feels, as D. always has, that the *fellah* (peasant) is the rock of ages of Algerian society. The discussion between Waëd the technocrat and Madjar the mystic escalates to a confrontation over governmental priorities and the prospects of an irrigation project, and Madjar is killed when an army detachment tries to prevent him from leading the peasants in the quest for water. The novel, couched in a hard-edged idiom akin to Arabic, is nevertheless the vehicle for a highly lyrical evocation of the eternal earth, which, with Madjar's dust, will somehow outlive even the most tenacious injustice.

D.'s poetry, ever since his first collection, *Ombre gardienne* (1961; guardian shadow), has been consistently hermetic, characterized by haunting ambiguity, dense and truncated syntax, and subtle eroticism. In many of the poems, the compact imagery and intricate semantics, although hypermodern, bring to mind traditional Islamic polygonal and foliate designs. Some of his later poems are spontaneous flashes from the unconscious, while other texts were revised for years until reduced to their essentials.

The heart of D.'s creative vision lies at the intersection of the particular plane of modern Algerian history and the universal plane of Jungian psychological insight.

FURTHER WORKS: *Au café* (1955); *Le talisman* (1966); *Formulaires* (1970); *Omneros* (1975); *Feu beau feu* (1979); *Mille hourras pour une gueuse* (1980)

BIBLIOGRAPHY: Ortzen, L., *North African Writing* (1970), pp. 20–43; Sellin, E., "Algerian Poetry: Poetic Values, M. D. and Kateb Yacine," *JNALA*, Nos. 9–10 (1971), 45–68; Déjeux, J., *Littérature maghrébine de langue française* (1973), pp. 143–79; Sari-Mostefa Kara, F., "L'ishrâq dans l'oeuvre de M. D.," *ROMM*, No. 22 (1976), 109–18; Junkins, D., ed., *The Contemporary World Poets* (1976), pp. 1–4; Salem, G., "The Algerian Writer: M. D. in the 'Algeria' Trilogy, the Life of a People in a Narrative Experiment," *LAAW*, 30, 4 (1976), 22–40; Déjeux, J. *M. D., écrivain algérien* (1977)

ERIC SELLIN

FERAOUN, Mouloud

Algerian novelist (writing in French), b. 8 March 1913, Tizi-Hibel; d. 15 March 1962, El Biar, Algiers

F., whose parents were poor peasants, was born and raised in the rugged mountains of Kabylia, east of Algiers. After secondary school he attended the teachers' college at Bouzaréah, outside Algiers. He then held a series of teaching and administrative positions in Kabylia and Algiers. In March 1962, three days before the signing of the cease-fire at the Évian negotiations, F. and five colleagues were assassinated in a suburb of Algiers by a terrorist squad of the illegal Secret Army Organization, which was bent on subverting the impending peace between France and Algeria.

From the mid-1930s on F. associated with Albert Camus, Emmanuel Roblès, and other writers of the so-called Algiers School. Roblès urged F. to tell the untold story of his own people. Indeed, F.'s major works all focus on himself, the territorial identity so important in Berber tradition, and the alienation of the emigrant worker.

F.'s first novel, *Le fils du pauvre* (1950; the poor man's son), was published at F.'s own expense and republished in 1954 by Éditions du Seuil. It has the distinction of being the first novel in the new wave of Algerian literature in French, which would become more readily identifiable when the first novels by Mohammed Dib and Mouloud Mammeri (qq.v.) appeared in 1952. *Le fils du pauvre,* whose protagonist bears the anagrammatic name Fouroulou Menrad, is an autobiographical novel about F.'s childhood and youth.

F.'s second novel, *La terre et le sang* (1953; earth and blood), explores the social consequences when an émigré returns with a French wife to his village in Kabylia and then falls in love with another woman. The passions, honor code, and sense of the immediacy of the earth are impenetrable to the outsider but have a firm hold on the Berbers of the area.

Les chemins qui montent (1957; the climbing roads) is ostensibly a fateful love story involving a man named Amer, a young orphan girl named Dehbia, and Amer's rival Mokrane; but it, again, examines Kabylian social constraints and the terrain that holds its inhabitants even as it repels them.

The three novels F. completed fall—as do the early novels of Dib, Mammeri, Malek Ouary (b. 1916), and others—into the category of the "ethnographic novel," written largely to explain to European readers the hidden, true side of Algeria. Because of their simple, naturalistic, accessible style, F.'s novels are more widely read in Algeria than are works by some of his more talented compatriots.

F.'s masterpiece, however, is his posthumously published *Journal 1955–1962* (1962; journal 1955–1962), which chronicles the physical horrors and cultural uncertainties of the Algerian war years (1954–62) and displays in its authentic humanity, quiet courage, and tragic dénouement qualities and a tone all too seldom achieved in fiction.

FURTHER WORKS: *Jours de Kabylie* (1954; new ed., 1968); *Les poèmes de Si Mohand* (1960); *Lettres à ses amis* (1969); *L'anniversaire* (1972)

BIBLIOGRAPHY: Khatibi, A., *Le roman maghrébin* (1968), pp. 49–52; Ortzen, L., *North African Writing* (1970), pp. 3–5, 100–111; Déjeux, J., *Littérature maghrébine de langue française* (1973), pp. 114–42; Déjeux, J., *La littérature algérienne contemporaine* (1975), pp. 62–66

ERIC SELLIN

KATEB Yacine

Algerian novelist, poet, and dramatist (writing in French and Arabic), b. 6 Aug. 1929, Constantine

The son of Islamic parents, K. was raised on tales of Arab achievement as well as on the legends of the Algerian heroes who had resisted the French invaders from the beginning.

After attending Koranic school (the elementary school of the traditional Arabic world), K. entered the French-language school system. When he was only sixteen years old, he took part in the demonstration in Setif on May 8, 1945, which resulted in the massacre of thousands of demonstrators by the police and the army. K. was jailed and reflected later that this period was crucial in his development, for during his imprisonment he discovered the two things closest to his heart. One was the Algerian struggle for independence from France, which was a struggle by those who had neither rights nor possessions against those who had both. The other was poetry; one of K.'s best-known poems, "La rose de Blida" (1963; the rose of Blida) was written about his mother, who, believing him to have been killed during the demonstration, suffered a mental breakdown. After K.'s release from prison, he embarked on what has since been basically an itinerant life.

The same themes and symbols, the same vision, are the subject of all of K.'s writings before 1970: poems, novels, plays, and criticism. As he himself has said, all of his works "are a single work written in one long breath and still in gestation." The first expression of his lifelong work was the powerful poem "Nedjma; ou, Le poème ou le couteau" (1948; Nedjma; or, the poem or the knife). The reader is introduced to the figure of Nedjma—the girl-spirit who will move hauntingly through K.'s work—and to the palm trees, the primeval desert, the archetypal ancestor who even in incestuous, moronic decadence contains a certain glory derived from the magnificence of accumulated victories and defiant inviolability.

The publication of the novel *Nedjma* (1956; *Nedjma*, 1961) was to assure K. his place in modern literature. So unusual is the form and structure of *Nedjma* that only an impression of it can be offered. The story involves Nedjma, the four men bonded by friendship and revolutionary ardor who love her, and a gallery of secondary characters of varying importance. The vitality of the work lies not in its narrative content, although it is a highly readable novel, but in the novel's structure, which is best described as radial. The action is not chronological. It moves out from a central point, returning time and again to that point only to move out on another radius. Universality is implied in the center and in the circumference and an infinite variety of shapes and repetitions are suggested by analogy to the arabesques and geometric forms of Islamic art.

Nedjma, the daughter of a French woman and an Arab from the Keblouti clan, becomes mythic through being portrayed in an ethereal way. As the star *(nedjma* in Arabic) she symbolizes the nationalism of the new nation, the importance of the desert in Algerian life, the quest of the unattainable. As a member of the Keblouti clan, she embodies the attachment of traditional Algerians to their clan, the strong emotional ties of those who can trace their kinship back to a legendary ancestor. *Nedjma*, widely considered a masterpiece, is the greatest French-language work to come out of North Africa. In it, the French language and the Arab soul have joined to achieve a new dimension in literature.

The impulsive flow of inspiration that produced *Nedjma* seems to have yielded to a more contrived and facile idiom akin to that of guerrilla street theater and the political cartoon. Representative of this later style is *L'homme aux sandales de caoutchouc* (1970; the man with the rubber sandals), a series of vignettes highlighting the military history of Vietnam and the plight of the transient Algerian labor force in Europe.

Since 1972 K. has lived in Algiers and has renounced French to devote his talents to the production of plays in the local Arabic dialect. Structurally these plays resemble *L'homme aux sandales de caoutchouc*.

K.'s works have been criticized as regressive by some Algerian critics who wish to see their country reject the heritage of the past in order to concentrate on becoming a modern technological nation. Most critics, however, both French and African, agree that K.'s major works masterfully blend past and present and successfully interweave personal vision—even hallucination—and cultural tradition.

FURTHER WORKS: *Soliloques* (1946); *Abdelkader et l'indépendance algérienne* (1948); *Le cercle des représailles* (1959); *La femme sauvage* (perf. 1963); *Le polygone étoilé* (1966); *Les ancêtres redoublent de férocité* (perf. 1967)

BIBLIOGRAPHY: Sellin, E., "Algerian Poetry: Poetic Values, Mohammed Dib, and K. Y.," *JNALA,* Nos. 9–10 (1971), pp. 45–68; Mortimer, M. P., "K. Y. in Search of Algeria: A Study of *Nedjma* and *Le polygone étoilé*," *ECr,* 12 (1972), 274–88; Déjeux, J. *Littérature maghrébine de langue française* (1973), pp. 143–79; Déjeux, J., "Les structures de l'imaginaire dans l'oeuvre de K. Y.," *ROMM,* Nos. 13–14 (1973), pp. 267–92; Déjeux, J., "K. Y., romancier, poète et dramaturge algérien," *PFr,* No. 15 (1977), pp. 127–47; Aresu, B., "Polygonal and Arithmosophical Motifs: Their Significance in the Fiction of K. Y.," *RAL,* 9 (1978), 143–75

ERIC SELLIN

MAMMERI, Mouloud

Algerian novelist, essayist, dramatist, and translator (writing in French), b. 28 Dec. 1917, Traourt-Mimoun

After attending the local primary school of his Berber village, where he learned French, M. pursued his studies in Rabat, Morocco, in Algiers, and in Paris. During World War II he fought in Algeria and later in Europe after the liberation of North Africa. After the war M. worked as a teacher. In 1957 he went to Morocco, returning after Algeria achieved independence in 1962 to Algiers, where he has been professor of ethnology at the University of Algiers and director of a research center at the Bardo Museum.

M. belongs to the first wave of major Algerian Francophone authors, called by some the "generation of '52"—for the year in which M. and Mohammed Dib (q.v.) published their first novels. M.'s novel, *La colline oubliée* (the forgotten hill), is set in a remote Kabyle village in the late 1930s and early 1940s. The book is presented in the form of a diary kept by Mokrane Chaalal. Near the end of the book, the diary breaks off and the narrator intervenes to tell what happens thereafter. The novel provides interesting sociological insights into such local customs as fertility rites and vendettas based on the male-honor code.

The action of M.'s second novel, *Le sommeil du juste* (1955; *The Sleep of the Just*, 1958), takes place during World War II; in it we see the notions of independence and an Algerian entity beginning to stir in the minds of the young Kabyles. M. shows greater technical mastery in this novel than in his first, which had numerous subplots; here he limits the number of major characters and increases the density of action. Much of *Le sommeil du juste* consists of a long letter the main character, Arezki, writes to his old French schoolteacher. The letter, like the novel in general, is an indictment of the inequality imposed by the colonial system.

M.'s third novel, *L'opium et le bâton* (1965; opium and the stick), although in some ways less unified in creative vision than M.'s earlier works, is nevertheless his most successful. It is an ambitious fresco of the liberation struggle in Algeria, presenting particular moments of the revolution.

In *La traversée* (1982; the crossing)—an impressionistic novel that makes frequent use of dreams, letters, and diary entries—the notion of "crossing" is explored on four levels: the title and theme of a controversial political fable by the journalist Mourad, which causes his resignation; an actual Sahara crossing; the trajectory of a human life; and the inexorability of historical movements: Mourad, cynical and alienated, tries to recover his Berber roots, but dies of a fever on arriving in his native village.

The evolution of M.'s protagonists—within each book, as well as from book to book—has been from rural security toward a vaster but more fragmented cosmopolitan humanism. Even as his protagonists have become more disenfranchised, M. has become increasingly aware of the implications of their loss and increasingly involved in a quest to preserve the cultural roots some of his younger characters have forsaken.

M.'s later works have addressed the possible decline of Berber civilization, owing to a worldwide trend toward uniformity of culture. In 1969

M. brought out *Les isefra: Poèmes di Si Mohand-ou-Mhand* (the *isefra:* poems of Si Mohand-ou-Mhand), a large bilingual collection of the traditional nine-line *isefra* by the great Kabyle wandering bard (1845–1906), who sang of, among other things, Kabylia's degeneration after French colonization. In 1980 M. published an anthology, *Poèmes kabyles anciens* (old Kabyle poems). A play, *Le banquet* (1973; the banquet), preceded by an essay entitled "La mort absurde des Aztèques" (the absurd death of the Aztecs), deals ostensibly with Cortés's destruction of Montezuma and his people, but it also explores ethnocide in general and the dual threat that European colonialism and Arab-Muslim nationalism pose to the traditional values of Kabyle society.

BIBLIOGRAPHY: Dembri, M. S., "L'itinéraire du héros dans l'oeuvre romanesque de M. M.," *CALC*, No. 3 (1968), 79–99; Ortzen, L., ed., *North African Writing* (1970), pp. 1–3, 90–99; Mortimer, M., "M. M. Bridges Cultural Worlds," *AfricaR*, 16, 6 (1971) 26–28; Yetiv, I., *Le thème de l'aliénation dans le roman maghrébin d'expression française, 1952-1956* (1972), pp. 114–33; Déjeux, J., *Littérature maghrébine de langue française* (1973), pp. 180–208; Adam, J., "Le jeune intellectuel dans les romans de M. M.," *RUO*, No. 46 (1976), 278–87; Déjeux, J., "*La colline oubliée* (1952) de M. M., un prix littéraire, une polémique politique," *O&C*, 4, 2 (1979), 69–80

ERIC SELLIN

ANGOLAN LITERATURE

In the latter half of the 19th c. the stirrings of protonationalist sentiment among black and mestizo (mixed-race) Angolans gave birth to a number of African-run newspapers in the capital, Luanda. A relatively small, but significant, educated elite expressed their social consciousness and reformist demands in editorials that echoed the strains of republican liberalism that drifted south from far-off Portugal. One of these early precursors of Angolan nationalism was Joaquim Dias Cordeiro da Matta (1857–1894), a journalist, poet, unpublished novelist, and collector of oral traditions in his native Kimbundu language, who first exhorted his fellow Angolans to devote their "leisure time to the founding of our literature."

Anything resembling a literary movement, however, had to wait until the second half of the 20th c. By the end of World War II the scene was set for a new militancy among educated Angolans. With the defeat of fascism in Europe and with the rising tide of national self-determination in Asia and elsewhere in Africa, social protest and cultural revindication contributed to the founding of a literary movement by a multiracial coalition that met on the common ground of anticolonialism and socialist ideology.

In 1950 a small nucleus of these mostly young intellectuals, belonging to the Association of Angola's Native Sons, founded the literary journal *Mensagem*. Although only two issues were published—one in 1951, another in 1952—this journal and a later one, *Cultura* (1957–61), challenged the colonial establishment and heralded the beginnings of a literature that would seek to reclaim Angola for its native sons and daughters. Ironically, but understandably, imaginative writing in the Portuguese language became the most accessible weapon against Western deculturation.

Contributors to *Mensagem* included António Agostinho Neto (1922–1979), of Kimbundu origin, Viriato da Cruz (1928–1973), a mestizo, and António Jacinto (b. 1924), of European descent. These poets, along with other militant writers, became political activists in the Movement of the Liberation of Angola (MPLA). Their literary activities, inseparable from a political consciousness that was strongly influenced by Marxist-Leninist thought, extended from Luanda to Lisbon and even to Paris, where

Mário de Andrade (b. 1928), a poet, literary critic, and one of the founders of the MPLA, lived in exile.

In Lisbon the House of Students from the Empire became, from 1944 to 1965, a spawning ground for progressive political ideas and a center of literary activities. Paradoxically, the Salazar government that had sanctioned the organization's founding ordered its closing by the secret police. But in the 1950s and early 1960s the group succeeded in editing two anthologies of Angolan poetry and a number of works by individual authors.

When guerrilla warfare erupted in Angola in 1961 political repression, the mass arrests of dissident intellectuals and writers, and the heavy hand of the censor all but silenced the more militant voices. Nevertheless, Angolan literature had gotten its start, and although the 1960s are often called the "decade of silence," writers did continue to produce in exile, at home for the desk drawer, or clandestinely in the quiet of a prison cell.

From their postindependence vantage point many Angolan writers like to claim that whereas Negritude (q.v.) was conceived in defeat and born in resignation, Angolan writing was cast in struggle and forged in victory. In truth, during the 1950s, and even beyond, the attitudes and images of such black ideologies as pan-Africanism, racial singularity, and Negritude did find expression in some Angolan writing. On the other hand, class struggle did indeed undermine the cause of racial exclusivity. Intellectuals from the three racial communities joined forces in an ideological pact predicated on a militant concern for the plight of the dispossessed masses of Angola.

Thus the themes of identity, identification, and alienation dominate much of the poetry of the 1950s and early 1960s. And in many works the problem of alienation comes across more in terms of class than of race, as in António Agostinho Neto's "Mussunda amigo" (c. 1957; Mussunda friend). In this haunting poem of collective conscience the educated persona addresses a former companion who cannot read the poem that evokes his name.

Other poets who reached a level of artistic competence in the 1950s and 1960s are Mário António (b. 1934), António Cardoso (b. 1933), Aires de Almeida Santos (b. 1922), Fernando da Costa Andrade (b. 1936). and Arnaldo Santos (b. 1936). Their poems combined the intimate "I" with the collective "we" to convey these militant writers' sense of social and political commitment. Many of the best of these poems are lyrical narratives, written in colloquial style, depicting daily life in the

African quarters that ringed the Europeanized central city of Luanda. Indeed, what developed in Angolan literature in general was a Creole and Kimbundu hegemony in which the poor neighborhoods and *musseques* (shanty towns) and their residents are the subjects of the poems and stories.

Love of Luanda also found expression in fiction, principally short stories. In the 1960s Arnaldo Santos was able to break the colonial cultural barrier with two collections of short stories: *Quinaxixe* (1965; Quinaxixe)—the title is the name of a Luanda neighborhood—deals mainly with the stresses of a racist environment on children, and *Tempo de munhungo* (1968; vertigo time) captures the social, cultural, and racial contradictions of preindependence Luanda.

But it was José Luandino Vieira (q.v.) who emerged as Angola's most prominent writer of fiction and chronicler of Luanda's Creole-Kimbundu hegemony. His *Luuanda* (1964—the archaic spelling of Luanda; *Luuanda*, 1980) marked a turning point in Angolan writing; for although ostensibly a Portuguese-language text, the three long tales simulate oral storytelling in form and language. Vieira invented a discourse that combines the creolized Portuguese of Luanda with the equally creolized Kimbundu of the *musseques*.

When independence came on November 11, 1975, Angola entered into what was almost a golden age of literary and editorial activities. Only one month after independence, and within earshot of a devastating civil war, the Angolan Writers' Union was proclaimed in Luanda; since its inception it has sponsored literature contests, organized colloquia, and launched an ambitious publishing program in conjunction with two Lisbon publishers.

As is the case with other emerging nations, Angolan writers have been called on to perform official functions that leave them little time to write. But until his untimely death in 1979, António Agostinho Neto, the poet-president of Angola and the president of the Writers' Union's General Assembly, led the way in stressing literature's role in the cultural revolution. Thus, with Neto's legacy and with the establishment of a literary and editorial base, Angola, despite its high illiteracy rate, is a country where imaginative writing is preeminent and writers are held in high esteem.

Not surprisingly, independence resulted in an outpouring of patriotism in the form of technically weak poems and stories. But out of this thicket emerged seasoned writers who applied their sense of craft to the production of literature at the service of the nationalist cause. Fernando da

Costa Andrade returned from his years as a guerrilla in the bush to write the poems collected in his *Caderno dos herois* (1977; sketchbook of heroes). Arlindo Barbeitos (b. 1940) drew on the experiences in the eastern zone of combat to fashion the poems in his *Angola Angolé Angolema* (1977; Angola, hail Angola, Angola the word). Another professional poet, Manuel Rui (b. 1941), came home to celebrate independence with his *11 poemas em novembro* (11 poems in November), the title of four different books published since 1976. Rui also published *Sim camarada* (1977; yes, comrade), a book of stories that captures the essence of the events and the language generated by the civil war that engulfed Angola after the coup in Portugal. Ruy Duarte de Carvalho (b. 1941), a Portuguese-born writer raised in southern Angola, has published sensitive poems and stories about that region in *A decisão da idade* (1976; decisions of the times) and *Como se o mundo não tivesse leste* (1977; as if the world had no east). And Pepetela (pseud. of Artur Pestana, b. 1941), another white writer from the south, wrote *As aventuras de Ngunga* (1977; the adventures of Ngunga), a didactic and patriotic novella that has sold over 75,000 copies in Angola alone.

Although most of the works published after the coup and since independence revolve around the same overworked themes of anticolonialism and cultural revindication, new forms and styles of writing have begun to appear. Vieira's pioneering example has influenced other writers to experiment with language and technique. Foremost among this new crop of writers is Uanhenga Xitu (Kimbundu name of André Agostinho Mendes de Carvalho, b. 1924). Xitu only began to write after the age of forty, while a political prisoner. Prison mates, including Vieira and António Jacinto, encouraged him to produce stories about the people and customs of his Kimbunda homeland. Thus far, Xitu, writing in Portuguese, has published seven books, the most masterful being *Manana* (1974; Manana).

In the early 1980s economic crises, military aggression from the outside, and the demands of building a new nation have curtailed the even greater flourishing of Angolan literature. But despite all, Angolans seem to take for granted that imaginative writing is an integral part of their cultural revolution.

BIBLIOGRAPHY: Moser, G. M., *Essays in Portuguese-African Literature* (1969); Hamilton, R. G., *Voices from an Empire: A History of Afro-Portuguese Literature* (1975), pp. 25–159; Hamilton, R. G., "Black from White and White on Black: Contradictions of Language in the

Angolan Novel," *Ideologies & Literature,* 1 (1976–77), 25–58; Burness, D., *Fire: Six Writers from Angola, Mozambique, and Cape Verde* (1977)

RUSSELL G. HAMILTON

VIEIRA, José Luandino

(pseud. of José Vieira Mateus da Graça) Angolan novelist and short-story writer (writing in Portuguese), b. 5 May 1936, Pôvoa do Varzim, Portugal

V. left rural Portugal at the age of three with his settler parents for Angola, where he grew up with black and mestizo (mixed-race) children in Luanda's *musseques* (African shantytowns that ringed the Europeanized city). Some outsiders are surprised to learn that a white man is independent Angola's greatest writer. But V. is living testimonial to the paradoxes of Portuguese colonialism, which, by means of social and economic neglect, permitted a measure of biracial creolization to occur in Luanda prior to a major influx of European immigrants around the time of World War II.

Luuanda (1964; *Luuanda: Short Stories of Angola,* 1980), V.'s first major work, was banned a year after its publication by the Portuguese authorities while the author was serving an eleven-year prison term for his nationalist activities. Since the overthrow, in 1974, of the Portuguese dictatorship, the book has gone through four editions in Portugal and Angola, and it has been translated into several languages. A turning point in Angolan writing, *Luuanda* simulates an African storytelling tradition while successfully combining a creolized Portuguese with an equally creolized Kimbundu (one of Angola's principal vernaculars).

The three long tales in *Luuanda* project the language and life style of the *musseques*. And in "A estória da galinha e do ovo" ("The Tale of the Hen and the Egg"), the best of the three stories, a dispute between two *musseque* women over the ownership of an egg frames the conflict between the colonizer and the colonized in terms that aggrandize the latter and challenge the hegemony of the former. In essence, the downtrodden rise above their petty differences to mobilize against the greater threat of intrusion by the hostile European power structure.

In 1961 V. wrote *A vida verdadeira de Domingos Xavier* (pub. 1974; *The Real Life of Domingos Xavier,* 1978), a novel that explicitly treats the subject of organized opposition to the colonial regime in Angola. Although the first Portuguese-language edition of the novel would not appear until thirteen years after it was written, the manuscript was spirited out of Angola to France, where, in the late 1960s, Sarah Maldoror, a Guadaloupan filmmaker, adapted the story to the screen under the title *Sambizanga* (the name of a *musseque*). The story takes place during the first months before the outbreak of armed revolt against the Portuguese, and it dramatizes the exploits and tribulations of a working-class black Angolan who joins the struggle only to pay with his life for his convictions.

Even while interned in Tarrafal, the Portuguese government's infamous concentration camp for political dissenters, V. managed to write several short stories and a novel, all of which add to the prestige of Angolan literature as the most mature imaginative writing of Lusophone Africa. After Angola became independent V. returned to his beloved Luanda, where he became secretary-general of the Angolan Writers Union; and although he has found little time to ply his craft as a writer, his works have profoundly influenced a new generation of Angolan writers.

FURTHER WORKS: *A cidade e a infância* (1960); *Duas histórias de pequenos burgueses* (1961); *Vidas novas* (n.d.; 2nd ed., 1976); *Velhas estórias* (1974); *No antigamente, na vida* (1974); *Nós, os do Makulusu* (1975); *Lourentinho, Dona Antónia de Sousa Neto e eu* (1981); *Joâo Vêncio: Os seus amores* (1982); *Macandumba* (1982)

BIBLIOGRAPHY: Figueiredo, A., "The Children of the Rape," *NewA*, Nov. 1965, 203–7; Hamilton, R. G., "Black from White and White on Black: Contradictions of Language in the Angolan Novel," *Ideologies and Literature*, 1 (1976–77), 25–58; Ngwube, A., on *The Real Life of Domingos Xavier, NewA*, Oct. 1978, 108; Bender, T., "Translator's Preface," in *Luuanda: Short Stories of Angola* (1980), pp. v–x; Jacinto, T., "The Art of L. V." in Burness, D., ed., *Critical Perspectives on Lusophone African Literature* (1981), pp. 79–87; Stern, I., "L. V.'s Short Fiction: Decolonisation in the Third Register," in Parker, C. A., et al., eds., *When the Drumbeat Changes* (1981), pp. 141–52

RUSSELL G. HAMILTON

BENINIAN LITERATURE

The written literature of the People's Republic of Benin (known as Dahomey until 1975) had its beginnings in the late 1920s. This small West African state became a French colony early in the 20th c., and writing by Beninians has been almost exclusively in the language of the colonizer. Over the years, Benin acquired the nickname of the "Latin Quarter" of French Africa, referring to its relatively large and active group of intellectuals, many of whom filled administrative positions throughout France's African colonial empire until independence in 1960; this may explain Benin's rather early start in the realm of creative literature in a non-African language.

Indeed, only four years after the publication in Senegal of the first French-African novel, Félix Couchoro (1900–1968), a Beninian writer later identified with Togo, published *L'esclave* (1929; the slave), the first of his many popular regional novels dealing with love, adventure, and the social problems of the coastal populations of Dahomey and Togo. Set in an earlier and more glorious time, the historical novel *Doguicimi* (1938; Doguicimi) by the teacher and scholar Paul Hazoumé (b. 1890) is one of the outstanding Francophone works of the pre-World War II era. Relating the tragic adventures of Doguicimi, a princess of the 19th-c. kingdom of Dahomey, this engrossing novel has the additional merit of being a storehouse of cultural information on one of the last of the great precolonial African kingdoms. Hazoumé is thus important as a pioneer in the revival of interest among African writers in their traditional cultures, a prominent feature of the Negritude (q.v.) movement.

It was during this prewar period in the realm of drama, as well, that Beninians were involved in early literary activity, for the genesis of African theater in French may be traced back to the plays written and performed by students of the William Ponty School, a colonial training college in Senegal. The first of these plays, all of which deal with the African past or traditional life, was *La dernière entrevue de Behanzin et de Bayol* (first performance Gorée, Senegal, 1933; the last conversation between Benhanzin and Bayol). Beninian students of the college wrote and produced at least three more plays during this period, one of which was performed in Paris in 1937.

The postwar years, so fertile for the novel elsewhere in Africa, have thus far produced only one true novelist in Benin, Olympe Bhêly-

Quénum (b. 1928). Eschewing the theme of culture conflict poetically treated in his *Le chant du lac* (1965; the song of the lake), he pessimistically explores the absurdity of existence in his best-known novel, *Un piège sans fin* (1960; an endless trap). *Liaison d'un été* (1968; a summer liaison) is a short-story collection of uneven quality.

Sharing recognition with Bhêly-Quénum beyond Benin's borders is Jean Pliya (b. 1931)—both have won literary prizes—who, in addition to an engaging collection of short stories, *L'arbre fétiche* (1974; the fetish tree), is known for two plays: *Kondo, le requin* (1969; Kondo the shark) deals with King Benhanzin's resistance to the French, while the satiric *La secrétaire particulière* (1973; the private secretary), echoing a new theme in African writing since independence, turns from history, traditional life, and confrontation with the West to criticism of the corruption of the new elite that has replaced the colonizer.

Among Benin's half-dozen good poets, Paulin Joachim (b. 1931) and Richard Dogbeh (sometimes Dogbeh-David; b. 1932) have earned recognition, the latter for his collection *Cap Liberté* (1969; Cape Liberty), the former especially for his *Anti-grâce* (1967; anti-grace). Both are "humanists," singing compassionately of their people, eloquently evoking their anger and despair but also their fervent hope of future liberation. Eustache Prudencio (b. 1924) and Agbossahessou (dates n.a.) certainly deserve mention, as does Émile Ologoudou (b. 1935), an extremely promising poet whose work has appeared thus far only in periodicals or anthologies.

Note must finally be taken of two essayists whose books, although not classifiable as creative literature, have had wide circulation and influence, embodying as they do two principal currents of pre- and postindependence African thinking. (Many of the writers already mentioned have also published in such diverse fields as literary criticism, politics, education, religion, and ethnography.) The first, Albert Tevoedjre (b. 1929), roundly condemns Western colonialism in Africa in his much discussed *L'Afrique révoltée* (1958; Africa in revolt), while Stanislas Spéro Adotevi's (b. 1934) *Négritude et négrologues* (1972; Negritude and negrologists) is an impassioned and scathing attack on Negritude as a smoke screen for neocolonialism.

Written literary activity in African languages has been very slight until recently. Since 1975, however, an effort has been made in their promotion, and a few school texts of tales from the oral tradition in Fon and other national languages have appeared. If this trend continues, a parallel literature in these tongues could, with time, become a reality.

BIBLIOGRAPHY: Herskovits, M. J., *Dahomean Narrative* (1958); Anozie, S. O., *Sociologie du roman africain* (1970), pp. 160–66; Jahn, J., and Dressler, P. D., *Bibliography of Creative African Writing* (1971), p. 397; Herdeck, D. E., *African Authors* (1973); Wauthier, C., *The Literature and Thought of Modern Africa*, 2nd ed. (1979); Baratte-Eno Belinga, T., et al., *Bibliographie des auteurs africains de langue française*, 4th ed. (1979), pp. 21–29

FREDRIC MICHELMAN

BOTSWANA LITERATURE

Botswana, under the colonial name Bechuanaland, was one of the Southern African territories directly administered by Great Britain. It could thus receive independence in 1961 although it remained within the orbit of South Africa's economic dominance.

The boundaries of Botswana literature are not yet clearly determined. Language association (commonly Tswana) has traditionally asserted more demonstrable allegiance than nationality, while education and business opportunity have often required extended residence in South Africa. Any sense of a national literature is in its infancy.

There were three earlier writers of note. Lettle Disang Raditladi (1910–1971) and Michael Ontepetse Seboni (b. 1912), although both educated in South Africa, preferred to write in Tswana. Raditladi was a playwright and poet: *Motswasele II* (1945; Motswasele II) and *Sekgoma I* (1967; Sekgoma I) and a prize-winning book of poetry *Sefalana sa menate* (1961; a granary of joy). (The publication dates are substantially later than the writing.) Seboni, with a doctorate in education, wrote in a more pedantic mode but produced several novels, including *Kgosi Isang Pilane* (1958; Chief Isang Pilane) and the collection of poetry *Maboko naloba le maabane* (1949; praise poems, old and new). He also translated Shakespeare's *The Merchant of Venice* and *Henry IV* into Tswana. In contrast, Moliri Silas Molema (1892–1965) preferred to write in English but produced less imaginative work: a book of Bantu history (1920) and biographies of two chiefs: *Chief Moroka* (1952) and *Montshiwa, Baralong Chief* (1966). These early works by the Botswana-born are restricted in topic and are handicapped by a certain pedantry necessitated by social conditions and publication options.

The contemporary writer whose work noticeably breaks from these limitations of formal style and historical themes is Bessie Head (b. 1931). She was born in South Africa but left for residence in Botswana. Her reversal of the movements of the earlier writers says much about changing conditions. Her first novel, *When Rain Clouds Gather* (1968), exhibits the clearest links to other contemporary African writing. It deals vigorously with the problems of black and white, and with the battle for progress against entrenched traditional chiefly authority. Her later works include the novels *Maru* (1971) and *A Question of Power* (1973), and some short stories, *The Collection of Treasures* (1977).

Other Botswana novelists are likely to follow the direction exemplified by Bessie Head and focus their plots on the subjects already familiar in West African novels: the conflict between tradition and change, in this case additionally affected by the extra difficulty of living close to the political and racial situation to the south.

Outside of this initial and minimal formal publication of international literature, there are other local lively manifestations of creativity such as the vigorous popular theater exemplified by the original Laedza Batanani group, who provide part real drama, part staged dissemination of public information. It may be out of these truly indigenous activities that a fresh literature will grow.

JOHN POVEY

CAMEROONIAN LITERATURE

The linguistic situation in Cameroon is unusual. Both French and English are official languages, although French is the dominant language of government, education, and commerce. The larger population centers are in former East Cameroon, which was under French colonial control; West Cameroon was under British colonial influence. The major African language groups are Bantu and are in southern Cameroon; Fulani is widely spoken throughout the north.

The folklore of Cameroon is rich and varied. Myths, legends, and folktales are important, particularly in the cultural life of the villages. They serve as entertainment and also instruct the young people about and initiate them into the social values and moral responsibilities of their people. The Pahouin troubadours are noted for their musical accompaniment on the *mvet,* a harp.

The Bamoun, western highlanders, are one of the few peoples of Africa to have a script. It was invented by the Sultan Njoya, enthroned in 1880, and has eighty-three signs and ten numbers. Writing was for the most part introduced by missionaries for the sole purpose of studying the Bible. In the early 1920s Jemba Medu, an elder in the Presbyterian church, wrote a chronicle in Bulu, one of the Bantu dialects of the Pahouin people: *Nnanga kon* (phantom albino), which tells of the arrival of the first white men in the southern forest region and enjoyed great popularity in the country.

Modern Cameroonian literature, written primarily in French, has been characterized by its strong condemnation of colonialism. The two best-known writers, Mongo Beti and Ferdinand Oyono (qq.v.), began publishing in the 1950s. Both make use of satire and irony, although Beti's satire of colonialism is less harsh in tone than Oyono's.

Oyono has written four novels to date: *Le vieux nègre et la médaille* (1956; *The Old Man and the Medal,* 1967); *Une vie de boy* (1956; *Boy!,* 1970); *Chemin d'Europe* (1960; road to Europe); and *Le pandémonium* (c. 1971, unpublished; pandemonium). In *Une vie de boy,* Oyono shows that the servant Toundi's contact with Christianity has taught him to believe that the "primitive" world is evil and that Europeans are bearers of good. As he matures, Toudi learns that the priest's teachings are to be interpreted in reverse. Contact with the white man leads eventually to Toundi's death.

Beti has also published four novels dealing with the conflict between traditional and Western values: *Ville cruelle* (1954; cruel town) published under the pseudonym Eza Boto; *Le pauvre Christ de Bomba* (1956; *The Poor Christ of Bomba,* 1971); *Mission terminée* (1957; *Mission to Kala,* 1958), winner of the Sainte-Beuve Prize in 1957; and *Le roi miraculé* (1958; *King Lazarus,* 1960). In *Mission terminée* Beti satirizes a confused youth caught in cultural conflict. Beti skillfully shows the dilemma of the individual out of step with a society because he has learned to live by a different set of standards.

Other Cameroonian literary figures writing French include Benjamin Matip (b. 1932), Francis Bebey (b. 1929), and René Philombe (b. 1934). Matip has published a novel, *Afrique nous t'ignorons* (1956; Africa, we do not pay attention to you), which deals with upheaval in Cameroon at the beginning of World War II. He has also published a collection of fables, *À la belle étoile* (1963, out under the stars) and a play, *Le jugement suprême* (1963; the highest judgment).

Bebey, who is well known as a musicologist, composer, and concert guitarist, has published a collection of short stories, *Embarras et Cie* (1968; Embarrassment and Company) and a novel, *Le fils d'Agatha Moudio* (1967; *Agatha Moudio's Son,* 1971), which won the Black Africa Grand Prize for Literature in 1967. It is the humorous account of a young man's struggle to marry the girl of his choosing.

Philombe has published an autobiographical work, *Lettres de ma cambuse* (1964; letters from my hovel) and two novels, *Sola, ma chérie* (1966; Sola, my darling) and *Un sorcier blanc à Zangali* (1969; a white witch doctor in Zangali), which tells of the mishaps of a European missionary.

The novelist Remy Gilbert Medou Mvomo (b. 1945) and the playwright Guillaume Oyôno-Mbia (b. 1939) write in English and French. Mvomo has published a novel, *Mon amour en noir et blanc* (1971; my love in black and white) and a short story, "Nancy in Blooming Youth" (1961).

Oyôno-Mbia has published two plays, *Trois prétendants, un mari* (1964; *Three Suitors, One Husband,* 1968), the first modern Cameroonian play to be performed in French in Yaoundé, in 1961, and *Until Further Notice* (1967), which was awarded the BBC African Service Prize the same year and was translated into French in 1970.

Cameroonian literature in French continues to flourish. A recent bibliography cites forty-two titles published in the 1970s in Cameroon and in France. Young Cameroonian writers are fortunate in having the Éditions Clé, an important African press, in Yaoundé. In addition, the playwright Oyôno-Mbia is perhaps setting a new Cameroonian tradition. His latest play, *His Excellency's Special Train/Le train spécial de son Excellence,* will appear in a bilingual edition, and he is preparing both the English and the French texts.

BIBLIOGRAPHY: Gleason, J., *This Africa: Novels by West Africans in English and French* (1965); Kesteloot, L., *Les écrivains noirs de langue française: Naissance d'une littérature* (1965); Jahn, J., *A History of Neo-African Literature* (1968); Cartey, W., *Whispers from a Continent* (1971); Palmer, E., *An Introduction to the African Novel* (1972); Gakwandi, S. A., *The Novel and Contemporary Experience in Africa* (1977)

MILDRED MORTIMER

BETI, Mongo
(pseud. of Alexandre Biyidi) Cameroonian novelist and essayist (writing in French), b. 30 June 1932, Akometam

Born in a small village, B. attended Catholic mission schools and a French lycée in nearby Yaoundé before going to France to study literature. Since 1959 he has not returned to his own country, for political reasons. He now teaches at a secondary school in Rouen.

B. was only twenty-one when his first short story appeared, and twenty-two when his first novel was published. Both were signed Eza Boto, a pseudonym he has since abandoned. In his novels written before 1960 B. offers his vision of the interplay of the two worlds of colonial Africa: the African society, the only one in which the natives can survive with integrity, and the colonial society, whose imperialist tentacles reach everywhere. These opposing forces generate violence of all sorts, and the effects of that violence in both the city and in the most remote country areas are demonstrated in B.'s novels. Those of his characters who try to meet the demands of both worlds inevitably fail and are condemned to a form of exile, to an "endless life of wandering."

B. shares with many other writers of his generation this sense of tragedy created by colonialism. The originality of his early novels, however, lies in his viewpoint and in the tone he adopted. He looks at the colonial world through the enlarging and yet selective prism of irony, showing a marked talent for parody.

The laughter of blacks in B.'s work, and the increasing importance it assumes as his literary production develops, bear witness to B.'s inner liberation and that of the African characters he portrays. In his first novel, *Ville cruelle* (1954; cruel town), the tragic tension is almost constant, leaving little room for the comic. On the other hand, in *Mission terminée* (1957; *Mission to Kala*, 1958) and *Le roi miraculé* (1958; *King Lazarus*, 1960), there is an explosion of healthy laughter, expressing the African's solid resistance to the white world.

In *Le pauvre Christ de Bomba* (1956; *The Poor Christ of Bomba*, 1971), B.'s masterpiece, irony is at the base of the presentation of the missionary world. In this novel B. did more than castigate the practices of colonialism—he showed that even well-meant intentions can cause disaster if an understanding of the values and particularities of the indigenous culture is lacking.

In 1958 B. decided to abandon writing as an anticolonial weapon and to become an activist in the African struggle for self-determination. (Two years later, in 1960, Cameroon became an independent republic.)

Since then, B. has concentrated upon the political problems of his own country and of Africa as a whole, particularly decolonization, which is either not being carried out at all or being carried out in the wrong way. After a long period of silence and thought, he decided to speak out again, first in a book-length political essay, *Main basse sur le Cameroun* (1972; the plundering of Cameroon), which denounces the injustices of a regime that he considered to be subservient to the former French colonial powers.

For Beti, political thought and fictional works are now more closely linked than ever, as can be seen in three new novels and in the periodical he founded in 1978, *Peuples noirs, peuples africains*. In the novel *Perpétue* (1974; Perpétue) the story of Essola and his sister Perpétue takes place against the backdrop of a supposedly independent society that yields to mediocrity and corruption, and in which the weak are oppressed by a police state. *Remember Ruben* (1974; title in pidgin English), is a re-creation of the period of resistance that led to independence, dramatizing the agitation of labor unions, urban guerrilla warfare, and political action. His latest novel, *La ruine presque cocasse d'un polichinelle* (1979; the almost laughable downfall of a buffoon) is a sequel to *Remember Ruben* and presents a second stage of resistance, which keeps its *raison d'être* even after independence.

No other black African writer has followed so closely the political evolution of Africa. Yet B. avoids the trap of producing works simply about immediate circumstances because he has succeeded in constructing a coherent fictional universe in which oppressed man searches, with numerous defeats and some successes, for the way to his liberation.

BIBLIOGRAPHY: Brench, A. C., *The Novelists' Inheritance in French Africa* (1967), pp. 63–74; Cartey, W., *Whispers from a Continent* (1969), pp. 32, 56-77; Cook, M., and Henderson, S. E., *The Militant Black Writer in Africa and the United States* (1969), pp. 23–31; Macaulay, J., "The Idea of Assimilation: M. B. and Camara Laye," in Pieterse, C., and Munro, D., eds., *Protest and Conflict in African Literature* (1969), pp. 81–92; Cassirer, T., "The Dilemma of Leadership as Tragi-Comedy in the Novels of M. B.," *ECr*, 10 (1970), 223–33; Melone, T., *M. B., l'homme et le destin* (1971); Lambert, F., "Narrative Perspective in M. B.'s *Le pauvre Christ de Bomba*," *YFS*, No. 53 (1976), 78–91

FERNANDO LAMBERT

OYONO, Ferdinand

Cameroonian novelist (writing in French), b. 14 Sept. 1929, N'Goulémakong, near Ebolowa

O.'s mother, a fervent Roman Catholic, left her husband because although professing to be a Catholic he continued to practice polygamy. O. was a choirboy and studied the classics with a priest; when he obtained his primary-school diploma, his father suddenly took pride in his son's education, sending him to the lycée of Ebolowa and urging him to study in France. Before going to France, O. worked for missionaries as a houseboy, a situation that served as the source of inspiration for his first novel, *Une vie de boy* (1956; *Boy!*, 1970). After receiving his diploma from the lycée of Provins near Paris, O. went on to study law and government administration. He has held several government positions.

O.'s three novels are rich in autobiographical material. *Une vie de boy* is the ironic tale of an innocent young African, Toundi, who works as a servant for a white missionary. After the missionary's death, Toundi is transferred to the service of the Commandant Decazy and his wife, a beautiful white woman whom Toundi idolizes, but who treats him with utter contempt. Like Voltaire's Candide, Toundi has an optimistic, easygoing nature and an unspoiled enthusiasm for life. His naïve frankness and sense of trust contrast sharply with the carefully calculated hypocrisy of the other Africans, who, while pretending to be subservient and obedient toward their masters, openly express their disgust and dissatisfaction when in their own private circles. Toundi's gradual awakening to the injustice of his colonial masters is pathetically demonstrated toward the end of the novel, but that awakening occurs too late for Toundi to save his own life.

His sad death is made known to the reader in an epilogue in which O., in his own voice, purports to be offering the reader Toundi's own diary. Since the narrative is presented as a translation into French from the unsophisticated houseboy's native Ewondo, its style is extremely simple and direct. *Une vie de boy* was one of the first novels to challenge openly the European's claim to being superior to the African.

In O.'s second novel, *Le vieux nègre et la médaille* (1956; *The Old Man and the Medal,* 1967), the satire is aimed not only at the whites but also at those blacks who fawn over and cringe before their masters. Meka, the old man of the title, is to be presented with a medal for his service to the administration. As naïve as Toundi, Meka is equally comical in his desire to impress his white superiors. His realization that he has been exploited also occurs late in the novel. Following the award ceremony, when Meka accidentally wanders into the white section of town, he finds himself suddenly imprisoned as a prowler and begins to rebel. He recognizes the meaninglessness of the sacrifices of his land to the Church mission and of his two sons, who died fighting in the French army. In the end Meka rejects European civilization and Christianity as he seeks to regain his original African identity.

O.'s third novel, *Chemin d'Europe* (1960; road to Europe) is his most ambitious. The subject is the many problems and frustrations a young native encounters when he seeks permission from the colonial authorities to study in Europe. *Chemin d'Europe* marks a departure from O.'s first two novels because it is sophisticated in tone and broader in scope. The protagonist, Aki Barnabas, is disillusioned and cynical from the start. He bitterly resents both Europeans who try to impose their culture upon Africans and those Africans who refuse to admit the need for change. Although skillfully written, this novel lacks the warmth, freshness, and humor of O.'s first two works.

O., committed to exposing the evils of colonialism, encouraged Africans to regain their native values. By blending humor with pathos, he awakens the reader to the oppression endured by blacks in the French African colonies just before those colonies gained their independence.

FURTHER WORK: *Le pandémonium* (c. 1971, unpublished)

BIBLIOGRAPHY: Diop, D., on *Une vie de boy* and *Le vieux nègre et la médaille, PA,* 11 (1956), 125–27; Moore, G., "F. O. and the Colonial Tragicomedy," *PA,* 18, 2 (1963), 61–73; Mercier, R., and Battestini, M. and S., *F.O.* (1964); Brench, A. C., *The Novelists' Inheritance in French Africa* (1967), pp. 47–63; Makward, E., Introduction to *Boy!* (1970), pp. v–xvi; Linneman, R., "The Anticolonialism of F. O.," *YFS,* 53 (1976), 64–77; Storzer, G. H., "Narrative Techniques and Social Realities in F. O.'s *Une vie de boy* and *Le vieux nègre et la médaille,*" *Crit,* 19, 3 (1978), 89–101

DEBRA POPKIN

CAPE VERDEAN LITERATURE

Claridade, a cultural journal published sporadically from 1936 to 1960, and the so-called *Claridade* movement owe their existence to a unique set of historical circumstances at work in the Cape Verde islands since their discovery. The ten main islands, lying some 350 miles off the coast of Senegal, became inhabited only after the Portuguese happened on them in the 15th c. Slaves from the nearby Guinea coast, plantation owners, administrators, and not a few Portuguese convicts lived in a close if socially stratified proximity that over the centuries worked to bring about biological and cultural creolization. Thus, in the 1930s, two decades before anything similar would occur elsewhere in Portugal's then colonies, members of the largely mestizo (mixed race) bourgeoisie began to produce poems and stories that qualify as the beginnings of a characteristic, uniquely Cape Verdean literature.

Jorge Barbosa (1901–1971), one of the first major island poets, established a style and tone for Cape Verdean writers with the collection *Arquipélago* (1935; Archipelago); its nostalgia and tropical melancholy reflect the solitude of the forgotten archipelago, and the poems romanticize the common people as stoically resigned to their fate on the drought-stricken islands.

Under the pseudonym Oswaldo Alcântara, Baltasar Lopes da Silva (b. 1907) has written poems in which he combines popular themes and the techniques of Portuguese "art" poetry. Under the shortened name Baltasar Lopes he produced *Chiquinho* (1947; Chiquinho); one of Portuguese Africa's earliest and most important novels. As a Romance philologist, he made an early contribution to the elevation of Cape Verde's Portuguese-based Creole language. Since the 19th c., Creole, while essentially the language of the common people, has been cultivated as a vernacular in all strata of society. By describing the language as merely an archaic dialect of Portuguese, intellectuals like Silva hoped to erase its pidgin stigma.

Manuel Lopes (b. 1907), although also a poet, is best known for his powerful social novels, *Chuva braba* (1956; wild rain) and *Os flagelados do vento leste* (1960; victims of the east wind).

In 1952, Amílcar Cabral (1924–1973), founder of the African Party of the Independence of Guinea and Cape Verde, called for a new literature, one that did not merely lament human suffering and accept the islands' problems with a faith in the people's capacity to survive while celebrating their Creole uniqueness, but a literature that identified with the Cape Verdean on the level of intervening to bring about change. Many young writers heeded Cabral's plea, and in 1962 Ovídio Martins's (b. 1928) "Anti-Evasão" (antievasion) raised a poetic call for the nonavoidance of Cape Verde's endemic social, economic, and political problems. Martins was joined by other militant poets like Gabriel Mariano (b. 1928) and Onésimo Silveira (b. 1937).

After the military coup that overthrew Portugal's right-wing dictatorship (April 24, 1974) and paved the way for independence, which came on July 5, 1975, dozens of patriotic poems were published by Cape Verdeans at home and in the immigrant communities of Europe and the Americas. Seasoned poets, like Oswaldo Osório (b. 1937), Arménio Vieira (b. 1941), and Tacalhe (pseud. of Alírio Silva, b. 1943), produced verse in praise of the new nation. As a kind of cultural and national affirmation, some poets turned to the use of a virile, defiant Creole language that had been first used by Kaoberdiano Dambara (pseud. of Felisberto Vieira Lopes, b. 1936?) in *Noti* (1968?; night), a book of protest poems tinged with the images of Negritude (q.v.).

In the late 1970s and early 1980s the literary scene in Cape Verde could best be described as at an impasse, and at worst as in crisis. Writers are struggling with the problem of little time to write as they join in the effort to build a new nation on top of the shambles of centuries of colonialism. Kwame Kondé, the defiant Creole pseudonym of Dr. Francisco Fragoso (b. 1940?), made a gallant but not totally successful attempt to launch a national Cape Verdean theater based on popular themes and agit-prop productions. João Varela (b. 1937), who had published hermetic poems in the tradition of European metaphysics, adopted the Creole pseudonym Timóteo Tio Tiofe to produce his *O primeiro livro de Notcha* (1975; Notcha's first book), an epiclike poem that seeks to mediate between European values and an African Cape Verdean historicity. Corsino Fortes (b. 1933), even before independence, wrote *Pão & fonema* (1974; bread & phoneme), also an epiclike attempt to place Cape Verde into the course of African and world history.

Despite the impasse, there are other promising signs. With the founding in 1977 of *Raizes,* a cultural and literary journal, members of several generations of Cape Verdean intellectuals have made a valiant attempt to lay the basis of a new literary movement. Henrique Teixeira de Sousa (b. 1926?), published *Ilhéu de Contenda* (1978; Ilhéu de Contenda), a novelistic saga that has whetted the appetites of younger Cape Verdeans eager to retell the history of their islands. Finally, Creole's newfound prestige as a national language has upgraded its use as a literary language and has already resulted in a play, *Descarado* (1979; the brazen man), by Donaldo Pereira Macedo (b. 1950), who immigrated to the U.S. in the mid-1960s, and whose new Cape Verdean theater has captured enthusiastic audiences in the Boston area.

BIBLIOGRAPHY: Araujo, N., *A Study of Cape Verdean Literature* (1966); Gérard, A. S., "The Literature of Cape Verde," *African Arts*, 1, 2 (1968), 66–70; Moser, G. M., "How African Is the African Literature Written in Portuguese?," *RNL*, 1, 2 (1971), 148–66; Hamilton, R. G., *Voices from an Empire: A History of Afro-Portuguese Literature* (1975), pp. 231–357; Hamilton, R. G., "Cape Verdean Poetry and the PAIGC," in Priebe, R. O., and Hale, T. A., eds., *Artist and Audience: African Literature as a Shared Experience* (1979), pp. 103–25; Hamilton, R. G., "Amílcar Cabral and Cape Verdean Poetry," *WLT*, 53 (1979), 49–54

RUSSELL G. HAMILTON

CONGOLESE LITERATURE

On August 15, 1960, after more than half a century of French colonial rule, the People's Republic of the Congo (Congo-Brazzaville) achieved independence. Although France generally encouraged a policy of cultural assimilation in its colonies, urging the native populations to adopt the French language and customs, it never did so in Equatorial Africa, of which the Congo (Middle Congo) was part. French education rarely extended beyond elementary school in this region, and Congolese were allowed to preserve their own indigenous traditions. Following World War II French political and social reforms in the African colonies contributed to a growing political consciousness. Yet when France left the Middle Congo, there was no true sense of national unity; political parties reflected ancient tribal rivalries. Moreover, the educated elite was a very small minority, and a middle class did not exist.

Although French is the official language of government and education in the nation today, only a small percentage of the African population can use it efficiently. All the ethnic groups in the Congo Republic except the Binga pygmies belong to the Bantu-speaking population of tropical Africa. There are four principal ethnic divisions: the Kongo, the Teke, the Mboshi, and the Sangha. To facilitate communication among more than seventy subgroups, two trade languages developed. Lingala is spoken in the region north of Brazzaville, and Monokutuba between Brazzaville and the Atlantic coast.

In a country in which ethnic groups have retained their own cultural traditions and European influence has been minimal, the oral tradition has continued to thrive. The art of storytelling plays an important role in community life. Oral historians and storytellers instruct the children in their history, family traditions, and social values. Often animals symbolize human beings and their characteristics. Gods and ancestors appear in tales as well, particularly in creation myths.

The Congolese were first taught to read and write in missionary schools. By the 1970s a number of Congolese were producing imaginative works in French. Jean Malonga (b. 1907), Guy Menga (b. 1940), Martial Sinda (b. 1930), and Tchicaya U Tam'si (b. 1931) are the best known.

Malonga has published *La légende de M'Pfoumou ma Mazona* (1954; the legend of M'Pfoumou ma Mazona) and *Cœur d'Aryenne* (1955;

Aryenne's heart). The first is a romantic tale of an African princess who moves from sin to salvation. The second is more a sociological than a literary work, which deals with the theme of racial prejudice.

Guy Menga, a dramatist and novelist, has written the plays *La marmite de Koko-Mbala* (1966; the pot of Koko-Mbala) and *L'oracle* (1969; the oracle). The latter won the Grand Prize of the Inter-African Theater Competition in Paris in 1968. His novel *La palabre sterile* (1968; worthless palaver) concerns the experiences of a young man who leaves his village for the city just prior to the country's independence.

Martial Sinda was one of the first Congolese poets to be published. *Premier chant de départ* (first song of departure) appeared in 1955.

The figure who dominates Congolese literature is Tchicaya U Tam'si. He left the Congo as an adolescent when his father was named a deputy to the French National Assembly. Thus, U Tam'si had a French secondary education in Paris. He has published six volumes of poetry to date: *Le mauvais sang* (1955; bad blood), *Feu de brosse* (1957; *Brushfire*, 1964), *À triche-coeur* (1960; a game of cheat-heart), *Epitomé* (1962; summary of a passion), *Le ventre* (1964; the belly), and *L'arc musical* (1970; bow harp). His poetry—highly symbolic, surrealistic, charged with emotion—expresses the tension felt by a man caught between two worlds, someone who has experienced an African childhood and who sees himself in exile in Europe. Like so many African writers, U Tam'si is in search of his identity. He expresses his own personal anguish and that of the uprooted African. Yet he does not speak for the majority of Congolese, who live within a traditional framework, one in which the spoken word is vibrant and still more meaningful than the written word.

BIBLIOGRAPHY: Gleason, J., *This Africa: Novels by West Africans in English and French* (1965); Beier, U., *Introduction to African Literature* (1967); Brench, A. C., *The Novelists' Inheritance in French Africa: Writers from Senegal to Cameroon* (1967); Brench, A. C., *Writings in French from Senegal to Cameroon* (1967); Larson, C., *The Emergence of African Fiction* (1972); Blair, D. S., *African Literature in French* (1976)

MILDRED MORTIMER

EGYPTIAN LITERATURE

As with other literary traditions within the Arab world, modern Egyptian literature is the product of two major forces: the revival of the great Arabic heritage of the past and the influence of modernization through contact with Europe and America. The force of the impact between these two phenomena varied considerably according to time and place. In the case of Egypt, the process was abrupt, resulting from Napoleon's invasion in 1798. This military incursion served both to rid Egypt of its Mamlūk rulers and to expose its intellectual leaders to European thought. The process was further stimulated after 1860 by the arrival of numerous writers from Syria, where civil war had forced many Christian families to flee to Europe and the Americas as well as to Egypt. Many members of those families had already been involved in the revival of interest in the Arabic language and its literature. These and other Syrians were now to join Egyptian writers in making major contributions to the emergence of an indigenous modern Arabic literature in Egypt and of the press (which has always been and remains the principal means of propagating literature in Egypt).

At the turn of the century, the prevalence of the "traditional" or the "modern" varied according to genre. It is hardly surprising that poetry, by far the most prevalent medium of literary expression in the "classical" period, should have produced a modern neoclassical revival, the more conservative proponents of which carefully watched and often vigorously resisted attempts at change well into the 1950s. Pride of place as pioneer in this movement must go to Mahmūd Sāmī al-Bārūdī (1839–1904), while the patriotic fervor and violent attacks on the British occupying forces guaranteed Hāfiz Ibrāhīm (1871–1932) a warm place in Egyptian hearts. However, it is Ahmad Shawqī (1868–1932) who is undoubtedly the greatest poet of the period. While some commentators have rightly drawn attention to glimmerings of a more individual vision that can occasionally be seen in poems of these and other poets like them, it remains true that the vast bulk of their writings are occasional verse *(shi'r al-munāsabāt),* a fact that elicited the wrath of later critics.

While both fiction and drama may have had precedents of one kind or another in the earlier tradition of Arabic literature, the beginnings of both genres in the modern period point to their derivative origins in the West. While poets were imitating the stentorian tones of earlier exemplars, pioneers in fiction and drama translated and imitated European models, before attempting their own creative offerings. 'Uthmān Jalāl (1828–1898) translated some of Molière's plays into colloquial Egyptian. An Egyptian Jew, Ya'qūb Sanū' (1839–1912), began to write a series of satirical playlets poking fun at the aristocracy and the Khedive Ismā'īl (ruled 1863–79). Drama at this time was very much a "popular" phenomenon, with much melodrama, and singing and dancing almost as a *sine qua non*. The tradition was carried on into this century by Najīb al-Rīhanī (1891–1949), who followed Sanū''s example by writing comedies that poked fun at the foibles of various segments of society.

The rise of fiction is closely associated with the rapid expansion of the press in the 1880s and 1890s. Newspapers would regularly publish stories and novels in serial form. It was in this way that Jurjī Zaydān (1861–1914) published a whole series of historical novels dealing with Islamic history; these had a plainly educational purpose, but were "spiced" with local interest and romance so as to make them at least somewhat similar to the love, murder, and intrigue narratives that characterized other fictional writings of the era. Equally educational but more topical was Muhammad al-Muwaylihī's (1868–1930) *Hadīth 'Īsā ibn Hishām* (1898–1902; *Hadīth 'Īsa ibn Hishām*, 1974), which provided a marvelous exposé of the many faults of Egyptian society and its institutions under British administration. More straightforward in both style and sentiment were the series of essays on a variety of topics by Mustafā Lutfī al-Manfalūtī (1876–1924), which have remained popular among adolescents for many decades.

These writers and others were to carry out the vital tasks of adapting the older tradition to the needs of modern times, of experimenting with new genres, and of applying new language to the older genres. All this was an essential preliminary to the emergence of an indigenous tradition of modern Egyptian literature.

Poetry

In 1908 Khalīl Mutrān (1872–1949), known as the "poet of the two countries" (Lebanon and Egypt), published a collection of poetry, *Dīwān al-Khalīl* (the diwan of al-Khalīl) with an important introduction, in which he stated that the poet should be able to express his own feelings and urged poets to devote more attention to the unity of their compositions. While some of his poems show signs of such precepts of romanticism, the bulk of Mutrān's poetry was as occasional as that of

Ahmad Shawqī and Hāfiz Ibrāhīm. The real motivating force toward romanticism was the émigré school in the Americas, where a group of poets experimented with form, language, and mood in surroundings essentially detached from the forces of conservatism that were so strong in the Middle East. In Egypt the advocacy of romanticism fell to the so-called "Diwan" school of poets, 'Abbās Mahmūd al-'Aqqād (1889–1964), Ibrāhīm al-Māzinī (1890–1949), and 'Abd al-Rahmān Shukrī (1886–1958), all of whom were strongly influenced by the English romantic poets and critics such as William Hazlitt (1778–1830). Of the three, Shukrī was the greatest poet, while the other two had more influence at the time through their critical writings, which appeared in a volume called *Al-Dīwān* (1921; the diwan). This work contained iconoclastic attacks on Shawqī for his occasional versifying and on al-Manfalūtī for his morbid sentimentality, but more vicious and destructive was al-Māzinī's attack on Shukrī himself, something that had a profound effect on the poet.

In the 1930s a new school of romantic poets emerged who took their name from the magazine *Apollo*, published under the aegis of Ahmad Zakī Abū Shādī (1892–1955). He and other poets like Ibrāhīm Nājī (1893–1953) and 'Alī Mahmūd Tāhā (1902–1949) introduced poetry of a new sensibility to Egypt, particularly during the 1930s. While Abū Shādī wrote a vast amount of poetry and Nājī also wrote a great deal, mainly about unrequited love, Tāhā is probably the most enduring poet of the group.

In a collection called *Plutoland* (1947; Plutoland) the litterateur and critic Lewis 'Awad (b. 1915), who terms the poetry of the romantics *"mal de siècle* poetry," made what some critics consider to be the first attempts at writing free verse; the earliest poem dates from the late 1930s. If this is so, he predates by almost a decade the efforts of Nāzik al-Malā'ika (b. 1923) and Badr Shākir al-Sayyāb (q.v.) in Iraq. At any rate, Egyptian poets have, since the end of World War II, joined their colleagues in other Arab countries in writing poetry outside the dictates of the classical metrical system, ranging from poems using some of the traditional feet in different combinations, to free verse and the prose poem.

The most famous of these poets is Salāh 'Abd al-Sabūr (1931–1981); his first collection, *Al-Nāsu fī bilādī* (1957; the people in my country), displays considerable commitment to the ideals of the emerging revolutionary society, with its realistic descriptions of life (as in the title poem). During the 1960s this vigorous posture changed to a more personal, melancholy vision. One of 'Abd al-Sabūr's most successful works is the verse play *Ma'sāt al-Hallāj* (1966; *Murder in Baghdad,* 1972), which recounts the story of the crucifixion of a medieval Islamic mystic with considerable skill and impact and with a not too covert contemporary import. Other poets have also made contributions to this genre: the yet more committed 'Abd al-Rahmān al-Sharqāwī (b. 1920), with such plays as *Ma'sāt Jamīla* (1962; the tragedy of Jamīla) and *Tha'r Allāh* (1969; God's revenge); and the very Brechtian contributions of Najīb Surūr (?– 197?) in the form of elongated poetic tableaux drawing their inspiration from popular tales of Egypt, such as *Yāsīn wa Bahiyya* (1963; Yāsīn and Bahiyya). Another Egyptian poet whose writings continue to capture the imagination of readers throughout the Arab world is Ahmad 'Abd al-Mu'tī Hijāzī (b. 1935), who, having come to the modern metropolis after a village childhood, depicted the depersonalization and crushing anonymity of the big city, as, for example, in *Madīna bilā qalb* (1959; heartless city). Thereafter, his poetry became more concerned with the cause of commitment to the Egyptian revolution and its leader, Jamāl 'Abd al-Nāsir (Gamal Abdel Nasser).

While Egyptian poetry has tended to stand apart from the more conspicuous attempts at innovation, such as those of Adūnīs in Lebanon, in recent times a small group of younger poets in Egypt has been experimenting with new forms and new language; among these we should mention Amal Dunqul (b. 1940) and Muhammad Abū Sinna (b. 1937). It remains generally true, however, that, in the Egypt of the early 1980s, poetry no longer commands the public attention it has traditionally held since the beginnings of Arabic literature. Its position as the preeminent genre has been taken over by fiction, particularly short fiction.

Fiction

The first work of fiction in Egypt that had any pretentions of depicting contemporary reality was the novel *Zaynab* (1913; Zaynab) by Muhammad Husayn Haykal (1888–1956), written in France and published under a pseudonym. By the time of the second edition of this work (1929), a whole school of Egyptian writers had begun producing short stories. It was between 1910 and 1920 that attempts had first been made to emulate the European short story, and especially those of France and Russia. The early efforts of Muhammad Taymūr (1892–1921) were followed by stories by his brother Mahmūd Taymūr (b. 1894), by one of

Egypt's major contributors to this genre, Maḥmūd Ṭāhir Lāshīn (1894–1954), by Yaḥyā Ḥaqqī (b. 1905), and by others. The efforts of this "new school" during the 1920s, as well as the great impact of the first volume of Ṭāhā Ḥusayn's (q.v.) *Al-Ayyām* (3 vols., 1925, 1939, 1967; *An Egyptian Childhood,* 1932; *The Stream of Days,* 1948; *A Passage to France,* 1976), fostered an increasing interest in fiction.

The 1930s saw tremendous activity in this genre. It began with a competition in novel writing, which was won by Ibrāhīm al-Māzinī with *Ibrāhīm al-kātib* (1931; *Ibrahim the Author,* 1976), which, in spite of the author's denials, seems to be an autobiographical piece. A major advance in the use of dialogue in the novel was achieved by Tawfīq al-Ḥakīm (q.v.) in his *'Awdat al-rūḥ* (1933; the return of the spirit), the first part of which gives a lively portrayal of a group of Egyptian characters within a limited environment. The psychological dimension is investigated by 'Abbās Maḥmūd al-'Aqqād in his *Sāra* (1938; *Sara,* 1978) to a degree which robs it of some of its artistic appeal but which was to serve as a model for later novelists. These and other experiments served to develop the different facets of this complex genre; the writers of the next generation were able to proceed on the basis of the successes and failures of their predecessors.

At the end of the 1930s there emerged the figure who has dominated Egyptian fiction for the last two decades, Najīb Maḥfūẓ (q.v.). With his series of novels set in the old quarters of Cairo, written in the 1940s and early 1950s, the Egyptian novel may be said to have achieved its full maturity. To a tremendous skill in construction is added great attention to detail, a clear, straightforward style typical of a well-read civil servant (his career until his retirement in 1971), and an underlying social-realist purpose of showing the gradual breakdown of the societal fabric in Egypt as mirrored in the antagonisms and violence preceding the revolution of 1952. By April of that year, he had completed his monumental *Al-Thulāthiyya* (1956–57; the trilogy), a trilogy tracing an Egyptian family through three generations, with a sweep worthy of a Galsworthy. During the 1960s, Maḥfūẓ produced a further set of novels of which *Al-Liss wa al-kilāb* (1961; the thief and the dogs) and *Tharthara fawq al-Nīl* (1966; chatter on the Nile) are probably the best. These concentrate more than his earlier works on the individual within society and his sense of alienation. After the debacle of the Six Day War in June 1967, he expressed his views in lengthy short stories and even a few plays, before returning to the novel during the 1970s.

In the realm of the short story, Yūsuf Idrīs (q.v.) has shown a particular talent. His works not only display a clear development in technique and themes, but also an adventurous attitude toward the use of language. Mahfūz's language tends to be relatively uncomplicated, even to the point of being occasionally colorless. Idrīs, on the other hand, sprinkles his style with colloquialisms and unorthodox syntax, which lend to his stories an attractive element of liveliness and innovation.

While Mahfūz and Idrīs have dominated Egyptian fiction, there are a number of other excellent writers of their generation. The novels of al-Sharqāwī, especially *Al-Ard* (1954; *Egyptian Earth*, 1962), present a realistic and obviously committed view of the Egyptian peasant. Fathī Ghānim (b. 1924) has written several fine novels such as *Al-Rajul alladhī faqada zillahu* (1960; *The Man Who Lost His Shadow*, 1962) and *Al-Jabal* (1957; the mountain). In the realm of the short story, Edward al-Kharrāt (b. 1926) and Yūsuf al-Shārūnī (b. 1924) both write with intense meticulousness.

Egyptian writers reacted with varying degrees of fury, sorrow, and contemplation to the events of June 1967. A younger generation of writers, who emerged in the 1960s, expressed these feelings with particular clarity. These younger writers have in many ways found their path blocked, not only by the tremendous popularity of the writers of older generations, who, with a few exceptions, have kept a hold on most of the positions of influence within the cultural sector, but also as a result of the cultural policies of the Sādāt government, which tended to offer publication opportunities in Egypt only to writers who were prepared to tolerate—or, at least, not express opposition to—the political and social status quo. Writing fiction has never been a full-time occupation in Egypt, and that is certainly more true today than ever before. Many of the younger authors do their writing in their spare time, and, with this in mind, the quality of work produced by such short-story writers as Majīd Tūbiyā (b. 1938) and Yahyā al-Tāhir 'Abdallāh (1942–1980) and novelists like 'Abd al-Hakīm Qāsim (b. 1935) and Jamāl al-Ghītānī (b. 1945?) is remarkable. The late 1970s offered signs of the revival of a vigorous fictional tradition.

Drama

The dramatic tradition in Egypt traces its origins back to the 19th c., although some critics find precedents of one kind or another in still earlier works of belles lettres or folk literature. The popular theater began with the works of Ya'qūb Sanū' and was carried on into this century by

Najīb al-Rīhānī. This tradition has continued with undiminished vigor to the present day, and its success can be attributed not only to the popular predilection for farce but also to its unabashed use of the colloquial language, which appeals to the broadest spectrum of society.

The development of "literary" or "serious" drama has been dogged by two issues. The first is the initial association of the genre with music and singing; the historical verse dramas of Ahmad Shawqī, which contain much fine poetry, have been preserved and even revived on the basis of certain songs that were made extremely popular by famous singers. The second issue is the much discussed question of language: particularly to conservative critics, anything not composed in the written language was not literature, whereas to practitioners of the drama, plays not in the spoken language were restricted in their possible themes and extremely difficult to act. It has been the great contribution of Tawfīq al-Hakīm to raise the status of the genre and provide it with plays of more stimulating intellectual content. To critics like Tāhā Husayn, al-Hakīm's first lengthy play, *Ahl al-kahf* (1933; *The People of the Cave*, 1971) is a major monument in the history of Arabic literature. Al-Hakīm has followed it with a whole series of similar intellectual plays, the latest of which is *Al-Sultān al-hā'ir* (1960; *The Sultan's Dilemma*, 1973). All these plays have proved difficult, if not impossible, to stage effectively, a fact that has led several commentators, al-Hakīm included, to retreat to a position that claims them as "plays to be read." Al-Hakīm has also produced a huge number of short plays, on social and political issues.

The revolution of 1952 saw the beginning of the two most productive decades in the history of Egyptian drama. A new generation of playwrights emerged who made sigificant innovations in both language and form. In a whole series of works, Nu'mān 'Āshūr (dates n.a.) brilliantly captured the combination of dynamism and uncertainty following the revolution at all levels of society within the new political structure and exposed many of the inherent problems by showing the clash of generations. In the 1960s Sa'd al-dīn Wahba (dates n.a.) began by describing society in realistic terms, although he concentrated initially on the countryside. Later, in plays such as *Kubrī al-nāmūs* (1964; mosquito bridge) and *Sikkat al-salāma* (1965; road to safety), a more symbolic trend can be seen. In two of his most recent works, *Al-Masāmīr* (1967; the nails) and *Sab' sawāqī* (1969; seven waterwheels), he discusses the implications of 1967 with a bitter frankness that led to the banning of the latter play.

Alfred Faraj (dates n.a.) drew the inspiration for his comments on the present from history and the folktale; his plays on historical subjects include *Sulaymān al-Halabī* (1965; Sulaymān from Aleppo) and *Al-Zīr Salīm* (1967; Prince Salim). From the famous *1001 Nights* Faraj took themes for two of his best and most popular works, *Hallāq Baghdād* (1964; the barber of Baghdad) and *'Ali Janāh al-Tibrīzi wa tābi'uhu Qufa* (1969; 'Alī Janāh from Tabriz and Qufa his henchman). Among the most important of Faraj's contributions is the use of the literary language in a way that permitted effective stage productions.

A number of other plays were performed with great success in the 1960s: Mahmūd Diyāb's (b. 1932) *Al-Zawba'a* (1964; *The Storm*, 1967); Rashād Rushdī's (b. 1915) *Rihla khārij al-sūr* (1963; *Journey outside the Wall*, 1974), with its heavy symbolism; Yūsuf Idrīs's *Al-Farāfīr* (1964; *The Farfoors*, 1974; also tr. as *Flipflap and His Master*, 1977), with its combination of folklore, slapstick, and the absurd.

The drama, being the most public of all literary genres, has in recent years been particularly subject to the vicissitudes of politics and cultural policy. The term "theater crisis" has become a stock phrase of the majority of commentators on the drama, and the forced or unforced absence from the country of a number of critics and directors, and the reticence of several prominent dramatists mentioned above suggests that the present cultural milieu will need to change before we may see a revival of the dynamic tradition of earlier decades.

Criticism

As is the case with the literature itself, the early criticism of the modern period harks back to the classical ideals, as is clearly seen in the writing of Husayn al-Marsafī (?–1889) and the celebrated criticism on the poet Ahmad Shawqī written by Muhammad al-Muwaylihī in 1898. The first signs of change can be seen in the writings of the Dīwan school. Al-'Aqqād, the most prominent critic in the group, was one of a select number of writers who contributed to the development of literary sensibilities and critical taste in Egypt during the first half of this century. Particular mention should be made of Tāhā Husayn, whose iconoclastic work *Fī al-shi'r al-jāhilī* (1926; on pre-Islamic poetry) was among the first to apply the objective principles of literary criticism to the earliest examples of Arabic literature; Muhammad Husayn Haykal, whose advocacy of objectivity in criticism and of the concept of national literature did much to foster a particularly Egyptian identity during the 1920s and 1930s; and Muhammad Mandūr (1907–1965), a disciple of Tāhā Husayn, whose brilliant studies of both literature and literary criticism were to lay the foundation for the emergence of a number of critics still writing today.

In the aftermath of World War II, 'Abd al-Azīm Anīs (dates n.a.) and Mahmūd Amīn al-'Ālim (dates n.a.) produced a famous work of criticism, *Fī al-thaqāfa al-Misriyya* (1955; on Egyptian culture), in which they advocated the need for commitment in literature. This book started a fierce debate among literary scholars, including Tāhā Husayn, who vigorously opposed this notion. During the 1950s and into the 1960s al-'Ālim remained a very prominent figure in Egyptian criticism along with Lewis 'Awad, the cultural editor of *Al-Ahrām*. Other writers tended to concentrate on one particular aspect of literature: 'Alī al-Rā'ī (dates n.a.), Rajā' al-Naqqāsh (dates n.a.), and Bahā' Tāhir (dates n.a.), for example, tended to deal with the theater, 'Abd al-Muhsin Tāhā Badr (dates n.a.) and Sabrī Hāfiz (b. 1941?) concentrated more on fiction, and 'Izz al-dīn Ismā'īl (dates n.a.) turned his attention to a number of studies on literary theory from a variety of viewpoints.

It is an apt reflection on the current milieu in Egypt that the majority of its more famous and productive literary critics, such as Mahmūd Amīn al-'Ālim, Ghālī Shukrī (dates n.a.), 'Alī al-Ra'ī, and Lewis 'Awad (dismissed from his post at *Al-Ahrām*), no longer publish in their homeland. A number of younger writers have made themselves known to a wide audience, but they suffer, along with their colleagues, from a lack of sponsorship and a dearth of criticism. It is to be hoped that their talents will not be stunted by the present difficult circumstances but that they will prove to be the vanguard of a new generation.

BIBLIOGRAPHY: Sakkut, H., *The Egyptian Novel and Its Main Trends 1913–1952* (1971); Kilpatrick, H., *The Modern Egyptian Novel* (1974); Semah, D., *Four Egyptian Literary Critics* (1974); Badawi, M., *A Critical Introduction to Modern Arabic Poetry* (1975), passim; Hafiz, S., "Innovation in the Egyptian Short Story," in Ostle, R. C., ed., *Studies in Modern Arabic Literature* (1975), pp. 99–113; Hafiz, S., "The Egyptian Novel in the Sixties," *JArabL*, 7 (1976), 68–84; Allen, R., "Egyptian Drama and Fiction in the 1970s," *Edebiyat*, 1 (1976), 219–33; al-Jayyusi, S., *Trends and Movements in Modern Arabic Poetry* (1977), passim; Allen, R., "Egyptian Drama after the Revolution," *Edebiyat*, 4 (1979), 97–134

ROGER ALLEN

al-HAKĪM, Tawfīq
Egyptian dramatist, novelist, and short-story writer, b. 9 Oct. 1898 (or 1902?), Alexandria

After graduating as a lawyer in Cairo, H. was sent by his father to Paris in 1925 to continue his legal studies and submit a doctoral thesis. Instead of devoting his energies to his studies, however, he was strongly attracted to the theater and deeply influenced by Shaw, Pirandello, and Ibsen, whose plays he read or saw. In 1928 he returned to Egypt without a doctorate, but with the skill and inspiration of a promising writer.

Although he had written some music-hall plays before leaving for France, H. came into prominence only after publishing his first novel, *'Awdat al-rūh* (1933; the return of the spirit), in which he tried to describe and account for the sudden awakening of nationalist feelings that led to the 1919 revolution. In this novel, which is in part based on H.'s own experiences, a symbolic layer is superimposed on the essentially realistic, day-to-day story. *'Awdat al-rūh* was meant to be a literary expression of the then-popular notion according to which Egypt has always retained a distinctive national and cultural identity.

Yawmiyyāt nā'ib fī al-aryāf (1937; *The Maze of Justice*, 1947) is a distinctive novel written in the form of diary and draws on H.'s personal experience as a public prosecutor in provincial towns. Autobiographical material is also found in his novel *'Usfūr min al-sharq* (1938; *A Bird from the East*, 1966), which depicts the emotional and intellectual reactions of an Easterner in his first encounter with the West. In spite of the personal material in these three novels, however, H. has repeatedly warned literary critics not to take them as autobiographical documents. Like all novels, he insists, they are fictional works of art and should, therefore, be read as such.

His fame as a novelist notwithstanding, it is in the realm of drama that H.'s talent is best manifested. He wrote scores of social plays and playlets in which the dialogue, often in colloquial Arabic, is full of wit and dramatic tension. But H. is at his best in intellectual plays, which he introduced into Arabic literature. As dramas of ideas, they ought to be considered in the light of H.'s world outlook. Man, he believes, is constantly at war with forces stronger than himself. In his perseverance lurk the secret of his greatness and the source of his tragedy. The heroes of *Ahl al-kahf* (1933; *The People of the Cave*, 1971), which is based on the Koranic version of the Christian legend of the Seven Sleepers of Ephesus, are engaged in a hopeless struggle against time, whereas

Shahriyār, the hero of his *Shahrazād* (1934; Scheherazade) aspires to free himself from the confinements of space.

H.'s tragic heroes are also subject to an inner conflict between various dualisms, such as life and art, as in his play *Pygmalion* (1942; Pygmalion), or strength and wisdom, as in *Sulaymān al-hakīm* (1943; Solomon the wise).

H. also wrote a number of experimental plays. In *Yā tāli' al-shajara* (1962; *The Tree-Climber*, 1966), he borrows some of the devices employed by the dramatists of the Theater of the Absurd (q.v.), although he does not share their sense of loss and despair: he still has faith in a meaningful and well-ordered universe. A play within a play is found in *Al-Ta'ām li-kull fam* (1963; food for every mouth), in which the characters in the outer play undergo exhilarating experiences under the impact of what happens in the inner one. In *Bank al-qalaq* (1967; the bank of anxiety), which is set against the political background of 1960s Egypt, the dramatic episodes are interspersed with narrative ones.

Although H. is often referred to as an artist shut up in his ivory tower, his literary production displays an acute awareness of Egypt's cultural and social problems, as well as deep concern over the present situation of mankind.

FURTHER WORKS: *Ahl al-Fann* (1934); *Muhammad* (1936); *Masrahiyyāt T. al-H.* (1937); *Al-Qasr al-mashūr* (1937); *Taht shams al-fikr* (1938); *'Ahd al-Shaytān* (1938); *Ash'ab* (1938); *Prāxā* (1939); *Rāqisat al-ma'bad* (1939); *Nashīd al-anshād* (1940); *Himār al-H.* (1940); *Sultān al-zalām* (1941); *Min al-burj al-'Ājī* (1941); *Taht al-misbāh al-akhdar* (1942); *Zahrat al-'umr* (1943); *Al-Ribāt al-muqaddas* (1944); *Shajarat al-hukm* (1945); *Himārī qāla lī* (1945); *Qisas T. al-H.* (1949); *Al-Malik Ūdīb* (1949); *Masrah al-mujtama'* (1950); *Fann al-adab* (1952); *'Adāla wa fann* (1953); *Arinī al-Lāh* (1953); *'Asā al-H.* (1954); *Ta'ammulāt fī al-Siyāsa* (1954); *Al-Aydī al-nā'ima* (1954); *Al-Ta'āduliyya* (1955); *Īzīs* (1955); *Al-Safqa* (1956); *Al-Masrah al-munawwa'* (1956); *Lu'bat al-mawt* (1957); *Ashwāk al-salām* (1957); *Rihla ilā al-ghad* (1957); *Adab al-hayāt* (1959); *Al-Sultān al-hā'ir* (1960; *The Sultan's Dilemma*, 1973); *Sijn al-'umr* (1964); *Rihlat al-rabī' wa al-Kharīf* (1964); *Shams al-nahar* (1965); *Laylat al-zifāf* (1966); *Māsir sarsār* (1966); *Al-Warta* (1966); *Qālabunā al-masrahī* (1967); *Qultu dhāt yawm* (1970); *Ahādīth ma'a T. al-H.* (1971); *T. al-H. yatahaddath* (1971); *Majlis al-'adl* (1972); *Thawrat al-shabāb* (1972); *Rāhib bayn nisā'* (1972); *Hadīth ma'a al-Kawkab* (1974); *Al-Dunyā riwāya hazliyya* (1974); *'Awdat al-wa'y* (1974); *Al-*

Hamīr (1975); Wathā'iq fī tarīq 'Awdat al-wa'y (1975); Safahāt min al-tārīkh al-adabī (1975); Mukhtār tafsīr al-Qurtubī (1977); Bayn al-fikr wa al-Fann (n.d.). FURTHER VOLUME IN ENGLISH: Plays, Prefaces, & Postscripts of T. al-H., Vol. I (1981)

BIBLIOGRAPHY: Landau, J. M., Studies in the Arab Theater and Cinema (1958), pp. 138–47; Long, C. W. R., "T. al-H. and the Arabic Theatre," MES, 5, 2 (1969), 69–74; Haywood, J., Modern Arabic Literature (1971), pp. 197–204, 219–34; Starkey, P., "Philosophical Themes in T. al-H.'s Drama," JArabL, 8 (1977), 136–52; Fontaine, J., Mort—Résurrection: Une lecture de T. al-H. (1978); Long, R., T. al-H.: Playwright of Egypt (1979)

DAVID SEMAH

HUSAYN, Tāhā

Egyptian novelist, short-story writer, critic, literary historian, and educator, b. 14 Nov. 1889, Maghāgha; d. 28 Oct. 1973, Cairo

H.'s loss of sight at a very early age had a deep effect on his life and his writing. In 1902 he went to Cairo and became a student at al-Azhar, Egypt's venerable institute of religious studies, but his disappointment with the traditional system of education brought him into conflict with his conservative teachers, At the newly established Egyptian University H. made his first acquaintance with modern scholarship. His thesis on the famous Arab poet Abī al-'Alā' al-Ma'arrī (973–1057), Dhīkrā Abī al-'Alā' (1915; the memory of Abī al-'Alā') earned him the first Ph.D. to be granted in Egypt. In France H. obtained from the Sorbonne his second Ph.D. for a dissertation on Ibn Khaldūn (d. 1406), the great Arab philosopher of history. Back home in 1919, he embarked on a university teaching career, and from 1950 to 1952 he was Minister of Education. He received honorary degrees from several European universities.

The publication of H.'s defiant book Fī al-shi'r al-jāhilī (1926; on pre-Islamic poetry), in which he claimed that the poetry attributed to the pre-Islamic period was forged in a later period and questioned some religious beliefs, placed him in the center of a public storm, and the teachers of al-Azhar accused him of heresy and tried to have him prosecuted. In retrospect, it is the intellectual courage displayed in his critical approach, rather than his actual conclusions, that earned H.'s study its prominent place in Arabic scholarship.

H. was a prolific writer whose output consists of six novels, as well as short stories, epigrams, and artistic paraphrasing of ancient Arabic poems. He also wrote books on Islamic history and Arabic literature, critical essays, translations of classical Greek and French plays, and innumerable journalistic articles on social and political topics.

H.'s autobiography, *Al-Ayyām* (3 vols., 1929, 1939, 1967; *An Egyptian Childhood,* 1932; *The Stream of Days,* 1943; *A Passage to France,* 1976), may be considered one of the finest works in modern Arabic literature. In addition to the insight it provides into the inner world of the blind youth, it sheds valuable light on Egyptian social and cultural life. The idiosyncratic style, which makes full use of the resources of the Arabic language, is extremely evocative. Its imagery shows that H.'s attitude toward people and things is determined by his reaction to the sounds they make rather than their appearance. This book, with its emotional appeal, helped mold the sensibilities of two generations of readers.

H.'s novel *Shajarat al-bu's* (1944; the tree of misery) depicts the life of a traditional family with great sympathy, whereas the short stories in *Al-Mu'adhdhabūn fī al-ard* (1949; the sufferers on earth) are symptomatic of growing resentment against social injustice prior to the 1952 revolution.

In his work as a literary historian and critic, a certain line of evolution is discernible. H. came to believe that criticism is an art, not a science. His book on the poet al-Mutanabbī (d. 965), *Ma'a al-Mutanabbī* (1936; with al-Mutanabbī), in which he laid greater emphasis on his personal taste, contrasts sharply with his earlier book on al-Ma'arrī, in which he tried to apply a rigid scientific method.

Although the Arabic cultural heritage ranked high in his esteem, H. was an admirer of Western civilization, and of French culture in particular. These meant for him not only material prosperity and scientific achievements, but also freedom of thought and respect for human rights. In his famous *Mustaqbal al-thaqāfa fī Misr* (1938; *The Future of Culture in Egypt,* 1954) he reiterated his adherence to the cause of Westernization, and exhorted the Egyptians to adapt themselves to the requirements of modern life.

An ardent lover of freedom, H. was opposed to a politically committed literature. His own writing, however, was motivated by a deep sense of mission and responsibility. His contribution, therefore, cannot be evaluated merely in terms of aesthetic excellence; it should also be taken in the context of the role he played in the emergence of a new culture.

During his lifetime H. gained general recognition as the most outstanding figure in modern Arabic literature.

FURTHER WORKS : *Étude analytique et critique de la philosophie sociale d'Ibn Khaldun* (1917); *Qādat al-fikr* (1925); *Hadīth al-arbi'ā'* (3 vols., 1925, 1926, 1945); *Fī al-Adab al-jāhilī* (1927); *Ma'a Abī al-'Alā' fī sijnihi* (1930); *Fī al-sayf* (1933); *Hāfiz wa Shawqī* (1933); *'Alā hāmish al-sīra* (3 vols., 1933, 1939, 1943); *Du'a' al-karawān* (1934); *Adīb* (1935); *Min ba'īd* (1935); *Min hadīth al-shi'r wa al-nathr* (1936); *Al-Qasr al-mashūr* (1937); *Al-Hubb al-dā'i'* (1942); *Ahlām Shahrazād* (1943); *Sawt Abī al-'Alā'* (1944); *Fusūl fī al-adab wa al-naqd* (1945); *Jannat al-shawk* (1945); *'Uthmān* (1947); *Rihlat al-rabi'* (1948); *Mir'āt al-damīr al-hadīth* (1949); *Al-Wa'd al-haqq* (1950); *Jannat al-hayawān* (1950); *Alwān* (1952); *Bayn bayn* (1952); *'Alī wa banūhu* (1953); *Khisām wa naqd* (1955); *Naqd wa islāh* (1956); *Ahādīth* (1957); *Min adabinā al-mu'āsir* (1958); *Mir'at al-Islām* (1959); *Min laghw al-sayf* (1959); *Al-Shaykhān* (1960); *Min laghw al-Sayf ilā jidd al-shitā'* (1961); *Khawātir* (1967); *Kalimāt* (1967); *Ma warā' al-nahr* (1976)

BIBLIOGRAPHY: Cachia, P., *T. H.: His Place in the Egyptian Literary Renaissance* (1956); Hourani, A., *Arabic Thought in the Liberal Age, 1798–1939* (1962), pp. 324–40; Semah, D., *Four Egyptian Literary Critics* (1974), pp. 109–50

DAVID SEMAH

IDRĪS, Yūsuf

Egyptian short-story writer, dramatist, and novelist, b. May 1927, al-Bayrūm

After a childhood spent in the Nile delta, I. came to Cairo to attend university. He studied medicine, and upon graduation (1951) became a medical inspector in the Department of Health. He had already been writing short stories for amusement as a student, and the requirements of his medical position that he visit the poorer quarters of Cairo served to strengthen and expand his innate ability to portray the living conditions of the poor in realistic detail. His first collection of short stories appeared in 1954 and was an instant success; between 1954 and 1958 he published five collections and three plays. His increasing fame as a writer led him to give up his medical career, and he has since worked as a full-time creative writer and journalist. During the 1970s he wrote relatively little, contenting himself with occasional articles for the newspaper *Al-Ahrām;* these pieces may not contain quite as much of the direct social and political criticism that made I. an enfant terrible earlier in his career and led to his imprisonment on more than one occasion, but they still succeed in penetrating to the core of the Egyptian character and in reflecting the concerns and aspirations of his fellow countrymen of all classes.

The short-story collections of the 1950s, beginning with *Arkhas layālī* (1954; the cheapest nights), describe in vivid and often gruesome detail the conditions of Egypt's poorest classes both in the towns and the countryside. In the majority of cases, the reader is introduced to the character within his surroundings and shown the routine of his life; little has changed by the end of the story. The title story of his first collection is typical. A man emerges from evening prayer in the mosque and has to wade through scores of children in order to proceed in any direction. He curses them and the hole in heaven through which they come. His mind is spinning because of a cup of strong tea he has been given. After despairing of finding any of his friends with whom he might spend the evening, he heads for home and makes love to his wife, if only to keep warm. In due time he is being congratulated yet again on the birth of a child. The way in which I., the doctor and short-story writer, projects the overwhelming problem of Egypt's birth rate with such force and clarity is exactly the quality that has made his works at once so popular and so important in the history of this genre.

During the 1960s I. began to write symbolic and surreal tales. Examples of these are "Al-Aurta" ("The Aorta," 1978) from *Lughat al-ay ay* (1965; the language of screams), a horrifying parable concerning the callousness of human beings spurred on by the herd instinct; "Alif al-ahrār" ("The Omitted Letter," 1978) from *Ākhir al-dunyā* (1961; the end of the world), an amusing yet poignant tale of bureaucratic man as victim; and "Mu'jizat al-'asr" (the wonder of the age) from *Al-Naddāha* (1969; the clarion). Another feature of I.'s recent writings has been a concern with the role of sex in society, explored, for example, in "Bayt min lahm" ("House of Flesh," 1978) from the collection *Bayt min lahm* (1971; house of flesh).

I.'s contributions to the novel and drama are also numerous, but, with a few notable exceptions, they tend to show a certain lack of affinity on the writer's part with longer genres. For example, by far his most successful play is *Al-Farāfīr* (1964; *The Farfoors,* 1974; also tr. as *Flipflap and His Master,* 1977), a brilliant attempt at combining elements of

Egyptian popular dramatic forms with the modern techniques of the Theater of the Absurd. Yet, the work suffers from an excess of padding and farce that lessens the total impact. Of I.'s novels, perhaps only *Al-Harām* (1959; the taboo), with its themes of moral hypocrisy among villagers faced with an annual visit of transhumants (people who move seasonally from one area to another in search of pasturage for their animals) avoids this same lack of cohesion or excessive concern with politics.

One of the most interesting aspects of I.'s craft is his style, which has reflected an adventurous spirit of growth during his career. When he began to publish his stories, I.'s language was criticized severely. Far from paying any attention to such views, I. has persisted in his distinctive style to such a degree that his most recent works are a blend of the written and spoken languages. I. himself admits that he writes in an impulsive fashion, and this may well account for his greater success in short stories than in other genres. As a short-story writer and as a brilliant and controversial innovator in language and form, I. is guaranteed a major place in the history of modern Arabic literature.

FURTHER WORKS: *Jumhūriyyat Farahāt* (1956); *Al-Batal* (1957); *A laysa kadhālika?* (1957); *Al-Lahza al-harija* (1957); *Hādithat sharaf* (1958); *Al-'Ayb* (1962); *Al-'Askarī al-aswad* (1962); *Al-Mahzala al-ardiyya* (1966); *Al-Mukhattatīn* (1969); *Al-Baydā'* (1970); *Al-Jins al-thālith* (1971). FURTHER VOLUMES IN ENGLISH: *In the Eye of the Beholder: Tales from Egyptian Life from the Writings of Y. I.* (1978); *The Cheapest Nights* (1978)

BIBLIOGRAPHY: Beyerl, J., *The Style of the Modern Arabic Short Story* (1971), passim; Cobham, C., "Sex and Society in Y. I.," *JArabL*, 6 (1975), 80–88; Somekh, S., "Language and Theme in the Short Stories of Y. I.," *JArabL*, 6 (1975), 89–100; Allen, R., Introduction to Y. I., *In the Eye of the Beholder* (1978), pp. vii–xxxix; Mikhail, M., *Images of Arab Women* (1979), pp. 77–89, 91–111

ROGER ALLEN

MAHFŪZ, Najib

Egyptian novelist and short-story writer, b. 11 Dec. 1911, Cairo

M. is the Arab world's most famous novelist, and he has also made contributions to the short story and drama. Born in Cairo, he has spent his entire life in Egypt, much of it as a civil servant within the cultural sector. At the University of Cairo M. studied philosophy, and it was while he was contemplating entering a graduate degree program that he began to write the series of short stories that appeared in his first collection, *Hams al-junūn* (1939; whisper of madness).

The stories in this earliest collection show clearly what has remained one of M.'s principal concerns: the individual and the question of the nature of the absurd. Following this volume however, M. pursued an earlier interest in the history of ancient Egypt by writing three novels set in that period and even made plans for a whole series of such works. It is the immense gain of the modern Arabic novel that he changed his mind and turned his attention to the circumstances of his own contemporaries within the older quarters of Cairo itself. The series of novels that appeared during the late 1940s and early 1950s demonstrated the maturity of the realistic novel in Arabic literature. This was a period of tremendous political unrest in Egypt, with terrorism and assassination being clear signs of the social turmoil preceding the revolution of 1952. M.'s novels succeed in capturing the atmosphere of these times, and no more brilliantly than in *Zuqāq al-Midaqq* (1947; *Midaq Alley,* 1966), *Al-Qāhira al-jadīda* (1946; modern Cairo), and *Bidāya wa nihāya* (1951?; beginning and end). This series of novels was to culminate in a huge project that took M. five years to complete, the monumental *Al-Thulāthiyya* (1956–57; the trilogy), consisting of three novels, *Bayn al-Qasrayn* (1956), *Qasr al-Shawq* (1956), and *Al-Sukkariyya* (1957), each named after a different quarter of Cairo. This huge work of over fifteen hundred pages presents three generations of the family of 'Abd al-Jawwād, seen during the period 1917–44. As the narrative moves from one part of Cairo to another, we witness through the infinite care and subtlety that M. applies to his task the way in which this family is a microcosm of the forces of change within Egyptian society as a whole.

M. has said that this work was completed just before the 1952 revolution, in which King Farouk was overthrown, and that he was uncertain about publishing it until the nature of the revolution itself was clearer. The publication of *Al-Thulāthiyya* brought him instant fame and the State Prize for Literature. In 1959 the newspaper *Al-Ahrām* serialized his most controversial work, *Awlād hāratinā (Children of Gebelawi,* 1981), which caused a sufficient outcry among the conservative religious establishment to prevent its publication in book form in Egypt (it was published in Lebanon in 1967). An allegory concerning the development of the great religions and man's attitude to them, it surveys the careers of Adam, Moses, Jesus, and Muhammad before posing in the fifth section the question of the relationship between science and religion, strongly implying that the former has destroyed the latter. While this work was satisfyingly controversial, it was not a success from a literary point of view: the level of allegory was too inconsistent and the major purpose of the entire work—to suggest that science might be the cause of the destruction of religion—was too obvious.

During the 1960s M. wrote another series of novels in which he is more concerned with the individual in society than he was in his earlier work. Descriptions are more economical than previously, the symbolism is more pronounced, and there is much use of interior monologue and stream of consciousness. Outstanding among these works are *Al-Liss wa al-kilāb* (1961; the thief and the dogs), with its scarcely veiled criticism of the fair-weather socialists and opportunists within society; and *Tharthara fawq al-Nīl* (1966; chatter on the Nile), in which a houseboat symbolizing Egypt itself is the setting for the meetings of a group of intellectuals and artists who have retreated from society because they feel that they have no role to play. The final novel in this series, *Mīrāmār* (1966; *Miramar,* 1978), is a yet franker exposé of corruption in the public sector of Egypt, but the kind of exploitation that M. describes seems insignificant in the wake of the circumstances surrounding the defeat by Israel in the 1967 Six-Day War.

Following this disaster, M. addressed himself to the issue of civic responsibility and the maintenance of values in a series of lengthy short stories, often cyclical in form, which were published in collections between 1967 and 1971. The publication of his novels had been interpersed previously with a few short-story collections, of which *Dunyā Allāh* (1963; God's world) and *Khamārat al-Qitt al-Aswad* (1968; Black Cat Tavern), contain some of the best examples of M.'s contributions to this genre.

In 1971 M. surveyed the course of his career and the intellectual life of Egypt in the first half of this century in a work entitled *Al-Marāyā* (1972; *Mirrors,* 1977), purportedly a series of fifty-five vignettes but actually a commentary on education, morals, religion, international relations, and a whole host of other topics. Since then, M. has written a number of other novels, of which the most famous, *Al-Karnak* (1974; Karnak Café), paints a gruesome picture of the methods of the secret police against various opposition groups during the 1960s.

M.'s style has changed relatively little during the course of his career, and his vocabulary is quite small in comparison with some other writers of fiction in the Arab world today. His mastery of the use of language to create scene and mood, more expansive in his realistic period, more economical and symbolic during the 1960s, is complete, and has allowed him to create some memorable pages of Arabic fiction. His total oeuvre is vast, and not all his works are of equal quality, particularly his more recent novels. When the history of 20th-c. Arabic fiction comes to be written, however, he will undoubtedly be regarded as the first Arab novelist to bring full mastery to the genre and to produce works of world stature.

FURTHER WORKS: *'Abath al-aqdār* (1939); *Radūbīs* (1943); *Kifāh Tībā* (1944); *Khān al-Khālīlī* (1946); *Al-Sarāb* (1948); *Al-Summān wa al-kharīf* (1962); *Al-Tarīq* (1964); *Bayt say' al-sum'a* (1965); *Al-Shahhādh* (1965); *Taht al-mazalla* (1969); *Hikāya bilā bidāya wa lā nihāya* (1969); *Shahr al-'asal* (1971); *Al-Hubb tahta al-matar* (1973); *Al-Jarīma* (1973); *Hikāyāt hāratinā* (1975); *Qalb al-layl* (1975); *Hadrat al-muhtaram* (1975); *Malhamat al-harāfīsh* (1977); *Al-Hubb fawqa hadbat al-haram* (1979); *Al-Shaytān ya'iz* (1979); *Afrāh al-qubba* (1980); *'Asr al-hubb* (1980); *Layālī alf layla* (1982); *Ra'aytu fīmā yarā al-nā'im* (1982).
FURTHER VOLUME IN ENGLISH: *God's World* (1973)

BIBLIOGRAPHY: Le Gassick, T., "The *Trilogy* of N. M.," *MEF,* 39, 2 (1963), 31–34; Milson, M., "N. M. and the Quest for Meaning," *Arabica,* 17 (1970), 177–86; Allen, R., "Mirrors by N. M.," *MW* 62, 2 (1972), 115–25, and 63, 1 (1973), 15–27; Somekh, S., *The Changing Rhythm: A Study of N. M.'s Novels* (1973); Sakkut, H., "N. M.'s Short Stories," and Le Gassick, T., "An Analysis of *Al-Hubb tahta al-matar,*" in Ostle, R. C., ed., *Studies in Modern Arabic Literature* (1975), pp. 114–25, 140–51; Milson, M., "Reality, Allegory and Myth in the Work of N. M.," *AAS,* 11 (1976), 157–79; Allen, R., "Some Recent Works of N. M.," *JARCE,* 14 (1977), 101–10; Allen, R. M. A., *The Arabic Novel: An Historical and Critical Introduction* (1982), pp. 55–62, 101–7

ROGER ALLEN

ETHIOPIAN LITERATURE

Ethiopia possesses a rich and ancient literary tradition, yet only in recent decades has a truly modern Ethiopian literature begun to evolve. This literature, unlike that of most African countries, has emerged under noncolonial conditions, and thus is not a literature of protest against foreign domination. Instead it has drawn heavily upon centuries of religious and moral writings in Ge'ez, the old Ethiopic literary language which still survives as a liturgical language in the Ethiopian Orthodox Church but which is now meaningless to all but a small number of Church-educated Ethiopians.

Ethiopia's official language, Amharic, existed for centuries as a vernacular before finally becoming in the 20th c. an accepted literary language. The early 1900s saw the beginnings of Amharic literature, even though it had to compete initially with Ge'ez. Earliest Amharic writing tended to be infused with stock moral didacticism, and often still is, influenced as it has been by the traditional association of Ge'ez literature with ethical instruction.

The first Amharic novel, *Lebb wallad tarik* (1908; *Tobbya,* 1964), by Afawarq Gabre Yesus (1868–1947), clearly presented its moral purpose with the introductory comment that "much is due to him who is kind to others, much is lost to him who does evil to others." Other early writers, such as Makonnen Endalkachew (1892–1963) and Kebebe Mikael (b. 1915), concentrated on moral edification and glorification of Ethiopia's past in their short fiction and plays.

More recent Amharic writing has frequently remained in line with tradition or else risked government suppression, and as yet consists largely of short pamphlet-novels, some didactic poetry, and short patriotic plays.

Unfortunately, only a handful of non-Ethiopians can read Amharic, with its unique syllabic script, and Ethiopians have felt the same artistic and economic impulses to write in a language of wider currency that have motivated other African authors. After World War II English became the accepted second language of Ethiopia, and English translations of Amharic and Ge'ez works soon became popular. Such translations directly preceded significant creative work in English. In 1964 the *Ethiopia Observer* published in translation *Marriage by Abduction,* a short play, first published in Amharic in 1955, by Menghistu Lemma (b.

1925), and thus brought this notable author to the attention of the English-speaking world.

This play breaks with traditional Ethiopian sermonizing drama by being a comedy of manners based on reconciling tribal marriage customs with modern ones. It sets the tone for a longer and more important play by the same author, first published in Amharic in 1957 and in English as *The Marriage of Unequals* (1970), whose satire focuses on social and economic inequality, highlighted by the main character, Baharu, an Ethiopian version of the "been-to" who instead of using his foreign education to get the usual cushy administrative job in Addis Ababa, goes to live in a remote village, where he starts a school and a number of self-help programs.

Abbe Gubegna (b. 1934) is well known in Ethiopia for his popular moralistic Amharic writing. Unfortunately his *The Savage Girl* (1964), the first Ethiopian play written in English, does not possess the technical qualities of Menghistu Lemma's drama. An allegory based on history, the play teaches the virtues of isolationism and hatred of change; a forest girl living an idyllic natural life—she has a Bible, however, symbolizing Ethiopia's sixteen centuries of Christianity—finds the impact of the outside world to be fatal.

The weaknesses of *The Savage Girl* are not to be found in the drama of Tsegaye Gabre-Medhin (b. 1936), Ethiopia's leading playwright. He has written and directed over twenty Amharic plays dealing with social and historic themes, and has also written some internationally noted English poetry and drama. His short historical play *Tewodros,* first performed in 1963, led to the opening of the Creative Arts Center in Addis Ababa. Emperor Tewodros (fl. 1855–68), a popular figure in Ethiopian literature and art, is here portrayed as a heroic visionary dreaming of a homeland free of factionalism who is prepared to sacrifice all to this end, beset as he is on all sides by foreign intrigue and local warring chieftains.

Tsegaye Gabre-Medhin's more recent play, *Collision of Your Altars* (1977), turns to a more ancient historical period, that of the disintegration of Emperor Kaleb's Auxmite Ethiopia (A.D. 587–629), but this author's best-known English work, *Oda-Oak Oracle* (1965), has found its popularity at least partly because of its more universal and archetypal plot, which includes an ancestoral command, an obligatory sacrifice, and a tribal "strong son" who has been blessed with a strength that is also a great curse.

In 1961 the *Ethiopia Observer* published "Truth," an English translation of an Amharic short story (1958) by Alamayyawh Mogas (dates n.a.). Although strictly in the moralistic tradition, relating how a successful man rejects true friendship for a false lover, this story was the harbinger of a series of stories soon to be written in English. Unfortunately, few are available outside of Ethiopia, mostly appearing in *Something*, a transitory journal of the English department of what was then Haile Sellassie I University. Most are concerned with moral instruction, although some venture into social criticism—as does Tesfaye Gessesse's (dates n.a.) "Ayee My Luck," which attained wider recognition through its publication in *African Arts* (1971).

Amharic poetry has as yet shown only limited development, in the work of Menghistu Lemma and Solomon Deressa (b. 1937). Deressa's "Legennaat" (1968; childhood) might be considered the beginnings of modern Amharic poetry. Poetry in English ranges from weak, amateurish attempts published locally by their authors to the inspired work of Tsegaye Gabre-Medhin and Solomon Deressa. A weighty awareness of their country's ancient heritage permeates the work in both English and Amharic of Ethiopia's poets; this heritage is frequently judged an albatross to be rid of, as, by implication, are the traditional ideas of Ge'ez and Amharic literature. Fiercely contrasting images depict Ethiopia; it is a nation with a rich and ancient heritage perhaps, yet also a land of hideous poverty, feudal exploitation, and numbing lethargy. Modernism might be shunned, yet like it or not, after centuries of slumber the nation must awaken, no matter how uncertain the world it awakens to might be.

The artistic limitations of didacticism often found in Ge'ez and Amharic writing are also evident in *Confession* (1962), the first English-language novel by an Ethiopian. Yet its author, Ashenafi Kebede (b. 1937), effectively presents a picture of the problems of an Ethiopian student abroad in race-conscious America—a new theme for Ethiopian literature. Another writer, Sahle Sellassie (b. 1936), places his novels only in indigenous settings. After his successful translation (from his Chaha-language original) of *Shinega's Village* (1964), dealing with village life and the inevitable conflicts with modern influences, Sahle Sellassie wrote his next novel, *The Afersata* (1968), in English.

The Afersata suffers from a thin plot resting on the burning of a villager's hut and an ensuing investigation carried out by a local committee, or *afersata*, yet the author achieves an effective feeling for the highly communal and self-sufficient nature of peasant society. In his next novel, *Warrior King* (1974), he turned to the ever-popular Emperor Tewodros and the sense of patriotism and pride evoked by this historical figure.

Any technical shortcomings in these novels are more than compensated for in *The Thirteenth Sun* (1973), written in English by Daniachew Worku (b. 1936), an author who has also written some Amharic plays, short stories, and poems. Taking its title from the Ethiopian calendar, which consists of a thirteen-month year, the novel is set in the present yet is full of an awareness of the past—a past seen with the critical eye of recent poets rather than traditional or patriotic authors. The past is the pollutant of contemporary life. Goytom's pilgrimage up Mount Zekwala to Abbo Shrine with his half-sister and dying father allows to unfold a broad panorama of the brutal realities of present-day Ethiopia, rooted as they are in the medieval nature of that society. Violence and exploitation overwhelm the reader; the Church is the great profiteer of the poor, the sick, and the superstitious. The land, long ravished by an unenlightened peasantry, now enslaves them; their ignorance, poverty, and the feudal system that victimizes them all work to transform them into callous, sullen, and brutish creatures.

It is not yet evident that *The Thirteenth Sun* is the precursor of a new, sophisticated Ethiopian novel aimed at an international audience. Time may prove it to be, but so far it has been succeeded only by Sahle Sellassie's *Warrior King* and by Abbe Gubegna's *Defiance* (1975), two novels primarily concerned with extolling Ethiopia's past. Set in Addis Ababa in 1937 during the Italian occupation, *Defiance* focuses on an old patriot, Fitawrari Abesha, and his family's resistance to their Italian persecutors. It is clear from the handling of his material that the author has matured considerably since the publication of his drama *The Savage Girl* a decade earlier. Some effective description brings to life a Fascist dungeon for Ethiopians, atrocities, and a hillside battle. If *Defiance* is a timely reminder to Ethiopians of hardships suffered once before under an oppressive rule, it is also an indication, along with the best of Sahle Sellassie, Daniachew Worku, Tsegaye Gabre-Medhin, and others, that Ethiopian writers possess the resources and potential for significant literary contributions to African literature.

BIBLIOGRAPHY: Harden, J. M., *An Introduction to Ethiopic Christian Literature* (1926); Gérard, A. S., *Four African Literatures: Xhosa, Sotho, Zulu, Amharic* (1971), pp. 271–376; Huntsberger, P. E., comp., *Highland Mosaic: A Critical Anthology of Ethiopian Literature in En-*

glish (1973), pp. 1–13, 28–47, 72–82, 106–15; Beer, D. F., "Ethiopian Literature and Literary Criticism in English: An Annotated Bibliography," *RAL,* 6 (1975), 44–57; Kane, T. L., *Ethiopian Literature in Amharic* (1975); Beer, D. F., "The Sources and Content of Ethiopian Creative Writing in English," *RAL,* 8 (1977), 99–124; Molvaer, R. K., *Tradition and Change in Ethiopia: Social and Cultural Life as Reflected in Amharic Fictional Literature, ca. 1930–1974* (1980)

DAVID F. BEER

GAMBIAN LITERATURE

Gambia is Africa's smallest country, situated along the banks of the Gambia River. A classic illustration of colonial indifference to natural boundaries, it is totally surrounded by its larger and weathier French-speaking neighbor, Senegal. Having few resources, it is developing into a Caribbean-type winter resort for Scandinavians.

There is here only minimal basis for any identifiable or sustained national literature. Nevertheless it has, surprisingly, produced two major writers: William Conton (b. 1925) and Lenrie Peters (q.v.). Conton has lived long enough in Sierra Leone to have rather a marginal residual allegiance, and the themes of both writers are as much contemporary West African as definably Gambian.

William Conton made his name through one influential novel, *The African* (1960); its early date makes him a pioneer in contemporary African literature. The novel proffers a rather awkward mixture. It opens with a conventional portrayal of an African coping with the problems of being educated in Britain, includes several amusing, probably autobiographical, anecdotal incidents to give it reality, and concludes with events after the hero's return when, having achieved political success, he makes a curiously symbolic voyage to a mythic country, presumably South Africa. The novel cannot be critically admired for its technical qualities, but its influence has been considerable. Its fame is apparent from its translation into Arabic, Russian, and Hungarian. It is less regularly read at present, but it is so well known that it has encouraged several African writers to attempt similar exercises.

Lenrie Peters is a doctor by profession and spent many years away from Gambia earning degrees at Cambridge and the University of London. He is a far more subtle and sophisticated writer than Conton. His first novel, *The Second Round* (1965), is set in Sierra Leone, but it could be equally appropriately located in either country, having the common semiautobiographical plot. It details the difficulties, both social and personal, that confront the well-educated doctor on his return to his traditional life at home. Peters's handling of this idea is more sensitive to the psychological complexities of the protagonist's dilemma than is usual in African fiction. Most African novelists choose to blame the external social pressures for their hero's difficulties.

This topic of the anxiety and alienation of the returnee is a regular theme in Peters's volume of poetry, *Satellites* (1967). His verse is highly sophisticated and urbane, sometimes appearing only minimally African. It remains aways keenly aware of the core of the African cultural dualism.

Gambia suffers, like all small countries, from the dispersal of its more able people to other places offering more rewarding opportunities. For this reason its literature is for some time likely to appear only as the works of isolated, if individually impressive, writers—too isolated and exceptional to form any markedly national tradition.

BIBLIOGRAPHY: Cartey, W., *Whispers from a Continent* (1969), passim; Dathorne, O. R., *The Black Mind* (1974), passim

JOHN POVEY

PETERS, Lenrie
Gambian poet and novelist (writing in English), b. 1 Sept. 1932, Bathurst

In 1952 P. left Africa to study medicine at Cambridge, eventually going on to specialize in surgery. He now resides in Gambia.

P.'s one novel, *The Second Round* (1965), is important as one of the first African novels to turn from the theme of colonial protest and culture conflict to that of self-criticism—the African's criticism of his own country. In this book a doctor returns to his home in Freetown after studying and then practicing medicine for several years in England. He finds himself to be an objective observer, unable to engage himself fully in the lives of his friends, who are being torn apart as they fail to adjust to, or even to recognize, the values of their changing society. Despite several passages of a fine lyrical quality, the novel is marred by excessively sentimental scenes and a contrived plot.

P.'s forte is clearly his poetry. In *Satellites* (1967), his best collection to date, he draws together his experience of living in two worlds, the African and the Western, and analyzes both worlds in fine, almost microscopic detail. The particular confusion, frustration, and alienation he finds in his own soul is seen to be representative of Everyman's malaise in the face of technology and its suffocation of human values. P.'s medical training informs the poetry in this volume with a precision that the reader finds not only in his short, tight stanzas, but also in the incisive, at times surgical, images he employs.

This analytical introspection is continued in much of the poetry in *Katchikali* (1971), but the collection as a whole lacks the vitality of *Satellites*. Nevertheless, in a few of the poems P. made some interesting experiments with form, breaking away from the tighter structures of his earlier verse.

P.'s total output has been small, and he has published nothing since *Katchikali*. He remains, however, one of the finest contemporary African poets. No other living African poet has, in fact, so consistently displayed such control of form or created such startling images. Concerned with the spirit no less than the flesh, P. has effectively married his concerns in a poetry that addresses the social and economic problems of contemporary Africa and reasserts the aesthetic principles he finds threatened in his society.

FURTHER WORKS: *Poems* (1964); *Selected Poetry* (1981)

BIBLIOGRAPHY: Moore, G., "The Imagery of Death in African Poetry," *AfricaL,* 38 (1968), 57–70; Theroux, P., "Six Poets," in Beier, U., ed., *Introduction to African Literature* (1970), pp. 110–31; Knipp, T. R., "L. P.: The Poet as Lonely African," *SBL,* 2, 3 (1971), 9–13; Larson, C. R., "L. P.'s *The Second Round:* West African Gothic," *The Emergence of African Fiction* (1972), pp. 227–41; Egudu, R. N., *Four Modern West African Poets* (1977), passim

RICHARD PRIEBE

GHANAIAN LITERATURE

Ghana has one of the longest written literary histories in Africa, extending back into the 18th c., when Antonius Guilielmus Amo (c. 1703–c. 1750) studied in Germany and produced a powerful theological study in Latin, and Ottobah Cugoano (c. 1745–c. 1790) wrote a bitter antislavery tract in England.

During the 19th and early 20th cs., there was considerable publication in English, but most of these books were rather pedantic volumes of history or anthropology. Carl Reindof (1834–1917), Raphael Armattoe (1913–1953), and Adelaide Casely-Hayford (1868–1959) were typical. Their works emulate British styles and attitudes. These were sarcastically pilloried by Kobina Sekyi (1892–1956) in *The Blinkards,* a play produced as early as 1915. In addition, and this is not common in Africa, there has been a considerable publication in local languages—Fanti, Twi, Ewe—often sponsored by missionaries.

There was little that could properly be called creative literature until 1946, which saw the publication of Michael Francis Dei-Anang's (1909–1978) first collection of poetry, *Wayward Lines from Africa.* Although he must be regarded as the first Ghanaian poet, his work is strongly influenced by the conventions of British Victorian poetry. Such literary borrowing is characteristic of many lesser poets who published in this period, who emulated the colonial culture even while they made gentle professions toward nationalism.

Significant literature of international stature developed only in the years following the 1966 coup against Kwame Nkrumah's restrictive socialist government. Since then, writing in all genres by numerous gifted writers has been published. Their themes cover the subjects found regularly in other West African countries that have shared a similar colonial experience, but with a specifically Ghanaian emphasis.

Today many novels record the past fondly while describing the process of inevitable change. They often include substantial autobiographical details, especially of growing up in a traditional or transitional society. This theme is exemplified in such novels as Joseph Abruquah's (b. 1921) *The Catechist* (1965), Amu Djoleto's (b. 1929) *The Strange Man* (1967), Asare Konadu's (b. 1932) *A Woman in Her Prime* (1967), and Francis Selormey's (b. 1927) *The Narrow Path* (1966). These novels often show reverence for traditional life even when they deal with the personal impact occasioned by its inescapable destruction. The conflict of generations in the division of spiritual beliefs brought about by Christianity, and in the division of mind brought about by education, are persistently expressed.

In contrast, there are the novels that deal with more recent history and focus upon the frenetic experience of the rapidly developing (and deteriorating) city life, which is simultaneously attractive and shocking. Cameron Duodu's (b. 1932) *The Gab Boys* (1967) typifies this theme, describing the delinquencies of unemployed school dropouts who lounge around town in their fancy gabardine trousers looking for excitement and trouble, an international subject surprising only in coming from Africa.

In this vein is one of the most powerful novels yet produced by an African: Ayi Kwei Armah's (q.v.) *The Beautyful Ones Are Not Yet Born* (1969), with its sardonic implication that those who have been born are marked by a spiritual ugliness. It is a scarifying attack on corruption during the Nkrumah regime, blazing with profound anger at the way in which independent Africa has been seduced by the modern toys of Western capitalism, just as were the old chiefs by gifts of beads and mirrors. This novel had international impact; it raised the whole standing of African fiction.

Armah went on to write four more distinguished novels: *Fragments* (1970), *Why Are We So Blest?* (1972), *Two Thousand Seasons* (1973), and *The Healers* (1975). His analysis blames the new elite not only for their greedy arrogance but for their deeper spiritual corruption deriving from their infatuation with things European and the shame they feel for their African heritage.

The only Ghanaian writer of similar stature is Kofi Awoonor (q.v.), whose political views have brought him to prison. His complex novel *This Earth, My Brother* (1971) repeats Armah's critical challenge to Ghana's rulers. Awoonor is also a critic and a poet. His poetry is marked by its originality and sensibility, and shows his unusual determination to maintain his Ewe inheritance in his English verse. He regularly takes the pose of oral narrator, his themes often derive from Ewe culture, and his style forces English to adapt to some of the forms of Ewe oral verse. In *Rediscovery* (1964) and *Night of My Blood* (1971) he confronts the continual problem of the cultural dualism that afflicts African writers. By asserting the importance of tradition, he separates himself from another major poet, Albert Kayper-Mensah (b. 1923), whose collection *The Drummer in Our Time* (1975) seems as close to Europe as to Africa.

The last fifteen years have seen a large new group of published

Ghanaian poets. The most significant is Atukwe Okai (b. 1941), who, like Awoonor, is committed to his inheritance, an attitude demonstrably more fruitful than emulation of foreign writers. Okai has become highly popular as a public reader, thus restoring poetry to the oral mode. *Call of the Fonton-fron* (1971) occasionally lapses into mere rhetoric, but it indicates a direction that other Ghanaian poets followed.

There is the beginning of a Ghanaian drama. Drama can be argued to be relatively free from the stigma of primarily seeking international appeal, since it initially requires a local audience. Nevertheless, there is a clear distinction between plays written for educated audiences who patronize the theater, and the local vaudeville-type comedy of the ever-popular concert parties (traveling singing and acting troupes). Ama Ata Aidoo (b. 1942), well known for her realistic short stories, has written a conventional play on an important theme, the problems of the black American "returning" to Africa—*Dilemma of a Ghost* (1965). Joe de Graft (b. 1924), who is deeply involved in the theater, began his career as a dramatist with *Sons and Daughters* (1963), a conventional enough social comedy. However, he became more ingeniously experimental with *Through a Film Darkly* (1970), which suggested options for the African playwright to escape from the borrowed format of the formal well-made play. His ideas have been augmented in a different vein by Efua Sutherland (b. 1924), who helped found the Ghana Drama Studio. Her most famous published play is *Edufa* (1964), but she has written numerous other plays for local radio broadcast.

Ghanaian literature flourishes sufficiently to be able to support the irregularly published literary journal *Okyeame*. The country also sustains a printing industry that frees at least some authors from dependence on foreign publication. Locally published short novels may be considered unworthy of critical analysis, but they delight a broad readership. Cofie Quaye's (b. 1947) amusing if derivative detective stories, such as *Sammy Slams the Gang* (1970), and Asare Konadu's intense love stories like *Come Back Dora* (1966) have a substantial sale. These books, which satisfy readers on a fairly elementary level of English literacy, may well form the basis for an indigenous readership out of which could grow a literature more truly Ghanaian than the writings of those who are admired abroad and whose audience is limited to an intellectual elite.

BIBLIOGRAPHY: Cartey, W., *Whispers from a Continent* (1969), passim; Roscoe, A., *Mother Is Gold* (1971), passim; Senanu, K. E., "Creative Writing in Ghana," in Kayper-Mensah, A. W., and Wolff, H., eds.,

Ghanaian Writing (1972), pp. 13–31; Dathorne, O., *The Black Mind* (1974), passim

JOHN POVEY

ARMAH, Ayi Kwei
Ghanaian novelist (writing in English), b. 1939, Takoradi

In 1959 A. went to the U.S. to study at Groton School in Massachusetts, and later received a degree in sociology from Harvard. He worked as a translator for the periodical *Révolution Africaine* in Algiers and taught English at the Navarongo School in Ghana in 1966. He subsequently served on the staff of the magazine *Jeune Afrique* in Paris, and on the faculty of the University of Massachusetts. In 1972 he moved to Dar es Salaam, Tanzania.

A. published poems and short stories in the Ghanaian magazine *Okyeame*, and in *Harper's, The Atlantic Monthly,* and *New African* before his first novel, *The Beautyful Ones Are Not Yet Born,* appeared in 1969. Its simple, spare style evokes the smells and pain of living in the slums of Accra. Pitted in the daily struggle for survival against poverty on one side and high crime and the "high life" on the other is the major character, simply called The Man, and his family. The Man resists the temptations of bribery and corruption, but his virtues go largely unrewarded. His wife thinks him a fool, and his more sophisticated acquaintances mock him. Using images of excrement to symbolize the state of corruption in Ghana, A. nevertheless expressed hope in the faith of honest, simple men. At the end of the novel, The Man proves stronger than the once-powerful politician who has been deposed in a military coup. This novel is allegorical and poetic in its compressed style.

A.'s second novel, *Fragments* (1970), is realistic and possibly autobiographical. The protagonist is a "been-to," a man who has been to America and studied at one of the leading universities there. On his return to Ghana, he is welcomed as a hero, but he proves unable to live up to the expectations of the villagers. The irony in A.'s portrait is strong: the protagonist fails his villagers because they want him to shine, to flaunt his abilities, like a warrior chief. He prefers solitude and withdrawal. The young intellectual finally cracks under the strain of trying to live in and up to two worlds, and his mother has to commit him to an institution.

A.'s lyric tone becomes angry, and at times shrill, in his third novel,

Why Are We So Blest? (1972). Its action is set largely in a famous American university. The protagonist, a student, feels he must abandon the humanistic principles that he believes are constraining his revolutionary plans of action. To establish his independence—and that of Africa— he believes he must reject Western values, even Western kindness. The protagonist also suffers because his passion for an American girl gives him the feeling of losing his individuality. These conflicts drive him to despair.

A.'s work shows throughout an emphasis on the conflict between integrity and expediency, responsibility and amorality, commitment and withdrawal. The simple man in *The Beautyful Ones Are Not Yet Born* survives his ordeal. But the sensitivity of the intellectually more gifted protagonists of A.'s next two novels makes them vulnerable to the painful awareness of the gap between the real and ideal, the ugly realities and the desired harmonies.

In *Two Thousand Seasons* (1973–74) A. finds a way out of his dilemma. His fourth novel spans a thousand years, or two thousand seasons—the wet and dry reapings of African history. The narrator might be defined as the collective African consciousness. He indicts Arab and European exploiters, and denounces African imitators of Western ways. He describes the "predators," "destroyers," "parasites," and "zombies" who have raped Africa over the centuries. But he also prophesies a new age in which Africans will regain their identity and glory. Counseling against despair, he cries: "What suffering is there in our hearing only this season's noise, seeing only the confusion around us here. . . . That is not the nature of our seeing." This novel is mythic and close to the density of epic poetry. It shows less interest in characterization and more in allegorical tone. This wide shift from autobiographical and realistic detail to symbolist prose and generalized statements on human nature is a striking departure from his earlier style.

FURTHER WORK: *The Healers* (1975)

BIBLIOGRAPHY: Aidoo, C. A. A., Introduction to *The Beautyful Ones Are Not Yet Born* (1969), pp. viii–xii; Larson, C. R., *The Emergence of African Fiction* (1972), pp. 113–19, 245–68; Palmer, E., *An Introduction to the African Novel* (1972), pp. 129–42; Mphahlele, E., *The African Image* (rev. ed., 1974), pp. 270–75; Owomoyela, O. *African Literatures: An Introduction* (1979), pp. 104–11; Fraser, R., *The Novels of A. K. A.* (1980)

MARTIN TUCKER

AWOONOR, Kofi

(formerly George Awoonor-Williams) Ghanaian poet, novelist, dramatist, critic, and folklorist (writing in English), b. 13 March 1935, Wheta

A. attended the University of Ghana and upon graduation became a research fellow and lecturer in African literature at the school's Institute of African Studies. Later he served as managing director of the Ghana Film Corporation and as an editor of the Ghanaian literary review *Okyeame*. In 1967 he studied language and literature in England. From there he went to the U.S., where he continued his literary studies. A. returned to Ghana in 1975 and took up a position as chairman of the Department of English at Cape Coast University. He was arrested by the military government and detained for nine months in 1976 for allegedly aiding an officer who was planning a coup d'état.

During his student years in London, A. wrote several radio plays for the BBC. While only two of these plays have been published—*Ancestral Power* and *Lament*, in *Short African Plays* (ed. C. Pieterse, 1972)—they are important pieces in terms of the traditional imagery A. has consistently employed.

Despite his studies abroad, A.'s work has very strong links with his own Ewe culture. He writes mostly in English, but retains the rhythms and tonal quality of his native language as few other contemporary African writers have done.

Primarily through his poetry, A. has established himself as one of the most significant contemporary African writers. His first two books of poetry, *Rediscovery* (1964) and *Night of My Blood* (1971), show a powerful progression from a fascination with his roots, through an uncertain poetic and cultural synthesis with the West, to a voice that is confidently his own. More than any other western-African poet, with the possible exceptions of the Nigerians Christopher Okigbo and Wole Soyinka (qq.v.), A. has succeeded in transcending the raw tensions of culture conflict. His poetry should be read as a series of attempts to find in the history and poetry of his people correlatives to his own personal anguish as a modern African. Poems that serve to accentuate the anguish and give definition to the progression may appear to be difficult, or simply uneven and rough, when removed from this context.

In both form and imagery A.'s poetry has been heavily influenced by the Ewe dirge. According to traditional Ewe beliefs, those who have just died and are entering another existence represent potential danger to those left behind, for the physical loss interrupts the continuity of society and threatens it with dissolution. Yet good may also come out of a death, for a successful transition ends with the dead individual becoming an ancestral being who can be a beneficial force in the community. The purpose of the Ewe dirge is to aid the individual in making this transition.

For A., the dirge becomes symbolic not only of an individual and societal process but also of the poet's passage from insufficiency to fulfillment, from chaos to order, from alienation to integration. Death and anguish pervade his poetry as mediating agents that force the continual restructuring, refocusing, and revitalizing of individual and communal order. In effect, A. explores the relationship between contemporary society and traditional myth and ritual.

A.'s novel, *This Earth, My Brother* (1971), is an allegorical exploration of the ideas he developed in his poetry. Influenced by James Joyce no less than by the Ewe dirge, this highly lyrical novel is a re-creation of an Ewe funeral celebration. Alternating poetic and prose sections, A. writes of the anguish of a young African lawyer who ritually purifies his society, carrying the weight of its corruption with him into his own death.

In *Ride Me, Memory* (1973), a collection of poetry he published before returning to Ghana, A. looks at his sojourn in America. This examination is accomplished through a series of incisive images presented in the manner of traditional African praise and abuse poetry—the types of poetry through which the poet-priest could criticize the politically and socially powerful. Irony is present in many of his earlier works, but nowhere is it as pervasive or well controlled as in this collection.

Since his imprisonment A. has become more directly involved in the politics of Ghana, and this involvement is clearly reflected in his most recent collection of poetry, *The House by the Sea* (1978). The title is an ironic reference to the old slave castle (originally a fort, but still referred to as a "castle") in which he was imprisoned and a metaphysical reference to a place where he sees all his people held captive. In fact, the magic of these poems lies in the manner he has transfigured the "I" of the personal experience of imprisonment to the "we" of all humanity.

A. has shown a remarkable accomplishment in leading us into the world of the poet-priest and the African dirge, where the gaps between man and man, as well as those between man and his gods, must be continually confronted and bridged.

FURTHER WORKS : *Breast of the Earth: A Study of African Culture and Literature* (1973); *Ewe Poetry* (1973)

BIBLIOGRAPHY: Moore, G., "The Imagery of Death in African Poetry," *AfricaL,* 38 (1968), 57–70; Theroux, P., "Six Poets," in Beier, U., ed., *Introduction to African Literature* (1970), pp. 101–31; Priebe, R., "Escaping the Nightmare of History: The Development of a Mythic Consciousness in West African Literature," *ArielE,* 4, 2 (1973), 55–67

RICHARD PRIEBE

GUINEA-BISSAU LITERATURE

The tiny west African country of Guinea-Bissau lags far behind other Portuguese-speaking African nations in imaginative writing. In colonial times the small enclave was little more than a neglected trading outpost of the far-flung Portuguese empire. The absence of anything approaching the indigenous bourgeoisie that in other lusophone African colonies gave rise to small but significant elites of black and mixed-race intellectuals explains why little Portuguese-language and Creole writing emerged in preindependence Guinea-Bissau.

Not to be discounted, of course, is the rich oral expression in indigenous languages and in the region's Portuguese-based Creole. But what little Portuguese-language writing did appear in colonial times was chiefly quasi-ethnographic and mainly produced by Europeans and Cape Verdeans.

Fausto Duarte (1903–1955), a Cape Verdean who lived most of his life in Guinea-Bissau, can, by default, be called the first important writer of Guinea-Bissau. His five novels, published between 1935 and 1945, depict indigenous cultures in somewhat exotic terms.

In 1974 Guinea-Bissau gained its hard-fought independence amidst a surge of cultural and literary activity. A prime mover was Mário de Andrade (b. 1928), a distinguished Angolan intellectual and writer who was eventually appointed Guinea-Bissau's Minister of Culture. Andrade played an important role in the publication of *Mantenhas para quem luta!* (1977; hail to those who struggle!), a landmark anthology of poems in Portuguese by fourteen Guineans, most in their twenties. This historically important collection was followed by *Antologia dos jovens poetas* (1978; the young poets' anthology), comprising thirty-eight poems, almost equally divided between those in Portuguese and those in Creole.

With independence, the Creole lingua franca came to play a major role in literacy campaigns and primary education. Moreover, a project aimed at collecting Creole oral traditions resulted in *'N sta li'n sta la* (1979; I'm everywhere) and *Junbai* (1979; togetherness), both attractively illustrated, bilingual (Portuguese/Creole) collections of traditional riddles and stories.

In November of 1980 the cultural-literary impetus suffered a setback when the government was overthrown. The cultural leadership of Andrade ended, and several promising writers fled into exile. This setback notwithstanding, a national literature has definitively come into being in Guinea-Bissau.

BIBLIOGRAPHY: Bull, B. P., *Le Créole de la Guiné-Bissau* (1975); Hamilton, R. G., *Voices from an Empire: A History of Afro-Portuguese Literature* (1975), pp. 358–62; Moser, G. M., on *'N sta li 'n sta la, RAL*, 11 (1980), 402–3

RUSSELL G. HAMILTON

GUINEAN LITERATURE

Although Guinea, which achieved independence from France in 1958, consists of twenty-four ethnic groups, three predominate: the Malinké in Upper Guinea, the Peul in Middle Guinea, the Soussou in Lower Guinea. With this mosaic of ethnic diversity, Guinea acknowledges eight national languages: Poular, Soussou, Malinké, Kissi, Guerzé, Coniagui, Toma, and Bassari. A program initiated in 1962 encourages Guineans to learn to read and write in their national tongues, using a modified Latin alphabet for transcribing their oral languages. Devoutly Muslim, the Peuls have used Arabic script to translate the Koran into Poular and to write religious poetry and prose. French, the legacy of colonialism, is the tool of communication for all administrative, commercial, and technical tasks, and as the lingua franca of educated Guineans, is the official language. Yet it is understood by barely one fifth of the population.

The first modern Guinean literary works appeared in the 1950s, all of them in French, with the exception of the writings of Modupe Paris (b. 1901), a Guinean who studied in the U.S. and published his autobiography, *I Was a Savage* (1957), in English.

Guinean literature bears the stamp of history, both modern and traditional. Mamadou Traoré's (b. 1916) *Vers la liberté* (1961; toward liberty) and Sadan-Moussa Touré's (b. 1932) *Les premières guinéades: Contes, légendes de chez nous* (1961; the first Guineads: stories, legends of our homeland) celebrate Guinean independence in verse. Condetto Nenekhaly-Camara's (b. 1930) two plays, *Continent-Afrique* (African continent) and *Amazoulou* (Amazulu), published in one volume in 1970, present historical figures; the first play portrays Antar, a 6th-c. Arab warrior, and the second, Chaka, the 19th-c. Zulu king. Alpha Sow (b. 1935) has published an anthology of Peul folklore, *Chroniques et récits du Fouta Djalon* (1968; chronicles and tales of the Fouta Djallon mountains).

The Guinean literary scene has been largely dominated by Camara Laye (q.v.), whose first novel, *L'enfant noir* (1953; *The Dark Child*, 1954), was awarded the Charles Veillon Prize in 1954 and brought international recognition to its author. This work, profoundly poetic, recounts the life of a boy growing up in an African village, learning about his ancestors, appreciating his father's skills as a goldsmith. Camara's next novel, *Le regard du roi* (1954; *The Radiance of the King*,

1956), highly symbolic, presents a French protagonist unequipped for life in black Africa. Political difficulties with President Sekou Touré sent Camara into exile from 1965 until his death in 1980, first to Ivory Coast, then to Senegal, an exile made all the more painful when Sekou Touré detained Camara's wife in Guinea for several years. After leaving Guinea, Camara published *Dramouss* (1966; *A Dream of Africa,* 1968), a novel highly critical of Guinea's present political regime. Shortly before his death, he published an ethnographic work, *Le maître de la parole* (1978; the wordmaster), a transcription in French of the Malinké epic recounting the legend of Soundiata.

Djibril Tamsir Niane (b. 1920) had also published a version of this epic, entitled *Soudjata; ou, L'épopée mandingue* (1960; *Sundiata: An Epic of Old Mali,* 1965), in which he relates the tales of the crippled boy who grew up to rule the Mali empire (1230–55). Although the two versions are similar, Niane and Camara had based their work upon the accounts of different *griots,* or Malinké oral historians. In his introduction, Niane defines the role of the griot: "In the very hierarchical society of Africa before colonization, where everyone found his place, the griot appears as one of the most important men in this society, because it is he who, for want of archives, records the customs, traditions, and governmental principles of kings." Niane, who has griot ancestors, has also collaborated with the French historian Jean Suret-Canale (b. 1921) on an illustrated history of West Africa, *Histoire de l'Afrique occidentale* (1960; history of West Africa), and written two plays, *Sikasso* (1971; Sikasso) and *Chaka* (1971; Chaka), both with historical subjects.

As interested in Malinké history and tradition as Niane, but choosing a different vehicle of expression, Fodéba Keita (b. 1921), also of griot background, has composed music, poetry, and dance based on traditional sources. Keita's Ballets Africains, the Guinean national dance troupe, toured the globe in the early 1960s. After serving in the government from 1968 to 1971, Keita was imprisoned and disappeared. He is presumed dead.

One can only hope that Guineans in the future will have greater freedom of expression—both artistic and political—than they do at present, and that their rich oral tradition will continue to provide inspiration. It is unfortunate that talented artists such as Camara and Keita fell victim to repression. It is everyone's loss that their talents were not nurtured in their homeland.

BIBLIOGRAPHY: Gleason, J., *This Africa: Novels by West Africans in*

English and French (1965); Brench, A. C., *The Novelists' Inheritance in French Africa: Writers from Senegal to Cameroon* (1967); Larson, C., *The Emergence of African Fiction* (1972); Olney, J., *Tell Me Africa: An Approach to African Literature* (1973); Blair, D., S., *African Literature in French* (1976); Cook, D., *African Literature: A Critical View* (1977); Owomoyela, O., *African Literatures: An Introduction* (1979)

MILDRED MORTIMER

CAMARA Laye

Guinean novelist (writing in French), b. 1 Jan. 1928, Kouroussa; d. 4 Feb. 1980, Dakar, Senegal

C.'s formal French education began in local schools; he went on to a technical high school in Conakry and then left for France on a government scholarship. After earning a certificate of automotive technology at Argenteuil he moved to Paris, where, while continuing his studies toward a degree in automotive engineering, he held odd jobs and experienced great privation until he found employment in an automobile factory.

In 1956 C. returned to Guinea and worked there in a technical capacity for the French colonial regime. With the establishment of an independent Guinea, he was sent to several African countries on diplomatic missions and was named director of Sekou Touré's study and research center in the Ministry of Information in Conakry.

With other young intellectuals he had hoped that newly won independence would bring about greater personal freedom, but this was not to be. He fell out of grace with President Touré, partly because he attempted to withdraw from public service, partly because his writing became increasingly critical of the regime. In 1965 C. found it necessary to flee into exile in Senegal, where he lived until his death, working at the research institute commonly known as IFAN and trying to cope with failing health and the responsibility of raising his seven children by his first marriage and two by his second.

When still struggling in Paris C., feeling alienated and overwhelmed by homesickness, began to write, which sustained him in those trying days. A series of nostalgic reminiscences from his earliest days in the family compound at Kouroussa to the time he left for Paris became his first book—*L'enfant noir* (1953; *The Dark Child,* 1954). The romantic, even rhapsodic, evocation of daily life in the village and the rituals of growing up, and especially the often quoted description of C.'s father, a goldsmith, who saw himself as working mystically with his raw materials, recognizing a snake as his protective spirit, caused *L'enfant noir* to be championed as a major prose example of the Negritude (q.v.) movement. *L'enfant noir* is the most famous African novel in French.

C.'s finest work, *Le regard du roi* (1954; *The Radiance of the King*, 1956), is a surreal allegory whose most conspicuous attributes are (1) a reversal of the colonial racial roles in which the white protagonist must endure humiliation and loss of identity before he is accepted by the Africans; and (2) cinematographic effects, including repetitions, dissolves, flashbacks, shifts of place and time, and the like. The many layers of the novel admit of the most different interpretations: suggestions of Christian redemption and Islamic mysticism appear alongside reverberations of Kafka's fictional concepts and African animism.

After a long silence broken only by the publication of a short story, "Les yeux de la statue" (1957; "The Eyes of the Statue," 1959), which is a pessimistic variation of *Le regard du roi*, C. brought out the hastily written novel *Dramouss* (1966; *A Dream of Africa*, 1968). *Dramouss* takes up where *L'enfant noir* ends, telling of C.'s trials and tribulations in Paris and his return after six years to newly independent Guinea. But nostalgia has turned to bitterness. He finds a ruthless political party in complete control, whose rulers have thrown overboard all African traditional values and those of France as well. Noteworthy is the description of a dream in which the totemic snake-woman Dramouss holds forth the hope of a liberated Guinea, whose people, secure in their autochthonous traditions, may once again enjoy the time-honored brotherhood of men. It is these traditions that C. felt had been destroyed by corruption and greed for power in the new Republic of Guinea. The book earned C. a death sentence *in absentia* from the Guinean authorities.

After another decade of silence, dictated in part by a lingering serious illness, C. published *Le maître de la parole* (1978; the wordmaster). Although admittedly the retelling from existing chronicles of the story of the childhood and rise to power of the ancient emperor Sundiata Keita, the work is, in a sense, a broadening of the basic preoccupations that always haunted C., for the emphasis is on Sundiata's long and painful exile, and the two main themes running through C.'s overall literary work are those of exile and the quest for fulfillment.

BIBLIOGRAPHY: Brench, A. C., "C. L.: Idealist and Mystic," *ALT*, No. 2 (1969), 11–31; Sellin, E., "Alienation in the Novels of C. L.," *PAJ*, 4 (1971), 455–72; Larson, C. R., *The Emergence of African Fiction*

(1972), pp. 167–226; Palmer, E., *An Introduction to the African Novel* (1972), pp. 85–116; King, A., "C. L.," in King, B., and Ogungbesan, K., eds., *A Celebration of Black and African Writers* (1975), pp. 112–23; Bernard, P. R., "C. L.: A Bio-Bibliography," *AfrLJ,* 9 (1978), 307–21; Sellin, E., "Trial by Exile: C. L. and Sundiata Keita," *WLT,* 54 (1980), 392–95

ERIC SELLIN

IVORY COAST LITERATURE

The age-old traditional literatures in African languages of the Ivory Coast, indeed of most of sub-Saharan Africa, have been primarily oral. The colonization of this now-independent West African country by France early in this century was accompanied by a forceful imposition of the French language from elementary school on. This, coupled with the presence of a multiplicity of African languages (making the choice of any one as a national tongue difficult), has resulted in a written literature that is overwhelmingly in French.

Generally speaking, criticism of colonial excesses, cultural self-assertion, the conflict between tradition and modernism, and, more recently, disenchantment with independence and the new leadership have been the major themes.

Perhaps because of the low literacy rate, it is in the theater—with its roots in traditional spectacle and its ability to reach a broad audience—that the Ivory Coast has shown the most vitality. Born in 1932 in a school setting, dramatic activity was brilliantly fostered through playwriting and the organization of theater troupes by Ivoirian students of the celebrated William-Ponty School and others. The theater was early dominated by three graduates of that school, François-Joseph Amon d'Aby (b. 1913), Germain Coffi Gadeau (b. 1915), and Bernard Binlin Dadié (q.v.), the last the most outstanding, prolific Ivory Coast writer.

Two tendencies dominate this theater: (1) historical or legendary themes based on the oral tradition, e.g., Dadié's *Assémien Déhylé* (1936; Assémien Déhylé), Amon d'Aby's *L'entrevue de Bondoukou* (1939; the Bondoukou interview), and Gadeau's *Kondé Yao* (1939; Kondé Yao) and (2) more modern preoccupations, to be found in plays dealing with certain social ills inherited from tribal life, or in comedies of manners and political criticism reflecting a widespread disaffection with contemporary abuses, e.g., Amon d'Aby's *Kwao Adjoba* (1953; Kwao Adjoba) or Gadeau's *Nos femmes* (1940; our wives). In this vein, Dadié's very popular *Monsieur Thôgô-gnini* (1970; Mr. Thôgô-gnini) is exemplary.

Many talented younger playwrights have become active, often centering their dramas around great figures of the past. Thus, for example, Charles Nokan (b. 1936) re-creates (taking considerable liberties) the Baoule legend of Queen Pokou in his *Abrah Pokou* (1970; Abrah Pokou), while Bernard Zadi Zaourou (b. 1938) chronicled the career of the 19th-

c. Mandingo (Malinké) leader Samori Touré, whose resistance to the French colonial armies has become legendary, in *Les Sofas* (1975; the Sofas [name given to Samori's soldiers]). Here, as elsewhere among dramatists of this generation, historical themes are rarely presented for their own sake, but rather as a reinterpretation of the past in the search for solutions to the problems of newly independent African states.

In keeping with their concern for the continuity of the oral tradition, Dadié and Amon d'Aby have also published collections of legends and tales: *Le pagne noir* (1955; the black loincloth) and *La mare aux crocodiles* (1973; the crocodile pond), respectively. Léon Maurice Anoma Kanié's (b. 1920) *Quand les bêtes parlaient aux hommes* (1974; when animals spoke to men) is a similar venture with a significant addition: the author has appended several of La Fontaine's fables translated into Ivory Coast Creole, a blending of French and local languages.

Although his forte seems clearly to be the theater, Dadié also stands out as the leading poet of the Ivory Coast. His three volumes of poetry reflect his evolving concerns over the years. Among other poets of note there is Joseph Miézan Bognini (b. 1936), whose sensitive exaltation of nature and "controlled fervor" in his collection *Ce dur appel de l'espoir* (1960; this harsh call of hope) make him one of the better Francophone lyric poets. The unclassifiable ("dramatic poem"?) *Le soleil noir point* (1962; the black sun dawns) by Charles Nokan, as well as his poetic "novel" *Violent était le vent* (1966; violent was the wind), both passionate pleas for a true liberation in post-independence Africa, are noteworthy in their sincerity and their formal and stylistic innovations.

Ivoirian writers came rather late to the novel. Their themes tend to parallel those of the dramatists: at the outset, we find a preoccupation with the colonial experience, depiction (and occasionally criticism) of traditional life, and the myriad problems—both individual and societal— implied in the conflict of cultures. This last theme has, of course, carried over into the postindependence period. A common characteristic of many of these novels is their autobiographical nature, following (with variations) a more or less set pattern from village to school, to the big city (African or European), and the final return home. Both Dadié's *Climbié* (1956; *Climbié*, 1971) and Aké Loba's (b. 1927) *Kocoumbo, l'etudiant noir* (1961; Kocoumbo, the black student) are important autobiographical works, the first tracing the moral and political itinerary of its hero during the late colonial period, the second vividly depicting the African student milieu in Paris during the same era.

The confrontation of the old and the new within an African village is the subject of Aké Loba's second novel, *Les fils de Kouretcha* (1970; the sons of Kouretcha), while his *Les dépossédés* (1973; the dispossessed) chronicles the life of a simple peasant and that of his adopted city, Abidjan, during sixty years of colonial rule. New political developments have engendered new themes: disaffection in the wake of independence is at the very core of the most interesting and best written Ivoirian novel to date, Ahmadou Kourouma's (b. 1927?) *Les soleils des indépendances* (1968; the suns of independence). The subject has appeared frequently in recent African fiction, but its treatment here results in a highly successful molding of a Western genre to the realities of African thought and speech. With *Wazzi* (1977; Wazzi) by Jean D. Dodo (b. 1919?) and Tidiane Dem's (date n.a.) *Masseni* (1977; Masseni), women for the first time became the chief protagonists of Ivoirian novels.

BIBLIOGRAPHY: Cornevin, R., *Le théâtre en Afrique noire et Madagascar* (1970), pp. 185–200; Jahn, J., and Dressler, P. D., *Bibliography of Creative African Writing* (1971); Bonneau, R., *Écrivains, cinéastes et artistes ivoiriens, aperçu bio-bibliographique* (1973); Herdeck, D. E., *African Authors* (1973); Blair, D., *African Literature in French* (1976); Baratte-Eno Belinga, T., et al., *Bibliographie des auteurs africains de langue française*, 4th ed. (1979), pp. 74–85

FREDRIC MICHELMAN

DADIÉ, Bernard Binlin

Ivory Coast novelist, short-story writer, poet, and dramatist (writing in French), b. 1916, Assinie

D.'s mother, a one-eyed woman who felt that her presence held a curse that had been responsible for the deaths of her first three children, decided to send away her fourth child, Bernard, to protect him from her evil spell. D. spent much of his childhood with his elderly uncle N'dabian, who told him many of the African folk tales that D. later adapted in his short-story collections. D. studied in Gorée, then served in the government administration for eleven years in Dakar, Senegal. A lover of the theater, D. set up an important center for dramatic arts. He served as director of fine arts and research in the government of the Ivory Coast at Abidjan, and is currently Minister of Culture.

D. first gained prominence with the publication of his short-story collections *Légendes africaines* (1953; African legends) and *Le pagne noir* (1955; the black loincloth), the latter featuring the exploits of the legendary spider Kacou Ananzè, a clever, tricky, and conceited rogue similar to Renard the Fox of French medieval tales.

In 1956 the poems in *La ronde des jours* (the circle of days) were hailed by the Haitian poet René Dépestre (b. 1926) as an expression of "tender humor and joy in living." Because of the way they combine religion (Dadié is a Catholic) and humor, D.'s poems have been compared with those of Langston Hughes.

D.'s first novel, the autobiographical *Climbié* (1956; *Climbié*, 1971), published in the same year as Camara's (q.v.) *L'enfant noir*, differs substantially from Camara's rosy picture of the joys of growing up in an innocent, unspoiled Africa. Unlike Guinea, D.'s homeland had already been corrupted by European rule. D. traces Climbié's development from passive acceptance of white rule to anger at white domination, an anger that emerges when he returns to the Ivory Coast from Senegal and is imprisoned for political reasons.

Un nègre à Paris (1959; a Negro in Paris) and *Patron de New York* (1964; boss in New York), two novels of cultural contrasts, written in the light, bantering style of Montesquieu's *Persian Letters*, demonstrate how odd and foolish the customs and behavior of Parisians and New Yorkers appear to a West African. With irony and false naïveté, Tanhoé, the narrator of *Un nègre à Paris*, concludes that the Parisian, despite his ridiculous customs and attitudes, is really a human being in his own right, with his own history, traditions, and gods.

In the late 1960s D. found his true vocation when he returned to his first love, the theater. *Monsieur Thôgô-gnini* (1970; Mr. Thôgô-gnini), a farce in the tradition of Molière's *The Would-be Gentleman* and Jarry's *King Ubu*, was critically acclaimed at the 1969 Pan-African Festival in Algiers. Monsieur Thôgô-gnini takes advantage of the arrival of the white traders and exploits his own people in an attempt to gain fame and fortune. Like Molière's gullible Monsieur Jourdain, D.'s protagonist accepts anything the white traders give him, including a suit made from sacking, as the latest European fashion. D.'s next two plays, *Les voix dans le vent* (1970; voices in the wind) and *Béatrice du Congo* (1971; Beatrice of the Congo), treat the theme of the corruption and exploitation of Africa in a more serious vein, with multidimensional characters torn between conflicting desires.

Îles de tempête (1973; stormy islands), D.'s most ambitious drama, focuses on the moral dilemma of Toussaint L'Ouverture, whose excessive admiration for the French and especially for Napoleon made him reluctant to declare Haiti's independence. D. uses the techniques of the experimental theater in depicting simultaneous, parallel scenes, concluding with Toussaint's exile in Fort de Joux and Napoleon's exile on Saint Helena. Like the Martinican poet and dramatist Aimé Césaire's (b. 1913) *The Tragedy of King Christophe, Îles de tempête* debunks the myth of a great Haitian revolutionary, but in D.'s drama the caricature of a legendary black hero is blended with warmth and compassion.

His simplicity and directness of style have made D. one of the best dramatists in French-speaking Africa. Without anger or hatred, D. demonstrates the evils of colonialism and gives hope for the Africa of the future through his message of peace, brotherhood, and love.

FURTHER WORKS: *Assémien Déhylé* (1936); *Les villes* (1939); *Afrique debout* (1950); *Hommes de tous les continents* (1967); *La ville où nul ne meurt* (1968)

BIBLIOGRAPHY: Mercier, R., and Battestini, M. and S., *B. D.* (1964); Quillateau, C., *B. B. D.* (1967); Brench, A. C., *The Novelists' Inheritance in French Africa* (1967), pp. 84–91; Wake, C., in Banham, M., ed., *African Theatre Today* (1976), pp. 74–79

DEBRA POPKIN

KENYAN LITERATURE

Kenya has produced written literature in five languages—English, Swahili, Kamba, Kikuyu, and Luo—but most Kenyan authors writing today express themselves in either English or Swahili.

In English

The earliest literary works in English were ethnographies and autobiographical narratives, the prototype being Jomo Kenyatta's (1893–1978) *Facing Mount Kenya* (1938), an anthropological account of traditional Kikuyu life and culture. Muga Gicaru (b. 1920) in *Land of Sunshine: Scenes of Life in Kenya before Mau Mau* (1958) and R. Mugo Gatheru (b. 1925) in *Child of Two Worlds* (1964) described growing up in a Kikuyu village during the interwar years, when educational opportunities were scarce and nationalistic feelings were beginning to spread throughout the country. The struggle for political independence, which precipitated a Kikuyu civil war in the 1950s known as Mau Mau, was recorded in autobiographical works by Josiah Kariuki (b. 1929), Karari Njama (b. 1926), and Waruhiu Itote (b. 1922). In all these life histories the experiences of the narrator were treated as if typical of the Kikuyu people as a whole; the individual was a representative of his community, his ethnic group, and, in a larger sense, his nation.

The emergence of James Ngugi, now known as Ngugi wa Thiong'o (q.v.), as Kenya's first novelist may have been the consequence of the same ethnic autobiographical impulse, for he too was a Kikuyu writing about the impact of Western education and colonial political unrest on the lives of his people, ordinary rural citizens who had been deprived of their land by white settlers. In *The River Between* (1965) he tells of the rise of Kikuyu independent schools under the leadership of a "man of two worlds" who tries to unite his community through mass education. In *Weep Not, Child* (1964) he portrays a Kikuyu family split apart by the pressures of Mau Mau; the hero, a young boy, is nearly driven to suicide when he loses his opportunity for further education. In both works Ngugi stresses the importance of fusing old and new, traditional and Western, so that Africans could progress politically without losing their cultural identity.

Ngugi's later novels, *A Grain of Wheat* (1967) and *Petals of Blood*

(1977), deal with postcolonial social problems in Kenya that have their roots in the past. Like Chinua Achebe (q.v.) of Nigeria, Ngugi attempts to understand present realities in his country by searching for their origins in earlier times. He has written fictional chronicles of his nation's history.

A number of Kenyan authors have followed in Ngugi's footsteps by writing nationalistic novels about Mau Mau and its aftermath. Of these, the most talented is Meja Mwangi (b. 1948), whose *Carcase for Hounds* (1974) and *Taste of Death* (1975) elevated the armed struggle to legendary status by focusing on the exploits of heroic freedom fighters. More recently Mwangi has turned his attention to urban problems in Nairobi, examining the human consequences of economic exploitation in the postcolonial era by detailing the lives of laborers, vagabonds, and slum dwellers, who face their daily battle for survival with ingenuity and resilient humor.

Mwangi's latest novels have less in common with Ngugi's sober historical reappraisals than they do with the humorous literature that emerged in Kenya in the 1970s. The book that started the trend toward lighter fiction was Charles Mangua's (b. 1939) *Son of Woman* (1971), a picaresque novel that pokes fun at every stratum of Kenyan society by viewing it from the gutter through the eyes of an opportunistic trickster. In *A Tail in the Mouth* (1972) Mangua went a step further in irreverence and satirized even the Mau Mau freedom fighters. Mangua's refreshingly flippant novels broke sales records in Kenya and encouraged the development of an indigenous popular literature.

The most successful popular writer to emerge in Kenya in recent years has been David Maillu (b. 1939), who built a publishing house, Comb Books, on earnings from his first "mini-novels," *Unfit for Human Consumption* (1973) and *Troubles* (1974), and his best-selling narrative poems, *My Dear Bottle* (1973) and *After 4:30* (1974). Although Maillu has been criticized for writing mildly pornographic works, he has maintained that he is a serious moralist who chooses to clothe his social messages in frank, sexually explicit humor. He has tended to concentrate on urban characters—civil servants, politicians, secretaries, prostitutes—who suffer misfortunes because they cannot purge themselves of bad habits and insatiable appetites. He is truly a writer for the masses.

Other writers of fiction worthy of mention are Grace Ogot (b. 1930), whose tales of traditional Luo life skillfully evoke the past; the half-brothers Leonard Kibera (b. 1942) and Samuel Kahiga (b. 1946), whose short stories and novelettes deal with psychological aspects of social change; and Mwangi Ruheni (b. 1934), who specializes in domestic comedies and crime fiction. Such writers have contributed thematic diversity to Kenyan fiction.

Kenya has not produced as many dramatists or poets as it has novelists, but the plays of Francis Imbuga (b. 1947) and the poetry of Jared Angira (b. 1947) have earned a measure of public recognition. Imbuga has explored poignant human dimensions of social and political turmoil in modern Africa, sometimes tracing the roots of a personal tragedy to profound changes in the cultural values of contemporary society. Angira has brooded on the predicament of modern man in the Third World; his verse has remained simple, direct yet quite resourceful in projecting sharp images in which the new generation of Africans can see themselves and their experience reflected.

In Swahili

Kenya is not as rich in Swahili-language literature as Tanzania *(see Tanzanian Literature)*, but a significant number of plays, poems, and novelettes are available. The oldest and possibly most famous work is James Juma Mbotela's (dates n.a.) *Uhuru wa watumwa* (1934; *The Freeing of the Slaves in East Africa,* 1956), a narrative based on reminiscences about the slave trade. More recent examples include Ahmad Nassir bin Juma Bhali's (b. 1936) *Poems from Kenya: Gnomic Verses in Swahili* (1966), short enigmatic poems published in a bilingual edition, and J. N. Somba's (b. 1930) novel, *Kuishi kwingi ni kuona mengi* (1968; to live long is to see much), a story about the life of an average man in modern society. Kenyan publishers have also been active in bringing out Swahili translations of literary works written by African authors in English.

In Kikuyu

Although the production of literature in other Kenyan languages has been negligible, a start has been made in Kikuyu with the publication of two new works by Ngugi wa Thiong'o: a play co-authored by Ngugi wa Mirii (b. 1951) about the exploitation of peasants and workers in independent Kenya, *Ngaahika ndeenda* (1980; I will marry when I want), the public performance of which in 1977 led to Ngugi wa Thiong'o's arrest and detention for nearly a year; and a protest novel about neocolonialism, *Caitaani mūtharaba-Inī* (1980; the Devil on the Cross), which was the first piece of full-length fiction to appear in Kikuyu. Because he now seeks to address himself primarily to a local audience, Ngugi has declared his intention to continue writing in his mother tongue rather than in English. If other writers follow suit, there may be a surge in the production of African-language literature in Kenya in the years to come.

BIBLIOGRAPHY: Liyong, T. lo, *The Last Word: Cultural Synthesism* (1969); Ngugi wa Thiong'o, *Homecoming: Essays on African and Caribbean Literature, Culture and Politics* (1972); p'Bitek, O., *Africa's Cultural Revolution* (1973); Gurr, A., and Calder, A., eds., *Writers in East Africa* (1974); Cook, D., ed., *In Black and White: Writings from East Africa with Broadcast Discussion and Commentary* (1976); Roscoe, A., *Uhuru's Fire: African Literature East to South* (1977); Wanjala, C., *The Season of Harvest: Some Notes on East African Literature* (1978); Wanjala, C., *For Home and Freedom* (1980); Lindfors, B., ed., *Mazungumzo: Interviews with East African Writers, Publishers, Editors and Scholars* (1980); Ngugi wa Thiong'o, *Writers in Politics* (1981)

BERNTH LINDFORS

NGUGI wa Thiong'o

(formerly James Ngugi) Kenyan novelist, dramatist, and essayist (writing in English and Kikuyu), b. 5 Jan. 1938, Limuru

After receiving a B.A. in English at Makerere University College (Uganda) in 1964, N. worked briefly as a journalist in Nairobi before leaving for England to pursue graduate studies at the University of Leeds. Upon returning to Kenya in 1967, he taught at the University of Nairobi, eventually becoming head of the literature department, a position he held until 1978, when he was put in detention for nearly a year by the Kenyan government. After being released, he was not reinstated in his university post; in recent years he has supported himself entirely by writing.

N. is known best for his novels, which have focused on colonial and postcolonial problems in Kenya. *Weep Not, Child* (1964), the first novel in English to be published by an East African, tells the story of a young man who loses his opportunity for further education when his family is torn apart by the violence of the Mau Mau rebellion. *The River Between* (1965), written during N.'s undergraduate years, deals with an unhappy love affair in a rural community divided between Christian converts and non-Christians; the hero is a young schoolteacher who is trying to unite his people through Western education. Both books end tragically, emphasizing the difficulty of reconciling the old with the new in a society undergoing the trauma of cultural and political transition.

N.'s later novels, written after Kenya attained independence, concentrate on the legacy of colonialism in a new nation-state. In *A Grain of Wheat* (1967) the people who sacrificed most during the liberation struggle discover that their future has been blighted by their past and that the fruits of independence are being consumed by predatory political leaders. *Petals of Blood* (1977) carries this theme further by indicting wealthy landowners as well as politicians who capitalize on the miseries of others, thereby perpetuating economic inequality and social injustice. N. always sides with the poor, weak, and oppressed, exposing the cruelties they suffer in an exploitative neocolonial world. His most recent narrative, *Caitaani mūtharaba-Inī* (1980; *Devil on the Cross,* 1982), an allegorical novel written in Kikuyu, is an effort to make peasants and workers aware of the powerful political forces that shape their lives.

N.'s plays display the same gradual shift from colonial cultural concerns to contemporary social preoccupations. The early plays deal mainly with conflicts between parent and child and between the old and the new, but N. later teamed up with Micere Githae-Mugo (b. 1942) to write *The Trial of Dedan Kimathi* (1977), a dramatization of an episode in the career of Kenya's most prominent Mau Mau leader, and in 1977 he coauthored with Ngugi wa Mirii (b. 1951) *Ngaahika ndeenda* (1980; *I Will Marry When I Want,* 1982), a play in Kikuyu that depicts social, economic, and religious exploitation in the Kikuyu highlands. It was the staging of the latter play in Limuru, his hometown, that led to N.'s incarceration for nearly twelve months. Although no formal charges were ever filed against him, he apparently had offended members of the ruling elite in Kenya.

N.'s essays express very clearly and concisely the ideas that have animated his fiction and drama. *Homecoming: Essays on African and Caribbean Literature, Culture and Politics* (1972) places emphasis on coming to terms with the past and resisting colonial domination. *Writers in Politics* (1981) speaks of the postcolonial struggle for a patriotic national culture and outlines the writer's role in combating political repression. *Detained: A Writer's Prison Diary* (1981) provides a detailed account of his own involvement in efforts to increase the political awareness of his people.

N. remains East Africa's most articulate social commentator, someone whose works accurately reflect the tone and temper of his time and place.

FURTHER WORKS: *The Black Hermit* (1968); *This Time Tomorrow* (c. 1970); *Secret Lives* (1976)

BIBLIOGRAPHY: Roscoe, A., *Uhuru's Fire: African Literature East to South* (1977), pp. 170–90; Githae-Mugo, M., *Visions of Africa: The Fiction of Chinua Achebe, Margaret Laurence, Elspeth Huxley and N.* (1978), passim; Moore, G., *Twelve African Writers* (1980), pp. 262–88; Robson, C. B., *N.* (1980); Killam, G. D., *An Introduction to the Writings of N.* (1980); Gurr, A., *Writers in Exile: The Creative Use of Home in Modern Literature* (1981), pp. 92–121; Killman, G. D., ed., *Critical Perspectives on N.* (1982)

BERNTH LINDFORS

LESOTHO LITERATURE

Lesotho (formerly Basutoland) is a mountainous independent state surrounded by South Africa. The dominant language is South Sotho. The country is remarkable for its long tradition of printed vernacular literature, uncommon in Africa, where vernaculars are usually associated with oral poetry and storytelling.

Such writing was originally encouraged by missionaries, who, as early as 1841, imported a press to print translations of the Bible (completed 1878) and religious tracts. The literary tradition begins with Azariele Sekese's (1849–1930) collection in South Sotho *Buka ea pokello ea mekhoa ea Basotho le maele le litsome* (1893; new ed., 1907; customs and proverbs of the Basuto). The most important Sotho writer is Thomas Mofolo (q.v.). His series of moralistic historical novels culminated in a genuine masterpiece, *Chaka* (written 1910, pub. 1925; *Chaka the Zulu*, 1931; new tr., 1981), which recounts the life of the great Zulu conqueror as a tragic epic. This work, widely translated, has been called by the scholar Albert S. Gérard the "first major African contribution to world literature." The publication of *Chaka* marked the beginning of modern Lesotho literature.

Another writer of this period was Mofolo's teacher, Everitt Segoete (1858–1923), who wrote a moralistic novel, *Monono ke moholi mouoane* (1910; riches are like mist, vapor). This work has the distinction of originating the most common plot in southern African writing: the trials of an innocent tribal youth encountering the dangers and temptations of Johannesburg. The South African writer Peter Abrahams's (q.v.) *Mine Boy* (1946) is a classic example of the genre, later scornfully called the "Jim goes to the city" theme. It is also the subject of the most famous modern Lesotho novel, Attwell Sidwell Mopeli-Paulus's (1913–1960) *Blanket Boy's Moon* (1953).

During the 1930s most books published were obliged to feature the Christian ethics demanded by the missionaries, but the 1950s brought a new spate of original Lesotho writing.

The past success of vernacular publication and its established readership caused most Lesotho authors to retain their own language rather than explore English. The themes continue to parallel those that commonly inspire other writers in southern Africa. Albert Nqheku's (b. 1912) novel *Tsielala* (1959; silence, please), about Sotho workers in the gold mines, is bitterly outspoken against the racist policies of South

Africa. Bennett Khaketla's (b. 1913) novel *Meokho ea thabo* (1951; tears of joy) is about the inevitable clash between the values of the rural tradition and the expectations of the city life of young migrant workers. Since his theme stresses love as a mode of selecting a bride rather than the customary arranged marriage, he presents cultural conflict in sexual as well as political terms. Khaketla and Michael Mohapi (b. 1926) have written in various genres, including drama and poetry.

Kemuele Ntsane (b. 1920) wrote a series of satiric poems that, uncharacteristically for South Sotho verse, attempt rhyme forms. He also wrote four novels, including *Makumane* (1961; tidbits) and *Bao batho* (1968; these people).

Two novels by Mopeli-Paulus—*Blanket Boy's Moon* and *Turn to the Dark* (1956), both based on his own documentary account *Liretlo* (1950; ritual murder)—are the only modern works that have achieved a widespread international readership. They strongly oppose the apartheid system. Their method of creation was unusual: they were told by the author and then written down by sympathetic translators Richard Lanham and Miriam Basner, who produced the admired English versions, to which they may have contributed new material.

The first book written directly in English was *Masilo's Adventures, and Other Stories* (1968) by Benjamin Leshoai (b. 1920). The use of English was justified by the intention to use this book as a school reader, and it is still not certain whether this is the forerunner of the kind of English-language literature that is encountered elsewhere in Africa or whether the vigorous Sotho-language writing will predominate.

BIBLIOGRAPHY: Franz, G. H., "The Literature of Lesotho," *Bantu Studies*, 6 (1930), 45–80; Beuchat, P.-D., *Do the Bantus Have a Literature?* (1963); Mofolo, B., "Poets of Lesotho," *NewA*, 6, 2 (1967), 19–23; Gérard, A. S., *Four African Literatures* (1971), pp. 101–81; Jordan, A. C., *Towards an African Literature* (1973), passim; Maphike, P. R. S., "On the Essay in Southern Sotho," *Limi*, 8 (1980), 35–49; Gérard, A. S., *African Language Literatures* (1981), pp. 190–223

JOHN POVEY

MOFOLO, Thomas
Lesotho novelist (writing in South Sotho), b. 2 Aug. 1875, Khojane, Basutoland (now Lesotho); d. 8 Sept. 1948, Teyateyaneng

When M. was five, his Christian parents moved to the Qomoqomong

Valley, Quthing District. There M. met the black Christian missionary teacher whose devotion to education M. was to idealize in the figure of Reverend Katse in the novel *Pitseng* (1910; Pitseng). M. became a houseboy to Alfred Casalis, who was the head of the Bible school, the printing press, and the book depot in Morija. Recognizing M.'s potential, Casalis sent him to the Bible School and then to the teachers' college, from which M. received certification. Casalis also encouraged him to write.

M.'s first novel, *Moeti oa bochabela* (1907; *The Traveller of the East*, 1934), had first been serialized in *Leselinyana,* a Sotho journal. It is probably the first novel by a black to be published in southern Africa. Set in Basutoland, the action of the morality tale centers around the quest of the young protagonist, Fekisi, for the causes of the presence of evil in the world. Although he does not find the answer, his journey ends in his ascent to a Christian heaven where all is honesty and virtue.

In this novel Christian morality is idealized, while that of the African is shown to be in decline. M. tried to integrate African values with Christian values in a harmonious synthesis; Christianity for him was a way of restoring the purity of ancient African civilization.

The plot of *Pitseng,* M.'s second novel, concerns the marriage between two young Christianized Africans. In showing the moderation, discipline, and patience of both Alfred and Aria, qualities that make their marriage bond secure, M. alluded to marriage as the symbol of the relationship between the Church and Christ. Much emphasis is given to the character portrayal of the simple people who live in the secluded valley of Pitseng. In contrast to the virtue and piety of Alfred and Aria, M. pictures the hypocrisies of many other Christian Africans, black and white. M. here focuses on the discrepancy between the teachings of Christianity and the behavior of many Christians.

M.'s masterpiece, *Chaka* (1925; *Chaka the Zulu,* 1931; new tr., 1981), the last of his three novels, was written in 1910, but it was considered unsuitable for publication by M.'s only recourse, the missionary press, which did not alter this position for fifteen years. Disillusioned, M. gave up writing at thirty-five and devoted the next years to building a successful business. In 1937 he retired to his farm. But he was not to be allowed to enjoy it. M.'s farm was expropriated in 1940 when the government proceeded to enforce a prohibition of the Land Act of 1914—that a black could not own land that abuts the property of a white. Thus victimized by the whites and having lost the financial security obtained by years of work, he became a broken man. His last years were redeemed from grim poverty only by a small pension.

Chaka, a dramatic departure from M.'s earlier books, is the tragic study of a man who, once accustomed to the gratifications of power, can no longer live according to common morality. The novel is based on the history of an African conqueror, the "black Napoleon," who in the early 19th c. amassed an army of close to a million Zulu warriors and ruled over half of Africa, from the Congo to South Africa. In M.'s version, Chaka becomes evil when he succeeds to the chiefdom at his father's death; from that point on Chaka develops from a moral man into a monster. He sinks into the dark world of sorcery and paganism, bartering his soul for power. There is no turning back for Chaka, and he goes on to extraordinary success on the battlefields. But the code of power and violence by which he lives in the end devours him as well, when he is assassinated by his two half-brothers.

The appeal of Chaka is mythic; about him is the light of the fallen prince; he is Satan, Tamburlaine, and Faust. Although he destroys himself, his is a magnificent adventure. There is poetry in his evilness, fascination in his decline. Chaka chose the way of power, violence, cruelty. M. was attracted to another way—that of love and trust in humanity—but he understood the frustration and rage at the root of Chaka's evilness, and as an African he could even glory in Chaka's magnificent conquests.

Soon after its publication *Chaka* was a best seller in Africa, both in South Sotho and in other African and European-language editions, and M., who by then had long stopped writing, enjoyed its success.

M., both in the virtues he exhibited during his lifetime and in the themes he conveyed through his novels, belongs to a transitional African period, one in which conflict between traditional and modern values resulted in a painful distortion of both value systems. His work illustrates the tragic irony that angels as well as monsters are swallowed up when violence overtakes the African terrain.

BIBLIOGRAPHY: Kunene, D. P., *The Works of T. M.: Summaries and Critiques* (1967); Gérard, A. S., *Four African Literatures: Xhosa, Sotho, Zulu, Amharic* (1974), pp. 125–30; Mphahlele, E., *The African Image,* rev. ed. (1974), pp. 206–10, 223; Ikonné, C., "Purpose versus Plot: The Double Vision of T. M.'s Narrator," in Heywood, C., ed., *Aspects of South African Literature* (1976), pp. 54–65; Burness, D., ed., *Shaka, King of Zulus* (1976), passim; Swanepoel, C. F., "Reflections on the Art of T. M.," *Limi,* 7 (1979), 63–76

MARTIN TUCKER

LIBERIAN LITERATURE

Liberia was founded as a nation in the 19th c. by the U.S. Congress to provide a land for freed black slaves who wished to return to West Africa. Unfortunately, the returnees, called "Americos," became a governing class as cruelly indifferent to the problems of the indigenous Africans as any colonial administration. Years of resentment culminated in a coup d'état in 1980. Restrictive rule did little for development of a significant literature.

The Liberian writing that has been published either has been highly derivative, borrowing outdated diction and form from earlier English poetry, or has drawn on the indigenous storytelling tradition. Little of incisive contemporary value has appeared.

Typical of the earlier style is the work of Roland Tombekai Dempster (1910–1965). His poems *Echoes from a Valley* (1947) and "To Monrovia Old and New" (1958) have a declamatory rhetoric and style that derive little from their supposed occasion and locality.

One unusual earlier work, unfortunately without successors, was the novel *Love in Ebony: A West African Romance* (1932) by Varfelli Karlee (b. 1900). If not of outstanding quality, it did at least deal with the issues of the African people outside the society of the Monrovian elite.

Of those writers closely linked with the oral tradition, Bai Moore (b. 1916) is the most distinguished and the most prolific. After spending time studying in Virginia, he returned to Liberia in 1938 and began to collect folktales and poems, particularly from the Golah society into which he had been born. He translated much of this material and incorporated some of it into his English-language writing. Also drawing on the oral tradition is Wilton Sankawulo (b. 1945), whose stories of the Kpelle tribe, including "The Evil Forest" (1971)—part translations, part adaptations—have been published in *African Arts*.

The problems of a writer in Liberia are exemplified by the experience Bai Moore encountered in publishing his work. His major collection of poetry, *Ebony Dust* (1963), in which he reflects on his travels in Europe, America, and Africa, had to be produced in mimeographed form. His more topical journalistic report on a true event, *Murder in the Cassava Patch* (1968), was distributed by Moore himself, who sold two thousand copies on a street corner in Monrovia. Not until it was selected as a school text were the remaining three thousand copies sold.

Despite obstacles, writers do struggle to find an outlet for their work. Doris Henries (b. 1930) is one of the more active of recent writers. She has not yet prepared a full volume of her own work, but she has been instrumental in publishing some important anthologies of Liberian writing: *Poems of Liberia: 1836–1961* (1966) and *Liberian Folklore* (1966). It must be acknowledged that this country has not yet produced a writer of the stature of those from other West African countries. Perhaps the new political situation will encourage the development of a more vital literature.

BIBLIOGRAPHY: *Liberian Writing: Liberia as Seen by Her Own Writers as Well as by German Authors* (1970); Henries, D., *The Status of Writing in Liberia* (1972); Singler, J. V., "The Role of the State in the Development of Literature: The Liberian Government and Creative Fiction," *RAL*, 11 (1980), 511–28; Gérard, A. S., *African Language Literatures* (1981), pp. 243–46

JOHN POVEY

MALAGASY LITERATURE

In Malagasy

Before European missionaries introduced the printing press in the 19th c., Madagascar possessed highly developed forms of oral art: the most widely practiced genres were the proverbs *(ohabolana),* public oratory *(kabary),* the folktale *(angano),* and the fashionable poetic competitions known as *hain-teny;* also popular were dramatic rituals and festivities in which dancing and music by professional performers called *mpilalao* were as important as plot and the spoken word.

In 1818 King Radama I allowed the London Missionary Society to settle on the island. The first printing press was built in 1827, and in 1835 the Bible was the first book to be printed; the first vernacular newspaper, *Teny soa,* came out in 1866. Since then journalistic life in Madagascar has always been uncommonly lively: no other area of the French empire could boast as large a number of vernacular newspapers and little magazines, which fostered the promotion of literature; indeed, most Malagasy novels were first printed in serial form.

Imaginative writing in Malagasy can be said to begin in 1889 with *Fanoharana* (fables), a free adaptation of La Fontaine's *Fables* by a French-educated Jesuit priest, Basilide Rahidy (1839–1883), and with the tales and *hain-teny* of an L.M.S.-educated Protestant minister, Ingahibe Rainitovo (1852–?).

Apart from the edifying sentimental novels of Rev. Andriamatoa Rabary (1864–1947), the next generation was remarkable principally for its theatrical achievements. Its best representatives were exceptionally versatile, being journalists, novelists, poets, and musical composers as well as playwrights. But the chief contribution of Alexis Rakotobe (dates n.a.), Justin Rainizanabololona (1861–1938), and Tselatra Rajaonah (1863–1931) at the turn of the century was the creation of Malagasy musical comedy, which fused the native tradition of the *mpilalao* and the influence of the French operetta; their favorite theme is love, but the plays usually end on a moralizing note. Further, they gave instruction and encouragement to such younger dramatists as Dondavitra (pseud. of Charles-Aubert Razafimahefa, 1880–1936), whose best-known play, *Peratra Mahavariana* (the magic ring) was performed in 1906; Wast Ravelomoria (1886–1951), who wrote comedies of manners; Romain Andrianjafy (1888–1917), who directed his own company, Tananarive-

Theatre; Jasmina Ratsimiseta (1890–1946), who imitated the French boulevard theater; and Naka Rabemanantsoa (1892–1943) and Justin Rajoro (1893–1949), the founders of the first Malagasy acting company, Telonorefy. Most of the early 20th-c. plays never reached print.

Madagascar became a French protectorate in 1895 and a French colony in 1905. All teaching was henceforth done in French; no native could be appointed to an official position if he did not know French. Although a number of writers were imprisoned in 1915 during the ruthless suppression of a plot engineered by the cultural association Vy Vato Sakelika, the colonial regime did not put an immediate end to the ebullient literary activity of the Malagasy people. Together with Justin Rainizanabololona, Edouard Andrianjafintrimo (1881–1972) experimented with rhyme and new metrical schemes based on French and Latin prosody. Rev. Maurice Rasamuel (1886–1954), chiefly known for his historical and oratorical works, wrote his novel *Tao Manjakadoria* (1942; formerly in Manjakadoria). Madagascar's first woman novelist, Charlotte Razafiniaina (b. 1894), who wrote plays, poems, and *hain-teny* as well, produced several social novels dealing with the problems of acculturation. This was also the generation of the greatest lyric poet in the Malagasy language, Ramanantoanina (1891–1940); his nostalgic work was studied by the first notable Malagasy critic, Charles Rajoelisolo (1896–1966), who was also a historian and a gifted short-story writer. Another prominent representative of this generation was Rodlish (pseud. of Arthur Razakarivony, 1897–1967), the author of serious dramas such as *Ranomody* (1926; the whirlpool) and *Sangy mahery* (1936; violent games), which deal with the theme of frustrated love and offer a critique of the native caste system; he also published in collaboration with Jean Narivony (b. 1898), two anthologies of Malagasy poetry, *Amboara voafantina* (1926; selected poems) and *Kolokalo tatsinana* (1929; songs from the east).

Among the writers born after Madagascar came under French authority, there was a noticeable estrangement from the use of the vernacular language for literary purposes. On the other hand, there arose a gifted school of French-writing poets. Although many popular novelettes were printed in the capital, Tananarive, there was a steady decline in the number of legitimate writers in the vernacular. Apart from the short stories of Elie Raharolahy (b. 1901), the bulk of later Malagasy creative writing consists of the lyric poetry of Fredy Rajaofera (1902–1968) and especially the plays of J. V. S. Razakandrainy (b. 1913), better known under the pseudonym of Dox. Madagascar shares with the Cape Verde

Islands and northern Nigeria the peculiarity of having bilingual poets, such as Fidelis-Justin Rabestimanandranto (b. 1907) and Régis Rajemisa-Raolison (b. 1913), who handle their mother tongue and French with equal ease.

After Madagascar became the independent Malagasy Republic in 1960, official encouragement given to the national language resulted in the rapid growth of the novel, examples of which are Alphonse Ravoajanahary s (dates n.a.) *Tao anatin' ny sarotra* (1967; in big trouble), Jean-Louis Rasamizafy's (dates n.a.) *Mandrakizay ho doria* (1967; forever), Michel Paul Abraham-Razafimaharo's (b. 1926) *Valin-keloka* (1968; the punishment of sin), and E. D. Andriamalala's (dates n.a.) *Fofombadiko* (1971; betrothal).

BIBLIOGRAPHY: Aly, J. M., "Où en est la littérature malgache depuis 1960?" and Andriantsilaniarivo, E., "Où en sont les lettres malgaches?" in *Réflexions sur la première décennie des indépendances en Afrique noire/Reflections on the First Decade of Negro-African Independence,* special issue of *PA* (1971), pp. 272–82, 343–56; Gérard, A. S., *African Language Literature: An Introduction to the Literary History of Sub-Saharan Africa* (1981), pp. 75–91

ALBERT S. GÉRARD

In French

Malagasy literature in French began in the 1920s, with the publication of Édouard Bezoro's (dates n.a.) novel *La sœur inconnue* (1923; the unknown sister); it celebrates the success of the French military conquest of Madagascar in the late 19th c., which resulted in the abolition of slavery, practiced until then by the Hova rulers of the island.

Bezoro's attitude was not, however, to become typical, and subsequent writing in French was to be almost wholly dominated by the cultural and political tensions created by colonialism. This became evident very early on in the work of the country's most outstanding poet, Jean-Joseph Rabearivelo (1901–1937), whose poetry reflects his deep distress at the undermining of traditional Malagasy literature and his equally sensitive appreciation of contemporary French poetry. Rabearivelo suffered greatly from the isolation of the black writer in colonial society of the interwar years, an isolation that seemed to be intensified by Madagascar's geographical distance from France and the poet's frustration at being cut off from the intellectual life of the French capital. *La coupe de cendres* (1924; cup of ashes), *Sylves* (1927; woods), and *Volumes* (1928; volumes) follow conventional French verse forms, but the mature poetry of *Presque-songes* (1934; near-dreams) and *Traduit de la nuit* (1935; translated from the night) combines a mastery of modern French free verse and the traditional *hain-teny* (a prose poem in the form of a dialogue) to achieve a thoroughly personal style that fully reflects the poet's sense of his inner tensions. The poems in his *Vieilles chansons des pays d'Imerina* (1939; old songs of Imerina) are entirely based on the *hain-teny*.

The two best-known writers of the post-World War II period are Jacques Rabemananjara (b. 1913) and Flavien Ranaivo (b. 1914). Rabemananjara's most forceful poetry, in volumes such as *Antsa* (1956; Malagasy: eulogy), *Lamba* (1956; Malagasy: strip of cloth used as traditional article of clothing), and *Antidote* (1961; antidote), was inspired by the anticolonial violence that erupted in Madagascar in 1947 and expresses his bitter disillusionment with French policies, largely prompted by his experience of prison at the time. Plays like *Les boutriers de l'aurore* (1957; vessels of the dawn) and *Agapes des dieux* (1962; love feasts of the gods) are an attempt to evaluate the Malagasy past in keeping with the Negritude (q.v.) ideals of the day. Flavien Ranaivo's *L'ombre et le vent* (1947; the shade and the wind), *Mes chansons de toujours* (1955; my everlasting songs) and *Le retour au bercail* (1962; return to the fold) are modeled almost entirely on the traditional *hain-teny* and show how effectively the subtleties of Malagasy poetry can be conveyed in French.

A number of minor writers, chiefly poets, have helped to sustain the vitality of Malagasy writing in French since the 1920s. The best-known among these are Michel-François Robinary (1892–1971), whose *Fleurs défuntes* (1927; dead flowers) has survived remarkably well in spite of its heavy reliance on French romantic models, and Régis Rajemisa-Raolison (b. 1913), who continued the very fruitful exploitation of the *hain-teny* in his collection *Les fleurs de l'île rouge* (1948; the flowers of the red island).

As in the case of the vernacular literature, the constant regeneration of ephemeral literary journals was of considerable importance in the stimulation of creative writing in French and in keeping alive critical reflection on the problems confronting writers caught between two cultures. Another factor has been the existence of small local printing firms and an enterprising official printing house (which also publishes the only longstanding journal, the influential *Revue de Madagascar*). Apart from Rabemananjara, whose work has been published in France by the Présence Africaine publishing house, the majority of Malagasy writers, including Rabearivelo, have been dependent on these local publishers.

Madagascar obtained its independence from France in 1960, becoming the Malagasy Republic. Unlike most of the black states on the African continent, independence did not bring with it a continuing expansion of creative writing in French, and, since the military coup of 1972, the two most prominent living Malagasy writers, Jacques Rabemananjara and Flavien Ranaivo, have lived in political exile in France.

BIBLIOGRAPHY: Wake, C. H., and Reed, J. O., "Modern Malagasy Literature in French," *BA*, 38 (1964), 14–19; Cornevin, R., *Le théâtre en Afrique noir et à Madagascar* (1970), pp. 263–87

CLIVE WAKE

MALAWIAN LITERATURE

Malawi, formerly Nyasaland, became independent in 1964 after the Federation of Rhodesia and Nyasaland (1953–63) fell apart. There has been some publication in indigenous languages. Samuel Ntara (b. 1905) has published several novels in Nyanja, most importantly *Mnyamboza* (1949; *Headman's Enterprise,* 1949), a fictionalized biography of a chieftain of the Cewa tribe. Several of English Chafulumira's (b. 1930) short narratives in Nyanja were published in London. There has also been creative writing in the Tumbuka language.

The limitations of publishing opportunities at home and the likelihood that literacy will be achieved in English reduce the options for writers in every formerly British African country who might prefer to write in an indigenous language. When English is elected, there is usually a transitional type of writing, which draws heavily upon the admired formal accomplishments of the language taught at school. The poet Katoki Mwalilino (b. 1942?) exemplifies this unselective borrowing; he takes the style and diction of British poetry and tries to apply its unsuitable qualities to topics of African content—even the subject of African nationalism. The nature of Mwalilino's verse can be surmised from the Poet Laureate-like title of one of his more famous poems, "The Awakening Malawi on July 6th 1964" (1966).

There are only three contemporary Malawian writers of serious consequence. Legson Kayira (b. 1940) first achieved recognition for an extraordinary account of his "walk": he hiked some 2,500 miles from Malawi north to the Sudan, where he was befriended by the U.S. consul, who arranged for him to come to America for education. His autobiography, *I Will Try* (1965), if lacking much literary merit, is an impressive account of determination and commitment. Subsequently, Kayira settled in England, from where he has written three novels with themes also applicable to other parts of Africa. *The Looming Shadow* (1967) deals with the complexities of traditional life and belief, while *Jingala* (1969) confronts the generational conflict in its story of a young man who wishes to become a Catholic priest. These works are readable enough, without suggesting that the writer has the ability to give Malawian writing an individual stamp.

More competent technically is Aubrey Kachingwe (b. 1926), whose single novel, *No Easy Task* (1966), makes very clear that his training is as a journalist. It touches upon the inevitable problems that arise when a nation confronts the barriers to independence. It is less an imaginative creation than a documentation drawn from experiences both in Malawi and elsewhere in Africa. It is not clear whether Kachingwe will be able to move beyond reportage to true novel writing.

Superior to both these writers is the poet, novelist, and critic David Rubadiri (b. 1930). He is the most original Malawian literary figure, although he has spent much of his adult life outside the country. His single novel, *No Bride Price* (1967), deals, as do so many African novels, with the problems of coping with the incompetence and corruption of many African governments. More generally, it deals with the issue of establishing appropriate moral values to be retained in a violently transitional society. In Rubadiri's novel there is a coup, and the protagonist is imprisoned. The personal disaster of losing his child compounds his political distress, but he learns to comprehend the advantages and virtues of the traditional beliefs. He discerns belatedly that it is the false expectations raised by independence that are responsible for many of the problems afflicting modern Africa. Rubadiri is also a significant poet. He has not yet had his poetry collected in book form, but his verse is regularly anthologized, not only for its inherent quality but also because it treats of some of the more crucial issues confronting contemporary Africans. "The Tide That from the West Washes Africa to the Bone" (1970) is a powerful denunciation of the despoiling of the continent.

More recently, in the areas of drama and poetry Malawi has shown a far livelier development than is apparent from international lists of publications. There is an ambitious traveling theater, sustained by the university, for which several authors, including James Mgombe (dates n.a.), Innocent Banda (dates n.a.), and Chris Kamlongera (dates n.a.) have written plays published in the local Malawian Writers Series. The most ambitious dramatist is Steve Chimombo (dates n.a.), whose play *The Rainmaker* (1975) deals with the early rituals of the M'bona cult.

Similarly, the impetus for poetry derives from an active university poetry workshop. Felix Mnthali (dates n.a.) and Steve Chimombo, both significant poets, are on the faculty. Among this highly eclectic group, Jack Mapanje (dates n.a.) and Lupenga Mphande (dates n.a.) are promising poets who write sensitively on local themes. Frank Chipasula (dates n.a.) is the only one yet to have published a volume of verse, *Visions and Reflections* (1973). This vigorous array of local talent suggests a potential for a broadly based, specifically Malawian literature, which is being furthered by a literary quarterly, *Odi*.

BIBLIOGRAPHY: Kerr, D., "New Writing from Malawi," *Afriscope*, 3, 12 (1973), 54–59; Roscoe, A. A., *Uhuru's Fire: African Literature East to South* (1977), pp. 134–49, 215–25, 267–73; Gibbs, J., "Theatre in Malawi," *Afriscope*, 7, 11–12 (1977), 69–71; Mapanje, J., "New Verse in Malawi," *Odi*, 2, 1 (1977), 24–28; Namponya, C. R., "History and Development of Printing and Publishing in Malawi," *Libri*, 28 (1978), 167–81; Calder, A., "Under Zomba Plateau: The New Malawian Poetry," *Kunapipi*, 1, 2 (1979), 59–67; Gérard, A. S., *African Language Literatures* (1981), pp. 204–7, 226–33

JOHN POVEY

MALI LITERATURE

Vast, sparsely populated, predominantly agricultural, Mali has an illustrious history going back to medieval times. Under French rule the territory was called French Sudan. An independent nation since 1960, Mali has launched various campaigns to fight illiteracy, educating the masses in both French and Bambara, a Mandé language spoken by the largest ethnic group in the country. As literacy increases, interest in the arts grows as well. The rich oral tradition has given rise to theater groups. Since the early 1970s the government-owned publishing company, Éditions Populaires, has published historical, anthropological, and literary works. It limits publication to noncontroversial subject matter, however, emphasizing the glorification of the past rather than the examination of the present with a critical eye.

Among the most renowned African historians is Amadou Hampaté Bâ (b. 1920), who has published important works in the field of African religion and Islamic theology. Having developed an Arabic script for the Fulani language, Bâ published *Kaidara* (1965; Kaidara), a traditional allegorical poem in a bilingual Fulani/French edition.

Emphasis upon history and Mali's rich oral tradition is also apparent in the work of Bâ's contemporary, Djibril Tamsir Niane (b. 1920), who was born either in Mali or northern Guinea and whose ancestors were Malinké *griots* (oral historians). Niane's version of the Malinké epic *Soundjata; ou, L'épopée mandingue* (1960; *Sundiata: An Epic of Old Mali*, 1965) retells the legend of the crippled boy who grew up to become an outstanding military and political leader and rule the Mali Empire (1230–55). In the introduction to the epic, Niane emphasizes the importance of the *griot;* "We are vessels of speech, we are the repositories that harbor secrets many centuries old."

A younger generation has taken up the same tradition of glorifying the past. Massa Maken Diabaté (b. 1936) has rewritten the Sundiata legend as *Kala Jata* (1965; Kala Jata). Combining his talents as a poet and an anthropologist, Diabaté uses words and expressions in the Malinké language interspersed within the French text in an attempt to capture the rhythms of Malinké poetry.

Seydou Kouyaté Badian (b. 1928) is known as a poet, playwright, and novelist. His novel *Sous l'orage* (1963; under the storm) examines the conflict between generations in a changing society. When two lovers challenge their parents by deciding to marry, they involve the entire village in the conflict. Badian has also turned to African history for inspiration. His play *La mort de Chaka* (1962; the death of Chaka) treats the theme of the Zulu king first presented in literature by the Lesotho writer Thomas Mofolo (q.v.), in his novel *Chaka* (1925; *Chaka the Zulu*, 1931), written in the Bantu language South Sotho.

Drawing upon ancient Mali history to challenge modern perceptions of Africa's past, Yambo Ouologuem (b. 1940) published an important and controversial novel, *Le devoir de violence* (1968; *Bound to Violence*, 1971), in which he created the fictional African kingdom of Makem, ruled by the violent despots of the Saif dynasty. He advances the thesis that violence and slavery existed long before the colonial powers' scramble for the continent. The first African novel to receive the Renaudot Prize in France, *Le devoir de violence* has been attacked by critics for its brutality, eroticism, and alleged plagiarism. Ouologuem uses violence to shock the reader. In addition, he blends legend with realism, African and Arabic expressions with French. He forces the reader to react to his prose, to come to grips with his expression of the eternal problem of man's inhumanity to man.

Mali is committed to affirming a rich cultural tradition. Its writers today reveal a genuine commitment to studying the present and the past and to synthesizing the old and the new.

BIBLIOGRAPHY: Larson, C., *The Emergence of African Fiction* (1972), passim; Rubin, J. S., "Mali: New Writing from an Ancient Civilization," *SBL*, 4, 3 (1973), 15–18; Olney, J., "Of Griots and Heroes," *SBL*, 6, 1 (1975), 14–17; Diawara, G., "Literature and the New Generations," *LAAW*, 31 (1977), 114–17; Singare, T., "Où en sont les lettres maliennes?" *Études maliennes*, 22 (1977), 1–23; Palmer, E., *The Growth of the African Novel* (1979), pp. 199–220; Decraene, P., "Le Mali: Tradition, arts et littérature," *FE*, 294 (1980), 34–37

MILDRED MORTIMER

MAURITIAN LITERATURE

For a long time, Mauritius, in the Indian Ocean—or Île de France, as it was called until it was ceded by France to Britain in 1814—remained culturally a distant province of France. During the first part of the 19th c. the group of the Oval Table, led by Thomi Pitot de la Beaujardière (1779–1857), reflected the style of the popular French poet and song writer Pierre-Jean de Béranger (1780–1857). The first poet to depart from exclusively French themes and style was François Chrestien (1767–1846), whose *Le bobre africain* (1822; the African guitar) even included poems in Creole.

The "father of Mauritian poetry," Léoville L'Homme (1857–1928), and the more important poet Robert Edward Hart (1891–1954) gradually moved from romanticism to symbolism. Over the course of thirty-three volumes, Loys Masson (1915–1969) achieved the transition to surrealism in poetry, while his *Le notaire des Noirs* (1961; the notary of Les Noirs) was a high point in the Mauritian novel. In poetry, Malcolm de Chazal (1904–1981) followed André Breton's surrealism, notably in *Sens plastique* (1947; plastic sense), while André Masson (b. 1927) veered toward esoteric themes, and Édouard J. Maunick (b. 1934) emphasized the African element in the inspired lyrics of *Ensoleillé vif* (1977; sunstruck alive). In fiction, Marcel Cabon (1912–1972) depicted indigenous life with realism and authenticity, even using local phrases occasionally in the novel *Namasté* (1965; Namasté).

Beginning with *Folklore de l'Île Maurice* (1888; folklore of Mauritius)—a collection of works, some in Creole, gathered by Charles Baissac (1831–1892), a white ethnographer—tales and *sega* (a local musical form) songs in Creole have been an important component of Mauritian literature. It took René Noyau (b. 1912), however, to "decolonize" such tales—that is, to use Creole as a challenge to French cultural ascendancy—and to assert the claims of the folk tradition in *Tention caïma* (1971; beware, crocodile), reworkings of folktales in Creole. Today, Dev Virshsawmy (b. 1940) is the major champion of Creole literature as a means of achieving cultural unity and as an alternative to the belles-lettres of the French-speaking elite. His best-known work, *Li* (1976; him), a play whose production was banned by the government then in power, blends cultural and political satire. Another Creole writer, Renée Asgarally (b. 1942), also denounced social barriers in *Quand montagne prend difé...* (1977; when the mountain catches fire...).

Writing in English has always been on a limited scale, although English is the official administrative and school language, even since independence in 1968. Two worthy writers have emerged: Azize Asgarally (b. 1933), whose plays, mostly political and metaphysical, earned him an international reputation before he turned to writing in Creole with *Ratsitatane* (1980; Ratsitatane), a play about the Malagasy leader of a 19th-c. revolt of native workers; and Deepchand Beeharry (b. 1927), whose novel *That Others Might Live* (1976) graphically evokes the plight of Indian indentured workers at the turn of the century.

Mauritian literature in English seems to have little future. There remains a strong French tradition—more than eighty percent of literary publications are still in French—but Creole writing is assuming an increasingly important position.

BIBLIOGRAPHY: Prosper, J.-G., ed., *Mauritius Anthology of Literature in the African Context* (1977); Hazareesingh, K., ed., *Anthologie des lettres mauriciennes* (1978); Prosper, J.-G., *Histoire de la littérature mauricienne de langue française* (1978); Furlong, R., ed., "La production littéraire à l'Île Maurice," special issue, *Journal of the Mauritius Institute of Education,* No. 3 (1979); Fabre, M., "Mauritian Voices: A Panorama of Contemporary Creative Writing in English," *WLWE,* 19 (1980), 121–37; Fabre, M., and Quet, D., "A Checklist of Mauritian Creative Writing in English (1920–1980),"*WLWE,* 19 (1980), 138–43

MICHEL FABRE

MOROCCAN LITERATURE

In Arabic

The modern Arabic literary renascence known as "The Awakening," which began in the Levant in the second half of the 19th c., had for a long time only a minor effect in Morocco—on the western limit of the Arab world. There was not even a printing press in the country until 1865, when a lithograph press was opened in Fez, and no Arabic newspaper until 1889.

For the first two decades of the 20th c., literary endeavor in Morocco was confined primarily to the age-old forms of classical Arabic poetry and to traditional works of scholarship, such as treatises on law and liturgy, scriptural exegesis, local histories, and hagiologies. Few of these works enjoyed any sort of wide readership or lasting impact. A singular exception to the general obscurity is Muhammad al-Kattānī's (1858/9–c. 1927) *Salwat al-anfās wa muhādathat al-akyās bi-man uqbira min al-'ulamā' wa al-sulahā' bi-Fās* (1899; solace for souls and discourses for the wise concerning the scholars and saints buried in Fez). The book is not only a biographical dictionary of the holy men of Fez, but a theoretical treatise on the doctrine of saint veneration and a defense of this typically Maghrebi (North African) form of Islam.

The earliest discernible influence of the Middle Eastern revival appeared in historical writing, the most important traditional Arabic literary genre after poetry. Muhammad al-Nāsirī's (1835–1897) *Kitāb al-istiqsā' li-akhbār duwal al-Maghrib al-Aqsā* (4 vols., 1894; 9 vols., 1954–56; a thorough investigation of the chronicles of the dynasties of Morocco), a monumental chronicle of Moroccan history from the Muslim conquest to the author's own time, had a profound impact upon the historical and national consciousness of the reading public and remains to this day the classic exposition of the national past. The *Kitāb al-istiqsā'* was followed by other works that tried to bridge the gap between traditional and modern Arabic historiography, such as 'Abd al-Rahmān ibn Zaydān's (dates n.a.) *Ithāf alām al-nās bi-jumāl akhbār hādirat Miknās* (5 vols., 1929–33; a presentation of the most learned men according to the finest accounts of the capital of Meknes), a history of the author's native city of Meknes and its elite. The first volume opens with a dedication to the young Sultan Sīdī Muhammad ibn Yūsuf (later Muhammad V), who had recently ascended the throne. Like the *Kitāb al-istiqsā'* the *Ithāf* had the effect of further strengthening a national-historical awareness among Moroccans.

The first attempts at adopting truly modern literary forms came in drama after the highly successful tour of an Egyptian theatrical company in 1923. The early plays, such as *Al-Fadīla* (virtue) by 'Abd Allāh al-Jarārī (b. 1905), which was performed in Fez in the mid-1920s, and *Intisār al-haqq bi al-bātil* (the triumph of right over wrong) by 'Abd al-Khaliq al-Tarīs (dates n.a.), which was staged in Tetuan in 1933, were didactic and rather primitive works of no lasting importance. They were, however, the forerunners of the nationalist literature that became dominant in Morocco from the mid-1930s to the mid-1950s.

The new Arabic journals of the period, such as *Al-Maghrib, Al-Atlas, Al-Sa'āda,* and *Al-Salām,* became organs for essays on cultural themes by 'Abd Allāh Guennoun (dates n.a.) and Ahmad Bahnīnī (?-1971), for essays of literary criticism by Muhammad al-Qabbāj (pseud.: Ibn 'Abbād, dates n.a.) and Ahmad Ziyād (dates n.a.), and for patriotic poetry and stories in verse and prose by 'Allāl al-Fāsī (1910–1974), who became the leader of the nationalist movement, Mukhtār al-Sūsī (dates n.a.), who promoted Berber ethnic pride, and 'Abd al-Qādir Hasan (dates n.a.). During this period a new poetry, known as *al-shi'r al-nidālī* (resistance poetry), developed. Written in the classical meters, it expressed the new themes of struggle, self-sacrifice, and the establishment of equity and justice, all of which were watchwords of the nationalists.

The most lasting body of literature to come out of the nationalist period consisted of short stories, again appearing mostly in journals. Sentimental vignettes of Moroccan life were in vogue. The bourgeoisie of Fez, which formed the backbone of the independence movement, was frequently depicted. Ahmad Bannānī's (dates n.a.) "Wafā' li-Fās wa-wafā' li al-hubb" (1940; fidelity to Fez and fidelity to love) was the first in a series of stories set in the author's native city. It is a work of pure, descriptive lyricism. The protagonist longs to return to his beloved Fez, "where everything talks of love," and to die there. Among the finest short stories of the period are those of 'Abd al-Majīd Ben-Jellūn (b. 1919). His collection of tales *Wādī al-dimā'* (1948; the valley of blood) depicts with great sensitivity the relations between Moroccans and Frenchmen at the time of the Protectorate. For example, in the pathetic story "Sā'id al-asmāk" (the fisherman) Ben-Jellūn relates the tale of 'Abbās, a simple fisherman who cannot comprehend the changes wrought by the conquerors. Ben-Jellūn is one of the few Moroccan writers whose works have enjoyed some popularity in the Arab East.

In French

Alone among the writers of the nationalist period, Ahmed Sefrioui (b. 1915) employed French as his language of expression. Nevertheless, his stories exhibit the same romantic, patriotic sentiment found in the works of Moroccans writing in Arabic. Sefrioui's collection of tales *Le chapelet d'ambre* (1949; the amber necklace) has Fez as its principal setting. The stories have an almost fairy-tale quality. For Sefrioui, Morocco is an enchanted land whose daily life is "assuredly all poetry."

The only Moroccan writer to receive truly international attention stands totally outside the main current of nationalist literature as it developed from the 1930s through the 1950s. In 1954 Driss Chraïbi (b. 1926), a young Moroccan chemical engineer living in Paris, published his first novel, *Le passé simple* (the simple past), an angry, rebellious work, in part autobiographical, expressing the author's disgust for and rejection of traditional Moroccan Islamic society. *Le passé simple* was disconcerting both to the liberal French intellectual establishment and to the Moroccan public. It was denounced in the Moroccan nationalist press, and for a short while Chraïbi recanted and apologized to his countrymen for the book. He later admitted that the denial of his own work was made in a moment of weakness. The following year he published *Les boucs* (1955; billygoats). The hero of the book, Yalann Waldik (whose name means "may his father be cursed!") is an Algerian—not a Moroccan—living in France. The novel deals in part with the problem of North Africans in European society. Other novels in the same nervous, angry style followed, culminating in *Succession ouverte* (1962; unclaimed inheritance), a sequel to *Le passé simple*, in which the hero finally achieves a certain peace of mind after visiting Morocco to attend his father's funeral.

In the 1960s, a number of young Moroccans followed the trail blazed by Chraïbi, using similar subject matter and evincing the same spirit of rebelliousness against traditional Moroccan values. The most notable among these is the avant-garde poet and novelist Mohammed Khair-Eddine (b. 1941), whose novels *Agadir* (1967; Agadir) and *Corps négatif* (1968; negative body) have been described by Moroccan critics as "savage literature." Khair-Eddine is a consummate rebel revolting against his family, his king, even his own blood. He calls for the complete destruction of the old in order to build anew.

Other young contemporary Moroccan authors writing in French, such as Abdelkébir Khatibi (b. 1938), Tahar Benjelloun (b. 1944), Zaghloul Morsy (b. 1933), and El Mostefa Nissaboury (b. 1943), who have chosen to remain in their native country, stand somewhere between the rebels Chraïbi and Khair-Eddine, on the one hand, and the senior establishment romanticists such as Sefrioui and Ben-Jellūn, on the other.

BIBLIOGRAPHY: Lévi-Provençal, E., *Les historiens des Chorfa* (1922); Germanus, A. K. J., "The Literature of Morocco," *IC*, 38 (1964), 213–41; Khatibi, A., *Le roman maghrébin* (1968); Ortzen, L., ed., *North African Writing* (1970); Yetiv, I., *Le thème de l'aliénation dans le roman maghrébin d'expression française* (1972); Déjeux, J., *Littérature mahgrébine de langue française* (1973); Lahbabi, M. A., "L'acculturation franco-marocaine en littérature," *Comptes rendus trimestriels des séances de l'Académie des Sciences d'Outre-Mer*, 37 (1977), 675–94; *La littérature maghrébine de langue française devant la critique*, special issue, *O&C*, 4, 2 (1979); special Moroccan issue, *Europe*, Nos. 602–3 (1979)

NORMAN A. STILLMAN

MOZAMBICAN LITERATURE

In the development of their respective indigenous, acculturated elites, Mozambique and Angola have much in common. But while Angolan intellectuals, starting in the late 19th c., had access, because of relatively open lines of communication with Portugal and Brazil, to many of the new, often progressive ideas generated in Europe and America, their counterparts in the east African colony of Mozambique were isolated from Europe and exposed to the conservative thinking of the ruling classes in South Africa and Rhodesia. The historical peculiarities of Portuguese settlement in Mozambique also contributed to greater separation of the races than in Angola, where the color line was more subtly drawn.

De facto racial segregation in colonial Mozambique resulted in the founding of three social clubs: the first, established in 1920, was made up almost entirely of mestizos; the second, founded in 1932, was composed of blacks; and the third, established in 1935, had a membership of native-born whites. The mestizo club, which eventually came to be known as the African Association, through *O brado africano,* its official news organ, promoted some of the first literary efforts by Africans in the form of poems and stories in Portuguese, with an occasional work in Ronga, one of the principal Bantu languages of southern Mozambique. The Association of Mozambique's Native Sons, made up exclusively of so-called second-class whites, Europeans born in the colony (beginning in the 1960s a few token blacks and mestizos were admitted as members), published *A voz de Moçambique* as its official newspaper. This newspaper and others, like *Itinerário,* became important outlets for the literary efforts of members of the three racial communities.

The Associative Center of the Colony's Negroes published no newspaper, but it did harbor a unique component known as the Secondary School Studies Nucleus. Eduardo Mondlane (1920–1969), the American-educated economist who headed the Mozambican Liberation Front (FRELIMO) until his assassination, founded the Nucleus in the early 1960s as an intellectual training ground for many of the militants, like Samora Machel, who would lead the rebellion against colonial rule. The Nucleus also served as a meeting place for writers.

Mozambique's acculturated literature, written in Portuguese, but from an African perspective, got under way with the posthumously published

Sonetos (1949; sonnets) of Rui de Noronha (1909–1943) and the likewise posthumous *Godido, e outros contos* (1952; Godido, and other short stories) by João Dias (1926–1949). But in the absence of a coordinated sociocultural movement, as in Angola, and of a creole-African ethos, present in Angola's capital city of Luanda, the literary scene in Mozambique was fragmented and unsure.

Beginning in the 1950s the subject of Mozambican literature versus literature for its own sake reached the level of often heated debate, a debate that reached its peak in the late 1960s. Euro-Mozambicans, members of a white-dominated intellectual and literary clique in the city of Lourenço Marques (now Maputo), struggled with their own provincialism while denouncing black specificity and proclaiming a cultural universality that transcended ethnic, geographical, and political boundaries. But as the tide of national liberation swept across Portugal's colonial empire, advocates of a politically committed, authentically Mozambican literature came forward to contest art for art's sake. Ironically, from the ranks of Euro-Mozambican intellectuals emerged a few writers who did assure themselves a place in the history of Mozambican literature. Thus, Rui Knopfli (b. 1935), in his *Mangas verdes com sal* (1969; green mangoes with salt), produced "art" poems that express aspects of a black cultural reality through the codification of the tensions and ambivalences of the European born in Africa.

Some Euro-Mozambicans may have been appalled by what they saw as Noémia de Sousa's (b. 1927) stammering artlessness, but they could not help take note of her full-throated, frequently moving poetry of African revindication. But Sousa, one of sub-Saharan Africa's first female writers, never published a book of her poems, and her poetic voice became silent when, in the 1950s, she went into voluntary exile.

Meanwhile, José Craveirinha (b. 1922) was gaining attention with his vigorous poems, collected in *Chigubo* (1965; chigubo [a traditional Ronga dance]) and *Karingana ua karingana* (1974; a Ronga phrase roughly equivalent to "once upon a time"). Craveirinha's militancy, couched in the style of Negritude (q.v.), earned him an honored place among Mozambican nationalists, and his poetic phrasing and sensitivity brought him the respect and admiration of Euro-Mozambicans.

Craveirinha emerged as *the* poet of Mozambique; his counterpart in fiction was Luís Bernardo Honwana (b. 1942), whose short stories, such as those in *Nós matamos a cão tinhoso* (1964; *We Killed Mangy-Dog, and Other Mozambique Stories*, 1969), are artful elaborations of colonial social realities in the rural and semirural south. Some of Honwana's stories are clearly autobiographical; all play on the contradictions inherent in the relationship between the colonized and the colonizer. Both Craveirinha and Honwana were imprisoned in the 1960s for alleged subversive activities. Their status as political prisoners further enhanced their works in the eyes of many readers; but their literary production was an isolated case in the generally depressed cultural climate of Mozambique in the decade or so before independence.

In 1963, with the outbreak of the war of independence, literary activity became even more fragmented as militant writers fled into exile, joined their guerrilla compatriots in the bush, were imprisoned as subversives, or simply became discreetly mute. Liberal, if not militant Euro-Mozambicans, who generally opposed the Portuguese dictatorship and its colonial policies, often collaborated with black and mestizo dissidents, at least on the level of civil rights. And this concern for individual freedoms and democratic institutions led some members of the European circle to take part in a kind of cultural resistance that incorporated elements of a more committed African perspective and that ultimately embraced the cause of Mozambican nationalism.

Meanwhile, a small corpus of patriotic and combative literature was being published in exile and distributed abroad and in the liberated zones of northern Mozambique. Chief among these combative writers was Marcelino dos Santos (b. 1929), who also wrote some of his pamphleteering but frequently powerful and widely anthologized poetry under the pseudonym Kalungano.

Unlike what occurred in Angola, independence in Mozambique did not bring about a flurry of literary activity. With the flight of most Euro-Mozambican intellectuals, the preindependence publishing base was all but obliterated, and the lines of literary continuity became tenuous. There were, however, isolated and often curious cases of literary activity. Orlando Mendes (b. 1916), for example, a white Mozambican and a prolific writer, published two volumes of patriotic poems, stories, and plays under the title of *País emerso* (1975, 1976; a country emerged). And in 1975, the year of Mozambican independence, a startling find was made in the form of a number of poems written by one Mutimati Bernabé João, presumably a guerrilla fighter who had died in battle. The poems, published under the title *Eu o Povo* (1975; I, the people) were actually the product of António Quadros (b. 1933), a Portuguese who had come to Mozambique in 1964 and who had actively participated in the cosmopolitan cultural activities of the circle of Euro-Mozambican intellectuals. Despite what would seem to amount to a hoax, the poems stand as something of a monument to the idea that there can be such a thing as "good" political literature; and Quadros, who has never openly admitted to being the author and who, in fact, uses several different names, continues to live and work in Mozambique.

Even without a coordinated literary thrust, there was considerable literary activity in Mozambique. This activity was not limited to the major cities, and much of it took the form of grassroots organizing by the government and FRELIMO, the ruling party. Literary contests for students and workers resulted in the publication of prize-winning, albeit mainly technically weak poems and stories. Their amateurishness notwithstanding, these works contributed to the propagation of a taste for literature among a populace that was just beginning to learn to read, and they helped form a base upon which a more substantial literature could be built. And finally, in December 1980, the proclamation of the Association of Mozambican Writers set the stage for that more coordinated effort from which, Mozambicans hope, will emerge a national literature of universal appeal. If one new voice of recognizable merit has emerged since independence, it is that of Luís Patraquim (b. 1953), whose poems, collected in the small volume *Monção* (1980; monsoon), qualify him as Craveirinha's heir in terms of artistic quality.

BIBLIOGRAPHY: Moser, G. M., *Essays in Portuguese African Literature* (1969), passim; Honwana, L. B., "The Role of Poetry in the Mozambican Revolution," *LAAW*, No. 8 (1971), 148–66; Hamilton, R. G., *Voices from an Empire: A History of Afro-Portuguese Literature* (1975), pp. 163–229; Burness, D., *Fire: Six Writers from Angola, Mozambique, and Cape Verde* (1977); Hamilton, R. G., "Cultural Change and Literary Expression in Mozambique," *Issue*, 8, 1 (1978), 39–42

RUSSELL G. HAMILTON

NEGRITUDE

Negritude emerged in Paris around 1934, among a group of Caribbean and African students including Aimé Césaire (b. 1913) from Martinique and Léopold Sédar Senghor (q.v.) from Senegal. The word itself first appeared in print in Césaire's poem *Cahier d'un retour au pays natal* (1939; *Memorandum on My Martinique,* 1947; later tr., *Return to My Native Land,* 1969). It was only after World War II, in the late 1940s and 1950s, however, that the term and the concept acquired extensive currency. In the minds of its founders, Negritude was a reaction against the French colonial policy of assimilation and especially against the readiness of the older generation to accept assimilation as a goal. Negritude writers asserted instead the existence of an independent African culture and sought to define its distinctive values. They argued that all cultures have distinctive characteristics owing to biological differences between the races.

Although the term has been applied, often very loosely, to a wide variety of French-speaking black writers, there has never been a Negritude school. The concept itself has very little substance, in fact, outside its use by its main founders, Senghor and Césaire, and a few of their contemporaries, such as Léon Gontran Damas (1912–1978) from French Guiana and Birago Diop (q.v.) from Senegal. It is Senghor alone who has, since the end of World War II, consistently developed and expounded Negritude as an ideology in his poetry, speeches, and essays. He has listed and defined the fundamental, permanent values of African culture—emotion, rhythm, religious spirit, community—contrasting them with the European values of reason, skepticism, and individualism.

At first, Senghor viewed these characteristics as conflicting opposites, with the virtue of creativity on the African side. Jean-Paul Sartre, in his important essay on Negritude, "Orphée noir" (1948; *Black Orpheus,* 1963), therefore described it as an "antiracist racism." Senghor was, however, more inclined by temperament to reconciliation, and increasingly stressed the complementarity and interdependence of cultures and their evolution toward the "civilization of the universal."

While Césaire, too, stresses some of the African values invoked by Senghor (especially the African's essential quality of emotion as opposed to the European's reason), he has concentrated more on attacking the European stereotype of the black man as a cultural and racial inferior and the black man's readiness to acknowledge this stereotype. In his poetry Césaire presents the black man as much closer to the natural, real world than the white man, and therefore as much more vital and creative. Unlike Senghor, Césaire has not sought to develop Negritude as an ideology and has even tended to avoid the use of the term itself.

Since the 1960s, Negritude has been increasingly criticized by black writers. This criticism has been partly directed against the Negritude definition of African culture, which is seen as being too simplistic and too close to Western racist ideologies, but also against the conservative and neocolonialist politics considered to derive from Senghor's concept of Negritude. It is now being acknowledged, however, that during the 1950s Negritude was very influential in changing black, as well as white, attitudes toward the black peoples of Africa and the Caribbean; Sartre was therefore right to see it, in his 1948 essay, as a crucial but passing historical phenomenon.

BIBLIOGRAPHY: Jahn, J., *Muntu: An Outline of Neo-African Culture* (1961); Jahn, J., *Neo-African Literature: A History of Black Writing* (1969); Moore, G., "The Politics of Negritude," in Pieterse, C., and Munro, D., eds., *Protest and Conflict in African Literature* (1969), pp. 26–42; Adotevi, S., *Négritude et négrologues* (1972); Kesteloot, L., *Black Writers in French: A Literary History of Negritude* (1974); Steins, M., "La Négritude: Un second souffe?" *Cultures et Développement,* 12 (1980), 3–43; Irele, A., *The African Experience in Literature and Ideology* (1981)

CLIVE WAKE

NIGERIAN LITERATURE

In addition to oral art, which has been produced in the course of the centuries in the more than two hundred languages and dialects spoken by a population of nearly eighty million, Nigeria has been a prolific producer of written poetry, which began in the Muslim north, in the Arabic language, in the 15th c. The late 18th c. saw the emergence of *ajami*-type literature—that is, literature written in Arabic script used for the transliteration of such non-Arabic languages as Fula and Hausa.

In Hausa

Hausa, which is the main language of northern Nigeria, became all the more important as Western missionaries adapted the Roman alphabet to it for printing. In the 1930s the Literature Bureau at Zaria encouraged young literati to create prose fiction in Hausa: one of these early writers, who signed himself Abubakar Bauchi, was to become the first prime minister of independent Nigeria as Sir Abubakar Tafawa Balewa (1912–1966). Nevertheless, poetry has remained the most widely practiced and respected genre, with such talented authors as Sa'adu Zungur (1915–1958), Mudi Sipikim (b. 1930), and Mu'azu Hadejia (1920–1955). Formal drama, which had been initiated in the 1930s by Abubakar Imam (b. 1911), does not seem to be very popular, although it is practiced by a few members of the younger generation, such as Shu'aibu Makarfi (dates n.a.) and Umaru A. Dembo (b. 1945). Significantly, the Hausa have produced hardly any imaginative writing in English.

In Yoruba

Literacy was brought to the Yoruba of western Nigeria in the mid-19th c. by one of their own, Samuel Crowther (1809–1891), a freed slave who had been educated in Sierra Leone; he put the language in writing in order to translate the Bible. Although Yoruba was used for writing purposes from the late 19th c. on, especially in local newspapers, it did not reach its literary maturity until Daniel O. Fagunwa (1910–1963) had his first, highly original works of prose fiction printed in the 1950s; often described as "romances," these are traditional oral tales woven onto a central narrative thread, and slightly modernized to bring them in harmony with the moral tenets of Christianity. One of them was translated into English by Wole Soyinka (q.v.) as *The Forest of a Thousand Daemons* (1968). Novels closer to Western models were produced almost simultaneously by Chief Isaac O. Delano (b. 1904). Two distinct trends were thus initiated: one, originating in the rich store of local lore, was pursued by Gabriel E. Ojo (1925–1962), Olaya Fagbamigbe (b. 1930), Ogunsina Ogundele (b. 1925), and D. J. Fantanmi (b. 1938). The other, which seeks to reflect the problems of contemporary life, has on the whole been less successful: its main representative is Femi Jeboda (b. 1933). But while most of those writers were trained as schoolteachers, after independence Yoruba literature was enriched by the emergence of a number of university-educated authors who gave it greater complexity: Adeboye Babalola (b. 1926), a playwright and a well-known student of oral art, Adebayo Faleti (b. 1935), a versatile writer who has been active in narrative poetry and prose as well as in drama, and Afolabi Olabimtan (b. 1932). Yet another strikingly original Nigerian contribution to African literature is the dramatic genre known as the "Yoruba opera" because of the strong admixture of music and dance. Rooted in the biblical plays that were performed in mission schools in the 1930s, it made its real beginning in the early 1940s when Hubert Ogunde (b. 1916) founded his Concert Company; he produced a satirical play with definitely political overtones that became well known throughout West Africa, and his example was soon followed by E. Kola Ogunmola (1925–1973) and his traveling theater, whose outlook was conspicuously Christian and moralizing. The most widely known representative was Duro Ladipo (1931–1978), who was chiefly inspired by Yoruba myths and historical legends: his company was famed even in Europe, and several of his works were translated into English *(Three Yoruba Plays,* 1964).

In English

While the Yoruba had started creating a written art in their own language by the middle of the century, they, unlike the Hausa, also contributed significantly to the emergence and growth of Nigerian literature in English. Until the late 1950s, this had been represented only by the mediocre versifying of Denis Osadebay (b. 1911). The first Nigerian writer to reach international fame was Amos Tutuola (q.v.), whose first piece of prose fiction, *The Palm-Wine Drinkard and his Dead Palm-Wine Tapster in the Dead's Town* (1952) was enormously successful throughout Western countries, not only because of the author's highly idiosyncratic style but also because of the striking originality of the tale itself, which was derived, in fact, from the oral tradition and from Daniel O. Fagunwa's own recordings of it. Timothy M. Aluko (b. 1918) with *One Man, One Wife* (1959) inaugurated a series of satirical novels of a more conventional type, which constitute an imaginative chronicle of the evolution of Nigerian society and mores. And on the occasion of independence in 1960, Wole Soyinka produced *A Dance of the Forests*, a powerful drama in which elements drawn from the Yoruba tradition are combined to convey a message of national unity.

Besides Yoruba folklore and satirical wit, modern Nigerian literature is also rooted in a different, urban form of popular art: the so-called "Onitsha chapbooks" of the Igbo people. Written in substandard but often picturesque English, printed mostly in the Igbo market town of Onitsha, these became exceedingly popular among the Igbo lower middle class during the 1950s. It was as a purveyor of such subliterary pamphlets that Cyprian Ekwensi (q.v.) made his beginnings with a mawkish novelette, *When Love Whispers* (1948); but his *People of the* City (1954) made him known throughout the English-speaking world as the novelist of Nigerian city life. Although there are nearly ten million Igbo people in southeastern Nigeria, hardly any creative writing has been produced in the vernacular in spite of the efforts of Peter Nwana (dates n.a.) with *Omenuko* (1933; Omenuko) and, three decades later, of Leopold Bell-Gam (dates n.a.) with *Ije Odumodu jere* (1963; Odumodu's travels).

There is no doubt that the element that was chiefly responsible for giving Nigerian writing the decisive impetus that was to win for Nigeria undisputed leadership in black African literature in English was the cluster of initiatives that were taken around 1960 in the university town of Ibadan. The university college had been created in 1947. Ten years later its English department had become a hatching place for young writers, who could find an outlet for their youthful efforts in the student magazine *The Horn;* contributors from 1957 to 1960 included John Pepper Clark, Christopher Okigbo (qq.v), Wole Soyinka, and several other Ibadan students and graduates. While these were trying their hand in *The Horn*, two Germans, Janheinz Jahn (1918–1973) and Ulli Beier (b. 1922), launched (also in 1957 at Ibadan) a literary periodical named *Black Orpheus* after the title of Jean-Paul Sartre's famous preface to the Senegalese poet Léopold Sédar Senghor's (q.v.) *Anthologie de la nouvelle poésie nègre et malgache de langue française* (1948; anthology of the new black poetry in the French language). The journal's first task was to make available, to African readers of English, the already abundant amount of creative writing that had been produced in French during the 1950s in Africa and in the West Indies. After a few issues, however, original African contributions in English became more and more numerous, coming not only from Nigeria but also from elsewhere in West Africa and other parts of the continent. These two modest streams coalesced more or less formally when Ulli Beier founded (still at Ibadan) the Mbari Club, the name of which (meaning a certain kind of shrine) was suggested by the novelist Chinua Achebe (q.v.); while spreading to other parts of Nigeria (Duro Ladipo founded a Mbari Club in his hometown of Oshogbo), Mbari generated its own publishing firm and issued, between 1961 and 1964, several plays, novels, and collections of poetry by writers who now appear as the founding fathers of modern English-language literature in Africa.

By the time the civil war broke out in 1966, Nigeria could boast impressive achievements in creative writing. Poetry was dominated by Christopher Okigbo, who was killed during the Biafra war; his two slender collections, *Heavensgate* (1962) and *Limits* (1964), contain poems of exceptional excellence, some of which had previously appeared in *The Horn* and in *Black Orpheus;* they focus on familiar areas of experience, such as nostalgia for the African past, the sociopolitical problems of the present, and the eternal theme of the nature of love; but in spite of their social and historical relevance, they are first and foremost works of art, whose incantatory quality owes much to the music of Igbo oral art, even though Okigbo's techniques in the use of imagery may have been partly derived from English poetry of the generation of Yeats and Eliot. Another promising poet was Michael Echeruo (b. 1937), who seems to have given up poetry in favor of scholarship and criticism after his only collection, *Morality* (1968).

During the early years of independence, drama was entirely dominated by Wole Soyinka, who easily outclassed James Ene Henshaw (b. 1924), a popular author of "well-made" comedies such as *This Is Our Chance* (1956), and even his contemporary John Pepper Clark, whose *Song of a Goat* (1961) was more successful perhaps as poetry than as tragedy; Clark soon turned to the study of his native Ijaw folk tradition, editing its oral epic and giving it dramatic shape in *Ozidi* (1966). But it was Soyinka who chronicled—not only in dramatic terms, but also in his novel *The Interpreters* (1965)—Africa's dizzy descent toward the murky depths of despotism or anarchy. Whereas his 1960 play *A Dance of the Forests* had been a celebration calling on traditional myth and performance practice, *Kongi's Harvest* (1967) and *Madmen and Specialists* (1971), "enriched" by direct experience of civil war, were, as Soyinka himself put it, "an ironic expression of horror at the universal triumph of expediency and power lust."

Meanwhile, the vitality and attractiveness of Yoruba culture were illustrated in a very odd way in *The Imprisonment of Obatala, and Other Plays* (1966), whose author, who called himself "Obotunde Ijimere," was none other than Ulli Beier, translating into modern drama in English episodes from Nigerian folklore. Until the late 1970s Yoruba playwrights maintained a privileged (although by no means monopolistic) position in Nigerian drama, with such younger authors as Ola Rotimi (b. 1938) and Wale Ogunyemi (b. 1939).

In the making of the Nigerian novel, however, Igbo writers, led by Chinua Achebe, provided the main impetus. Achebe's early novels either explored the weakness that had caused the traditional society to collapse so easily under the impact of Europe—*Things Fall Apart* (1958), *Arrow of God* (1964)—or else analyzed the inner culture clash tormenting the Westernized African—*No Longer at Ease* (1960). In some way, the conflict between native tradition and imported novelty was basic to the Nigerian novel of the early 1960s; some writers—like Onuora Nzekwu (b. 1928), Ntieyong U. Akpan (b. 1924), and Obi Egbuna (b. 1938), who is also a playwright—chose to lament, sometimes in a humorous way, the disappearance of age-old customs and beliefs, while others— such as Timothy M. Aluko and Vincent C. Ike (b. 1931)—chose to welcome the winds of change.

In the mid-1960s, while a number of other young Igbo novelists— Nkem Nwankwo (b. 1936), Flora Nwapa (b. 1931), and especially Elechi Amadi (b. 1934) with his second novel, *The Great Ponds* (1969)—turned to the tribal past for literary inspiration, setting their stories in rural communities that had little or no contact with the outside world, the moral, social, and above all political deliquescence of the country was increasingly preoccupying the more sensitive observers. Frank criticism of the corruption of the leading classes, which had played a peripheral role in some of Ekwensi's novels—*Jagua Nana* (1961), *Beautiful Feathers* (1963)—and in *The Voice* (1964), the strange allegorical and experimental novel of Ijaw writer Gabriel Okara (q.v.), became the main theme of more ambitious works with ironic titles such as Achebe's *A Man of the People* (1966) or Aluko's *Chief the Honourable Minister* (1970).

The Biafra war thus broke out in an atmosphere of disillusionment.

Its traumatic impact made itself felt throughout Nigeria's literature with unprecedented intensity. The death of Okigbo was felt as a symbol of Africa destroying the best of her own substance in old-fashioned tribal quarrels. Some of the major writers turned to new modes of expression: while Clark voiced his despair in poetry—*Casualties: Poems 1966–1968* (1970)—Achebe gave up the novel in favor of poetry—*Beware, Soul Brother, and Other Poems* (1971)—and the short story—*Girls at War, and Other Stories* (1972); besides *Madmen and Specialists,* Wole Soyinka expressed his own concern and experience in an autobiography, *The Man Died: Prison Notes* (1972) (as did Elechi Amadi with *Sunset in Biafra: A Civil War Diary* [1973]), in poetry in *A Shuttle in the Crypt* (1972), and in his second novel, *Season of Anomy* (1973).

With John Munonye's (b. 1929) novel *A Wreath for the Maidens* (1973) and Flora Nwapa's novel *Never Again* (1974), it became clear that the civil war was on its way to becoming a mere literary cliché. It had nevertheless provided genuine inspiration for a younger generation of writers, who had been in their twenties when it broke out. These included Sebastian O. Mezu (b. 1941), with *Behind the Rising Sun* (1971), and Kole Omotoso (b. 1943), with *The Combat* (1972). But the restoration of peace in 1970, the comparative orderliness maintained by moderate military regimes, and the economic prosperity resulting from the discovery of oil also had their literary aftermath throughout the 1970s. For the new generation of writers, born in the 1940s, who had little knowledge of the colonial regime and of the struggle for independence, who were thoroughly urbanized and found traditional mores and ideas totally irrelevant to life in a modern society, who had attended one or several of Nigeria's eighteen universities and/or foreign institutions of higher learning as a matter of course, and for whom the rapid growth of the educational system had prepared a sizable public of literate readers, the Biafra war belonged to an outdated tribal past, the obsolete tensions of which were profitably manipulated by foreign capitalistic interests. What they regarded as the elitist posture of their elders, who had been trying to graft their own work onto a venerable but alien tradition ranging from Shakespeare through Jane Austen to Yeats and Eliot, was as anachronistically irrelevant as their alleged veneration for the so-called "African" values, the legends, the memories, the myths, and the superstitious creeds of a society that Nigeria, they felt, had outgrown.

Although a playwright of such exceptional ability as Ola Rotimi successfully managed, in *The Gods Are Not to Blame* (1968) and in ensuing plays, to put modern scenic techniques and the manipulation of dramatic space to the service of a type of inspiration that remained recognizably Yoruba, the novel outpaced both drama and poetry in the 1970s. Given the rebellious outlook of the post-civil-war generation, it is not surprising that they should have chosen for their masters, guides, and models, two writers whom academic criticism had hitherto regarded as comparatively minor: Cyprian Ekwensi, the founder of the urban novel, and John Munonye, whose many novels, from *The Only Son* (1966) to *Bridge to a Wedding* (1978), had mostly been devoted to recording the condition of the common man. This revulsion from profundity led to a literature that was at the same time popular and populist, and whose diffusion was greatly helped by the multiplication of private publishing houses, aiming, perhaps, to fill the void created by the destruction of Onitsha during the civil war. Since 1956 Ogali A. Ogali (b. 1935) had been one of the most prolific purveyors of popular reading, and during the 1970s there were many who shared with him the rewards of this profitable branch of the entertainment business. Some of the novelists who had already emerged before the civil war, such as Nkem Nwankwo, Obi Egbuna, and Vincent C. Ike, turned their satirical glance toward the ebullient urban society of the new Nigeria, and so did (although with angrier overtones) the younger writer Femi Osofisan (b. 1946) in his novel *Kolera Kolej* (1975) and especially in his various plays, such as *The Chattering and the Song* (1975), which "offers a model of the new society as well as a condemnation of the old" (Gerald Moore). But others, like Isidore Okpewho (b. 1941) in *The Victims* (1970), I. N. C. Aniebo (b. 1939) in *The Journey Within* (1978), and many of their generation—for instance, Charles Njoku (dates n.a.) in *The New Breed* (1978) or Festus Iyayi (dates n.a.) in *Violence* (1979)—chose to offer a realistic depiction of the common town dweller's experiences and ordeals, as did Nigeria's first woman playwright, Zulu Sofola (b. 1935). The theme of the culture clash and the motif of the "been-to" (returnee), both of which had been prominent in pre-civil-war writing, received new dimensions with *The Edifice* (1971) by Kole Omotoso, who has since become one of the dynamic leaders of the new Nigerian literature, and with *Second Class Citizen* (1976) by Buchi Emecheta (b. 1944), whose later novels gave ever more compelling voice to the new militancy of African womanhood.

As the 1980s dawned, it was clear that Nigerian literature, having outgrown its pioneering period, still remained the herald and the model it had been (although with Kenya close on its heels): it provided articulate evidence that this enormous, populous, and resourceful new republic had at last joined the modern society of nations, the modern world of industrialization and urbanization, with its standardized universal conflicts and tensions taking the place of the futile idealizations, the pointless nostalgia, the small-scale, parochial-tribal confrontations that had provided earlier writers with their usual subject matter.

BIBLIOGRAPHY: Laurence, M., *Long Drums and Cannons: Nigerian Dramatists and Novelists 1952–1966* (1968); Klíma, V., *Modern Nigerian Novels* (1969); King, B., ed., *Introduction to Nigerian Literature* (1971); Roscoe, A. A., *Mother Is Gold: A Study in West African Literature* (1971); Obiechina, E., *An African Popular Literature: A Study of Onitsha Market Pamphlets* (1973); Udeyop, N. J., *Three Nigerian Poets* (1973); Lindfors, B., ed., *Critical Perspectives on Nigerian Literature* (1976); Momodu, A. G. S., and Schild, U., eds., *Nigerian Writing: Nigeria as Seen by Her Own Writers as Well as by German Authors* (1976); Emenyonou, E., *The Rise of the Igbo Novel* (1978); Baldwin, C., comp., *Nigerian Literature: A Bibliography of Criticism, 1952–1976* (1980); Booth, J., *Writers and Politics in Nigeria* (1981)

ALBERT S. GÉRARD

ACHEBE, Chinua
Nigerian novelist, poet, and short-story writer (writing in English), b. 15 Nov. 1930, Ogidi

In 1953 A. became one of the first graduates of University College, Ibadan. He began working for the Nigerian Broadcasting Service the following year, and in 1961 became Director of External Broadcasting for Nigeria, a position he held until 1966, when he returned to his home in eastern Nigeria. During the Nigerian-Biafran conflict (1967–1970), A. worked for the Biafran government and afterward became a research fellow in the Institute of African Studies at the University of Nigeria in Nsukka. In 1972 he was appointed visiting professor in the English department at the University of Massachusetts at Amherst. Four years later he returned to the University of Nigeria in Nsukka, where he is a professor of English.

Working within the conventions of the realistic novel, A. has succeeded in creating a very vivid picture of African society in the process of change. His first novel, *Things Fall Apart* (1958), deals with the human consequences of the collision of African and European cultures in Nigeria, a theme that has preoccupied Nigerian writers ever since. The story is set in a traditional Igbo community at the turn of the century, when the first European missionaries and administrative officials were beginning to penetrate inland. One of the strongest men in the community tries to arouse his people to oppose the white man, but some of them have been won over to the white man's faith, and the clan is no longer united. When his people refuse to follow the protagonist, he commits suicide in anger and despair; his death symbolizes the passing of the old order.

In his second novel, *No Longer at Ease* (1960), A. switched to a modern urban scene in order to focus on the life of an educated Nigerian in the late 1950s. The protagonist, an idealistic young man who returns from university education abroad with the ambition of reforming the Nigerian civil service, eventually succumbs to the temptation of accepting bribes. He also alienates his people by falling in love with a young woman they find unacceptable. Like his grandfather, the hero of *Things Fall Apart,* this headstrong young man can be seen as a victim of the conflict of cultures in Africa; westernization has made him confused, ill at ease in his own society, and vulnerable to corruption.

In *Arrow of God* (1964), A. moved back to an earlier era to tell the story of an old Igbo priest who tries to cope with the changing times by maintaining a flexible stance. He compromises with the new religion by sending his son to a mission school and cooperates with the British administration by testifying against his own people in a land dispute. But these actions subvert his authority in the community, and his people gradually turn away from him and his god and start worshiping at a mission church. Again Africa loses out to Europe; a traditional way of life is destroyed forever.

A Man of the People (1966) concludes A.'s tetralogy by bringing the historical record up to the present. The novel focuses on a corrupt politician who lives high for a while but finally is brought low by a military coup. The chaos in modern African society wrought by such politicians is seen to derive ultimately from an absence of stable values. The unprincipled politician is a product of the moral confusion created by the collision of African and European cultures. Even the relatively upright schoolteacher who functions as a foil to the corrupt politician in the novel cannot be said to be a model of virtue; he, too, has been twisted by the conflicting forces that swirl about him. Mere chaos is loosed upon the world.

A. has articulated his views on writing in a number of cogent literary essays, recently collected in *Morning Yet on Creation Day: Essays* (1975). He believes that the African writer should be a teacher dedicated to explaining to his people how and why their world came to be the way it is today. To offset the psychological damage done during the colonial era, the writers of the 1950s and 1960s had a duty to create a dignified image of the African past, so that Africans could learn to take pride in their own culture and traditions. By the mid-1960s, however, Africa had changed so much that it became necessary for writers to expose injustice and corruption in their own societies. Any serious writer had to be politically committed, but in the transition from colonialism to independence the target of his protest had been transferred from Europe to Africa itself.

A.'s own commitment is evident not only in his novels but also in the shorter fiction and poetry he has published since the Nigerian-Biafran conflict. *Beware, Soul Brother, and Other Poems* (1971) and *Christmas in Biafra, and Other Poems* (1973) contain poignant and bitter reflections on wartime experiences. Several short stories in *Girls at War, and Other Stories* (1972) also deal with the ironies and tragedies of war, as do the pieces he collected from other writers and edited in *The Insider: Stories of War and Peace from Nigeria* (1971). A.'s *How the Leopard Got His Claws* (1972), ostensibly a folktale written for children, has an allegorical dimension that made it possible for A. to comment both on the Biafran tragedy and on the international power struggles that lead to such situations in the Third World. As in his earlier works, A. constantly seeks to transcend the local and particular and point to matters of more universal significance.

A. has also been firmly committed to educating the young. He believes that the novelist in Africa today should deliberately attempt to regenerate his society by directing his message to impressionable young people, especially schoolchildren. A.'s novels have been widely read in high schools throughout Africa, and he has written several books expressly for use in African grade schools: *Chike and the River* (1966), *The Flute* (1977), and *The Drum* (1977). The emphasis that he places on sound moral education of the young is reflected in the high seriousness that permeates all his literary work.

A.'s writings not only chronicle seventy-five years of Nigerian history but reflect the dominant African intellectual concerns of the past twenty-five years. For this reason they are likely to be of enduring value. A.'s works seem destined to become classics of African literature.

FURTHER WORK: *The Sacrificial Egg, and Other Stories* (1962)

BIBLIOGRAPHY: Ravenscroft, A., *C. A.* (1969; rev. ed. 1977); Killam, G. D., *The Novels of C. A.* (1969; rev. ed. entitled *The Writings of C. A.,* 1977); Carroll, D., *C. A.* (1970); Melone, T., *C. A. et la tragédie de l'histoire* (1973); Böttcher, K. H., *Tradition und Modernität bei Amos Tutuola and C. A.: Grundzüge der westafrikanischen Erzählliteratur englischer Sprache* (1974); Turkington, K., *C. A.: Things Fall Apart* (1977); Peters, J. A., *A Dance of the Masks: Senghor, A., Soyinka* (1978), pp. 93–158; Githae-Mugo, M., *Visions of Africa: The Fiction of C. A., Margaret Laurence, Elspeth Huxley and Ngugi wa Thiong'o* (1978), passim; Mbock, C. G., *Le monde s'effondre de C. A.: Essai critique* (1978); Anafulu, J. C., "C. A.: A Preliminary Checklist," *Nsukka Library Notes,* 3 (1978), 1–52; Innes, C. L., and Lindfors, B., eds., *Critical Perspectives on C. A.* (1978); Wren, R. W., *A.'s World: The Historical and Cultural Context of the Novels of C. A.* (1980)

BERNTH LINDFORS

CLARK, John Pepper

Nigerian dramatist and poet (writing in English), b. 6 April 1935, Kiagbodo

While a student at Ibadan University, where he studied English literature, C. founded and edited the student literary magazine, *The Horn*. After receiving his degree, he pursued graduate studies in the U.S. at Princeton University (he wrote about his American experiences in his caustic travel book *America, Their America* [1964]). Since his return to Nigeria C. has served on the staff of the *Daily Express* in Lagos and now lectures on African literature at the University of Lagos.

C.'s first play, *Song of a Goat* (1960), is loosely based on an Ijaw legend and is in the tradition of the village storyteller. A chief sends his wife to a masseur for a cure for her supposed barrenness; in reality, it is the husband who is impotent. The masseur tells the wife that "another should take over the tilling of fertile soil." In this play, C. isolates two aspects of life—sex and heredity—and gives them a "popular treatment," as he does in the play's alleged sequel, *Masquerade* (1964), in which a father shoots his daughter for defying him and is in turn killed by her lover. Because both plays are melodramatic "love stories," where personal experience determines the activities of the group, a certain distortion of African life is evident.

On the other hand, *Ozidi* (1966), C.'s best play, returns to the prototype of traditional African drama—the myth. It is a contemporary political play based on an Ijaw saga, combining ritualistic elements of song, speech, and dance in a drama that is simultaneously concerned with ritual rebirth and the need for succession and moral growth and with a depiction of the corrupt politicians and the coups of a modern African state.

As a poet, C. is really a "versifier," because his concern with metrical technicalities frequently makes his work unspontaneous and artificial. Nevertheless, his purely descriptive poems sometimes succeed even though they are written in a fragmentary fashion, since he conveys accurate and personal observations and often imaginatively works folk beliefs into a significant whole. Many of his poems are about doom, the tragedy imposed by history. The way in which C. can be very close to his subject shows that he is not so much a reflective poet but rather one who observes what is near to him and reproduces it accurately. He is very much a poet of the active present, involved in what is near, and to him tradition is only real in a personal and contemporary situation.

FURTHER WORKS: *Poems* (1962); *Three Plays* (1964); *A Reed in the Tide* (1965); *Casualties: Poems 1966–1968* (1970); *The Example of Shakespeare* (1970)

BIBLIOGRAPHY: Beier, U., on *Poems, BO,* No. 12 (1963), 47–49; Esslin, M., "Two Nigerian Playwrights: Wole Soyinka, J. P. C.," in Beier, U., ed., *Introduction to African Literature: An Anthology of Critical Writing from "Black Orpheus"* (1967), pp. 255–62; Banham, M., on *Ozidi, JCL,* No. 7 (1969), 132–34; Thumboo, E., "At Ibadan Dawn: The Poetry of J. P. C.," *BA,* 44 (1970), 387–92; Izevbaye, D., "The Poetry and Drama of J. P. C.," in King, B., ed., *Introduction to Nigerian Literature* (1971), pp. 152–72; Roscoe, A. A., *Mother Is Gold: A Study in West African Literature* (1971), pp. 36–39, 200–18; Dathorne, O. R., *The Black Mind* (1974), pp. 285–91, 419–21, 427–28

O. R. DATHORNE

EKWENSI, Cyprian

Nigerian novelist and short-story writer (writing in English), b. 26 Sept. 1921, Minna

E. studied at Achimota College, near Accra, Ghana, and obtained a degree in pharmacy at the University of London. On his return to Nigeria, he taught science at colleges in Lagos and in Yaba. He joined the staff of the Nigerian Broadcasting Corporation in Lagos in 1951, later serving as director of information in the federal ministry of information in Lagos. In 1966 E., an Ibo, resigned his position to move to Biafra. When the Nigerian-Biafran conflict (1967–70) ended, he proclaimed that he was "happy to be a Nigerian again." E. is now a practicing pharmacist.

E.'s first two novels show his ambivaence to the city. The first, *People of the City* (1954; rev. ed., 1963), is an episodic work in which a newspaperman, Amusa Sango, serves as commentator on life in Lagos. E.'s view of Lagos is both grim and fascinating. Several of his characters are overwhelmed by the city, turning to prostitution and thievery or committing suicide. Amusa, the protagonist, must work through the "hell" of Lagos (E. uses Dantesque imagery) in order to gain a mastery of life. The destructiveness of the city is strongly presented in E.'s portrait of a beautiful woman, Beatrice the First, who comes to the city, has several lovers (in a descending order of wealth and status), dies unattended and loveless, and is buried in a pauper's grave. Amusa's salvation comes through another Beatrice—Beatrice the Second—who, in her quiet, simple way, provides stability for him.

E.'s second novel, probably his best-known and most influential work, *Jagua Nana* (1961), shows E.'s continuing fascination with the city and its women. A series of events, particularly a romance with a young political idealist, leads Jagua Nana, a sleek, beautiful prostitute, to a new awareness. Her road to understanding, however, is strewn with twists of fate. Unable to bear children for many years, the one thing Jagua wants desperately is a child. Finaly, at forty-five, she does give birth, but the child dies two days later. Jagua overcomes her sense of loss and sets off for a new life in a small country town.

E.'s first two novels have been criticized for sentimentality, romanticism, and journalistic exploitation of sensational events. Yet, even his detractors admit the vitality of his characterizations and his broad canvas of urban events. Some critics see in his work a Dickensian sense of comedy and a talent for reportage and the picaresque similar to that of Defoe. E. himself has said that he is less interested in literary style than in getting to the "heart of the truth which the man in the street can recognize." E. calls himself a "writer for the masses," and he prefers to "go down to the people." His stated allegiance to the masses and his fear of literary pretentiousness provide some of the reasons he regards Georges Simenon and the English writer Edgar Wallace as two great influences on his work. Both Simenon and Wallace wrote their novels quickly, disdaining any pretensions of precious writing.

E.'s third novel, *Burning Grass* (1962), was written before his two earlier published novels. It reveals his deep commitment to the countryside as a source of respite for the battered soul. In *Burning Grass,* the action of which takes place in the northern Fulani countryside, the sense of an older way of life that is passing is conveyed against the ominous undertones of an encroaching city life. In *Beautiful Feathers* (1963), E. shifted the setting to the city again and explored the life of a young, earnest, respected politician, Wilson Iyari, cuckolded by his wife.

E.'s later work shows an increasing concern with style and less reliance on the episodic and sensational. *Iska* (1966)—the title is the name given to the wind that blows through the countryside—is the story of a young girl tragically blown about by the inevitable raging winds of tribal conflicts.

E. is also a prolific writer of short stories and juvenile literature. His best-known collection of stories is *Lokotown* (1966). In a recent collection, *Restless City and Christmas Gold* (1975), E. utilizes sketches of modern conflict—the sophisticated "been-to" bored with his white wife; the innocent girl corrupted by jaded pleasure seekers; the pettiness of industrial society. Much of his children's literature utilizes the motif of a young wanderer through strange lands and forests, settings inspired by his own experience in the forestry service.

E.'s work, various in its moods, style, and genres, centers on the individual act of choice. Far from bearing only simple messages and moralisms, E.'s work suggests unending ambiguities in man. His conclusions are pat, but his people are real and complex.

FURTHER WORKS: *When Love Whispers* (1948); *The Leopard's Claw* (1947); *The Dummer Boy* (1960); *Passport of Mallam Ilia* (1960); *An African Night's Entertainment* (1962); *Rainmaker* (1965); *Juju Rock* (1966)

BIBLIOGRAPHY: Mphahlele, E., *The African Image* (1962), pp. 276–78; Gleason, J., *This Africa* (1965), pp. 118–30; Tucker, M., *Africa in*

Modern Literature (1967), pp. 73–82; Laurence, M., *Long Drums and Cannons* (1968), pp. 148–69; Cartey, W., *Whispers from a Continent* (1969), pp. 147–73, 193–95; Pieterse, C., and Deurden, D., eds., "Interview with E.," *African Writers Talking* (1972), pp. 77–83; Emenyou, E., *C. E.* (1974)

MARTIN TUCKER

OKARA, Gabriel

Nigerian poet and novelist (writing in English), b. 24 April 1921, Bumodi

O. attended school in Umuahia and then worked as a printer and bookbinder in Lagos and Enugu. In 1956 he studied journalism in the U.S. at Northwestern University and has been involved in information-media work ever since, most recently as editor of the newspaper *Nigerian Tide*.

O.'s first poems were published in the maiden issue of *Black Orpheus* (1957), an influential Nigerian literary magazine that later carried some of his fiction, translations of Ijaw myths, and experimental verse. His poetry and fiction have also appeared in numerous anthologies and literary publications outside of Nigeria and have won him an international reputation as one of Nigeria's most innovative stylists.

O.'s poetry tends to be simple, lyrical, and polyrhythmic. He writes free verse disciplined by subtly controlled metrics and amplified by sharply defined images and richly ambiguous symbols. In his early poetry he frequently combined native and nonnative imagery (oil palm and snowflake, drum and piano) as a metaphoric way of communicating the confused psychological state of the Westernized African. He was one of the first African writers to introduce into English verse uncompromisingly literal translations of metaphors, idioms, and philosophical concepts from an African vernacular language. His most recent poetry is his most explicitly political, reflecting his intense personal reaction to the horrors of the Nigerian-Biafran conflict (1967–70). The first collection of his poetry, *The Fisherman's Invocation* (1978), was awarded the Commonwealth Poetry Prize.

Although O. originally made his mark as a poet, he is perhaps better known as the author of *The Voice* (1964), an imaginative novel written in an unorthodox prose style simulating idiomatic expression in Ijaw. *The Voice* is a moral allegory about man's quest for faith, truth, and the meaning of life in a corrupted world. An idealistic hero discomfits leaders in his village by initiating a search for coherent moral values. Soon he is expelled from the village and sent into exile, but he defies the ban, returns home, and confronts those in power who had sought to obstruct his quest. He is put to death, but his words and deeds have made an impact on his people. A moral revolution has begun.

Some critics have been harsh on the radical verbal and syntactical innovations O. introduced in *The Voice*, but others think the strangeness of the style superbly suited to the strangeness of the tale. The unnatural inversions and neologisms tend to enhance the hallucinatory, dreamlike quality of the protagonist's quest, giving it an appropriate parabolic flavor. It is a poet's concern for form, awareness of symbol, and sensitivity to language that make O.'s novel a brilliant literary achievement.

O.'s experimental style and poetic vision place him in the forefront of the movement to indigenize African literature by investing it with local sonority as well as pan-African significance.

BIBLIOGRAPHY: Anozie, S. O., "The Theme of Alienation and Commitment in O.'s *The Voice*," *BAALE*, 3 (1965), 54–67; Shiarella, J.,"G. O.'s *The Voice:* A Study in the Poetic Novel," *BO*, 2, 5–6 (1970), 45–49; Palmer, E., "G. O.: *The Voice*," *An Introduction to the African Novel* (1972), pp. 155–67; Webb, H., "Allegory: O.'s *The Voice*," *EinA*, 5, 2 (1978), 66–73; Egudu, R. N., "A Study of Five of G. O.'s Poems," *Okike*, 13 (1979), 93–110

BERNTH LINDFORS

OKIGBO, Christopher
Nigerian poet (writing in English), b. 16 Aug. 1932, Ojoto; d. Aug. 1967, near Nsukka

O. studied in Umuahia and then went on to study classics at Ibadan University. Between 1956 and 1962 he worked in business and in government and as a teacher and a librarian. In the Nigerian-Biafran conflict (1967–70), he joined the Biafran army as a major in July 1967 and was killed in action the following month.

O. began to attract attention in 1962, when three publications of his appeared: a sequence of poems in Nigeria's influential literary magazine *Black Orpheus;* a pamphlet, entitled *Heavensgate*, in a poetry series published in Ibadan; and a long poem, *Limits*, in the Ugandan cultural magazine *Transition. (Limits* appeared independently in 1964.) During the next few years O. continued to contribute poetry to *Black Orpheus* and *Transition.*

In his earliest verse—"Moonglow" and "Four Canzones," written between 1957 and 1961—one finds echoes of T. S. Eliot, Ezra Pound, Gerard Manley Hopkins, and other modern poets, echoes that O. deliberately evoked in order to give greater sonority to the verbal music he was intent on creating. As he matured and discovered his own distinctive poetic idiom, the greatest influence on him may have been Peter Thomas (b. 1928), an English poet who taught at the University of Nigeria at Nsukka for several years and encouraged O. through discussion and enthusiastic readings of successive drafts of his poems. O. was also remarkably responsive to instrumental music, both African and Western, and he incorporated in his verse motifs inspired by symphonies, songs, and traditional percussive rhythms. Many critics have noted that O.'s work may appeal to the ear more than to the eye, for subtle nuances of sound meant more to him than mere certainties of sense.

In *Heavensgate* O. began to speak in a poetic voice informed by a judicious blend of African and Western poetic elements. This mature verse tends to be difficult, cryptically allusive, and sinuously musical, yet it achieves remarkably vivid pictorial effects by juxtaposing fresh images and compressing ideas into spare, metaphorical statements that have the lucidity of proverbs. *Heavensgate,* which O. said was originally conceived as an Easter sequence, traces the spiritual journey of a celebrant through several levels of ritual.

In *Limits* the same poet-protagonist sets out on a mystical quest for something unattainable and loses himself to his obsession. *Distances* (1964), described by O. as "a poem of homecoming," deals with the psychic and spiritual fulfillment that the writer must achieve before he can create. *Silences* (1965), inspired by tragic events in Nigeria and the Congo, is a poetic investigation of the music of mourning, with drums symbolizing the spirits of the ancestors. The poems in *Path of Thunder* (in *Black Orpheus,* 1968) reflect O.'s pessimistic response to the tensions in Nigeria in the mid-1960s, a crisis that he felt presaged war and possibly his own death. His last poems, by far his most political utterances, indicate that he was moving toward a less oblique mode of expression that could articulate moral and patriotic concerns in images accessible to the ordinary reader.

O. believed that his poems, although written and published separately, were organically related and could be read as one poetic statement. After his death, final versions of his poems, which he had himself edited, were published in the collection *Labyrinths with Path of Thunder* (1971). It has been reported that he had been working on a novel before his death, but the manuscript of this venture into prose apparently was lost during the Nigerian-Biafran war.

O.'s work defies easy explication and rational analysis. He was often more concerned with the resonance of sound and symbol than he was with communicating an intelligible meaning. His imagination played upon the rich suggestiveness of rhythm, image, and allusion, creating a subtle fusion of curiously disparate associations. He found trenchancy in obscurity, precision in ambiguity, form in formlessness. These qualities make him the most modern of African poets.

BIBLIOGRAPHY: Whitelaw, M., "Interview with C. O.," *JCL,* 9 (1970), 28–37; Anozie, S. O., *C. O.* (1972); Izevbaye, D. S., "O.'s Portrait of the Artist as a Sunbird: A Reading of *Heavensgate,*" *ALT,* 6 (1973), 1–13; Udoeyop, N. J., *Three Nigerian Poets: A Critical Study of the Poetry of Soyinka, Clark and O.* (1973), pp. 101–57; Anafulu, J. C., "C. O., 1932–1967: A Bio-bibliography," *RAL,* 9 (1978), 65–78; Achebe, C., Preface to Achebe, C., and Okafor, D., eds., *Don't Let Him Die: An Anthology of Memorial Poems for C. O. (1932–1967)* (1978), pp. v–ix; Nwoga, D. I., *Critical Perspectives on C. O.* (1982)

BERNTH LINDFORS

SOYINKA, Wole

Nigerian dramatist, poet, novelist, essayist, and translator (writing in English), b. 13 July 1934, Abeokuta

S. was educated at University College, Ibadan, and the University of Leeds, where he studied English literature. He has held teaching positions at the University of Ibadan, the University of Lagos, and the University of Ife, and has served as a visiting professor at Cambridge and the University of Sheffield in England and at Yale. During the Nigerian-Biafran war he spent twenty-two months in prison as a political detainee. Currently he is a professor of comparative literature at the University of Ife, where he is also closely associated with the department of drama.

One of the most versatile and innovative of African writers, S. is known primarily for his plays, which range from high comedy and burlesque to fateful tragedy, biting social and political satire, and the Theater of the Absurd. His plays reflect the influence of both traditional African and modern European drama, and they invariably contain penetrating social criticism based on a profound understanding of human nature. S. has been a vital, moving force in the development of contemporary Nigerian theater, often serving as director, producer, and actor in professional stage companies that perform in the Yoruba language as well as in English.

In S.'s lightest comedy, *The Lion and the Jewel* (perf. 1959, pub. 1963), tradition triumphs over modernity: a wily old chief outmaneuvers a foppish young schoolteacher to win the hand of the village belle. Cunning and wit are also well rewarded in *The Trials of Brother Jero* (perf. 1960, pub. 1963) and its sequel, *Jero's Metamorphosis* (pub. 1973, perf. 1974), farces built around the antics of a fraudulent beach prophet. A more trenchant kind of satire can be found in *A Dance of the Forests* (perf. 1960, pub. 1963), an ironic celebration of Nigeria's independence, and in *Kongi's Harvest* (perf. 1965, pub. 1967), an attack on tyranny and megalomania in postcolonial Africa. S.'s sourest satire, *Madmen and Specialists* (perf. 1970, pub. 1971), published after the Nigerian civil war, deals with man's inhumanity and rapacity in times of severe stress. There has been a tendency toward increasingly dark humor in S.'s comic drama.

His serious philosophical plays explore less topical issues. *The Strong Breed* (pub. 1963, perf. 1966) and *The Swamp Dwellers* (perf. 1958, pub. 1963) examine the integrity of tradition and the nature of social responsibility in a confused world. *The Road* (1965), an intriguingly enigmatic work, deals with the meaning of death in the context of a seemingly meaningless, transitory existence. *Death and the King's Horseman* (pub. 1975, perf. 1976) investigates the notion of self-sacrifice and loyalty to a long-established ideal even in the face of cultural transformation. All these works are concerned in one way or another with man's efforts to come to terms with change and transition.

In recent years S. has adapted a few European plays for the African stage, infusing them with local relevance while retaining their basic structure and moral thrust. *The Bacchae of Euripides* (1973) includes scenes modeled upon contemporary Nigerian happenings, and *Opera Wonyosi* (perf. 1977, pub. 1981), based on John Gay's (1685–1732) *The Beggars' Opera* and Bertolt Brecht's *The Threepenny Opera*, is set in a slick but tawdry African gangster world. S. adroitly uses these foreign vehicles to drive home important social messages.

S.'s poetry is equally wide-ranging and morally committed. In *Idanre, and Other Poems* (1967) he proves himself the master of many different poetic moods, some of them inspired by the events that led to the Nigerian civil war. Gloom, depression, and grief are balanced by comic invective, mordant irony, and tender, lyrical reflections on death. *Poems from Prison* (1969), a pamphlet published while he was in detention, contains thoughts on his loss of freedom, and *A Shuttle in the Crypt* (1972) extends such encapsulated ruminations into the domain of metaphysics, religion, and ritual. One finds a yearning for liberty and light in these solemn songs of incarceration. *Ogun Abibiman* (1976), a single long poem, is a panegyric celebrating Mozambique's declaration of war on white-ruled Rhodesia.

S.'s novel *The Interpreters* (1965) is the most complex narrative work yet written by an African. Frequently compared with works by James Joyce and William Faulkner, it has an intricate, seemingly chaotic structure, a dense and evocative verbal texture, and a throng of tantalizingly emblematic characters. It focuses on a group of Nigerian intellectuals—an engineer, a journalist, an artist, a teacher, a lawyer, an aristocrat—who meet fortnightly at clubs in Ibadan and Lagos and get drunk together. Between binges they lead ordinary disorderly lives that bring them into contact with people from all parts of Nigerian urban society. Together or alone, in unison or at odds, these six intellectuals interpret and reinterpret their experiences and the world in which they live, leaving the reader to interpret the interpreters and their interpretations.

His second novel, *Season of Anomy* (1973), contains a more straightforward story line but is enriched by symbolic associations with the Orpheus and Eurydice myth and with narratives about Ogun, a revolutionary Yoruba deity. Like much of his writing in the early 1970s, this book reflects a number of the social attitudes and ideals S. formed while in prison.

S. has written two autobiographical works: *The Man Died: Prison Notes* (1972), a record of his imprisonment, and *Aké: The Years of Childhood* (1981), a reconstruction of his early years. Some of his ideas about literature and drama are recorded in *Myth, Literature and the African World* (1975).

S.'s works provide a kaleidoscopic view of human life in modern Africa; they also serve as graphic illustrations of his belief that the African artist should function "as the record of the mores and experiences of his society and as the voice of vision in his own time."

FURTHER WORKS: *Before the Blackout* (perf. 1965, pub. c. 1971); *Camwood on the Leaves* (perf. 1965, pub. 1973); *Collected Plays* (2 vols., 1973–74)

BIBLIOGRAPHY: Moore, G., *W. S.* (1971); Jones, E., *The Writing of W. S.* (1973); Udoeyop, N. J., *Three Nigerian Poets: A Critical Study of the Poetry of S., Clark and Okigbo* (1973), pp. 19–56; Graham-White, A., *The Drama of Black Africa* (1974), pp. 117–45; Ogunba, O., *The Movement of Transition: A Study of the Plays of W. S.* (1975); Böttcher-Wöbcke, R., *Komik, Ironie und Satire im dramatischen Werk von W. S.* (1975); Bejlis, V. A., *W. S.* (1977); Page, M., *W. S.: Bibliography, Biography, Playography* (1979); Gibbs J., ed., *Critical Perspectives on W. S.* (1980); Larsen, S., *A Writer and His Gods: A Study of the Importance of Yoruba Myths and Religious Ideas to the Writing of W. S.* (1983)

BERNTH LINDFORS

TUTUOLA, Amos

Nigerian storyteller (writing in English), b. 20 June 1922, Abeokuta

T. had six years of formal education in mission schools, worked as a coppersmith, messenger, and stock clerk, and currently is pensioned and living in Ibadan.

In all his books T. uses the same basic narrative pattern. A hero (or heroine) with supernatural powers or access to supernatural assistance sets out on a journey in quest of something important but suffers incredible hardships before successfully accomplishing his mission. He ventures into unearthly realms, performs arduous tasks, fights with fearsome monsters, endures cruel tortures, and narrowly escapes death. Sometimes he is accompanied by a relative or by loyal companions; sometimes he wanders alone. But he always survives his ordeals, attains his objective, and usually emerges from his nightmarish experiences a wiser, wealthier man. The cycle of his adventures—involving a departure, an initiation, and a return—resembles that found in myths and folktales the world over.

T.'s first long narrative, *The Wild Hunter in the Bush of the Ghosts* (written c. 1948, pub. 1982), was originally submitted to a London publisher of photography books, from whose files it recently was recovered and put into print for the first time. Basically a Yoruba hunter's tale, it tells of marvelous adventures in bizarre bush towns and includes excursions to Heaven and Hell, the latter resembling a vast bureaucracy with an Engineering Department, Correspondence Section, and Employment Exchange Office. The story shows signs of having been influenced by the Yoruba narratives of D. O. Fagunwa (1903–1963) as well as by John Bunyan's *The Pilgrim's Progress,* but it is a bit cruder in conception and execution than T.'s later works.

T.'s first published book, *The Palm-Wine Drinkard and His Dead Palm-Wine Tapster in the Dead's Town* (1952), describing a hero's descent into an African underworld in search of a dead companion whom he wants to persuade to return to the land of the living, had a mixed critical reception. Written in a curiously expressive idiom that Dylan Thomas termed "young English," this unusual story delighted European and American critics who tended to look upon its author as an extraordinarily imaginative native genius. However, it offended many educated Nigerian readers who recognized T.'s borrowings from oral tradition and from Fagunwa, disapproved of his bad grammar, and felt he was being lionized abroad by condescending racists. In much of the criticism written on T. since, there has been controversy over the merits and faults of this book, but it is still regarded as his most significant work and has been translated into many languages.

T.'s later books confirmed his reputation as an interesting but limited author who specialized in transmuting oral narratives into episodic adventure fiction about the wanderings of a resourceful human being in extraterrestrial domains. In *My Life in the Bush of Ghosts* (1954) the narrator-hero spends twenty-four years in an interesting African spirit world replete with towns, law courts, royal palaces, barber shops, and even a Methodist church, until a "Television-handed ghostess" helps him to escape to the human world he came from. *Simbi and the Satyr of the Dark Jungle* (1955) is the same kind of story, the major difference being that the chief character is a young lady who sets out on a quest for worldly experience because she wants to know the difficulties of poverty and punishment. This book was the first by T. to be organized into chapters and to be written in the third person; it was also his first to be populated with a number of non-African creatures—satyr, nymph, phoenix, imp, and so forth—a clear indication that he was supplementing his stock of Yoruba oral lore with readings in world mythology.

T.'s mode of storytelling gradually became more literary as he continued writing: In *Feather Woman of the Jungle* (1962), his most stylized work, he created an Arabian Nights structure by having a seventy-six-year-old chief entertain villagers every night for ten nights with accounts of his past adventures. In *The Brave African Huntress* (1958) and *Ajaiyi and His Inherited Poverty* (1967), he adopted the practice of citing one or more proverbs at the head of a chapter and then using the action in that chapter to illustrate the proverbs. Both of these narrative techniques may have entered written literature from oral tradition, but T. appears to have picked them up from his reading. In any case, they suited his material perfectly, providing him with ready-made vehicles for weaving together a group of disparate tales. His adoption of such conventions made him no less an oral raconteur in print. His latest narrative, *The Witch-Herbalist of the Remote Town* (1981), manifests the same blend of African and Western stylistic and structural elements.

T.'s reputation is now secure both at home and abroad, for he has come to be accepted as a distinctive phenomenon in world literature, a writer who bridges two narrative traditions and two cultures by translating oral art into literary art.

BIBLIOGRAPHY: Moore, G., *Seven African Writers* (1962), pp. 39–57; Obiechina, E. N., "A. T. and the Oral Tradition," *PA*, No. 65 (1968), 85–106; Collins, H. R., *A. T.* (1969); Lindfors, B., "A. T.: Debts and Assets," *CEAfr*, No. 38 (1970), 306–34; Anozie, S. O., "A. T.: Littérature et folklore; ou, Le problème de la synthèse," *CEAfr*, No. 38 (1970), 335–51; Armstrong, R. P., "The Narrative and Intensive Continuity: *The Palm-Wine Drinkard*," *RAL*, 1 (1970), 9–34; Böttcher, K.-H., *Tradition und Modernität bei A. T. und Chinua Achebe: Grundzüge der westafrikanischen Erzählliteratur englischer Sprache* (1974); Lindfors, B., ed., *Critical Perspectives on A. T.* (1975); Dussutour-Hammer, M., *A. T.: Tradition orale et écriture de conte* (1976); Achebe, C., "Work and Play in T.'s *The Palm-Wine Drinkard*," *Okike*, 14 (1978), 25–33; Coates, J., "The Inward Journey of the Palm-Wine Drinkard," *ALT*, 11 (1980), 122–29

BERNTH LINDFORS

RÉUNION LITERATURE

In the 19th c. two Réunion-born poets achieved prominence in Paris: Charles-Marie-René Leconte de Lisle (1818–1894), leader of the Parnassians, and Léon Dierx (1838–1912), elected "prince of poets" after the death of Mallarmé. In the first half of the 20th c., however, there was little literary activity, although two Réunion-born literary historians, Joseph Bédier (1864–1938) and Louis Cazamian (1877–1944?), who lived and worked in Paris, became well known for their scholarly publications.

A few Réunion writers began publishing in the 1950s, and in the 1960s a new generation gave evidence of an underlying literary vitality. This phenomenon seems linked to an improved economy and to access to education by all social classes. Until then, poetry had been the only field in which Réunion writers excelled, and French the only acceptable language.

Nowadays, writers no longer regard French literature as the only model to imitate. Aware of their multiracial culture, with roots in Madagascar, Africa, India, China, as well as France, they see themselves as a distinct entity, the specificity of which should be reflected in their works. They have started to write, in Creole and French, novels and plays deriving from oral tales or reflecting striking historical events and the quest for their own heritage. Creole is no longer looked down on; nevertheless, writers are aware that any publication in Creole has a very limited readership.

Poetry is still the dominant genre. Some twenty-five writers have published between one and seven volumes of poetry. Most prominent are Boris Gamaléya (b. 1930), Jean Albany (b. 1917), and Jean Azéma (dates n.a.), who write in French. The island of Réunion is their focus. Gamaléya, in *Vali pour une reine morte* (1972; *vali* [a Malagasy musical instrument] for a dead queen) and *La mer et la mémoire* (1978; sea and memory), sees the island from a passionately political viewpoint; he advocates independence, so as to achieve an integration of the past with present aspirations and the creation of a distinct country. Albany, in such works as *Miel vert* (1966; green honey), *Outre-mer* (1967; overseas), *Bleu mascarin* (1969; mascarene blue), *Bal indigo* (1976; indigo dance), and *Percale* (1979; percale), presents the people in vivid settings, depicting delightful scenes of everyday life full of humor and tenderness. Some of Albany's poems have been set to music and have become very popular. He writes in Creole as well as French. Azéma, in *Olographes* (1978; holographs) and *D'azur à perpétuité* (1979; of azure forever), looks at the island with the eye of a lover and makes it part of himself. His elaborate and sophisticated style conveys his pure lyricism and sensuousness.

Other highly regarded poets are Gilbert Aubry (b. 1942), Alain Lorraine (b. 1946), and Jean-François Sam-Long (b. 1949), all of whom write in French.

BIBLIOGRAPHY: Cornu, M.-R., "Les poètes réunionnais du XXe siècle: Vue d'ensemble," *PFr,* 13 (1976), 129–37; Joubert, J.-L., "L'Océan Indien," in Reboulet, A., and Tétu, M., eds., *Guide culturel: Civilisations et littératures d'expression française* (1977), pp. 321–25; Aubry, G., and Sam-Long, J.-F., Introduction to *Créolies: Poésies réunionnaises* (1978), pp. 9–21; Sam-Long, J.-F., "Écrivains d'aujourd'hui," in *Le mémorial de la Réunion* (1980), Vol. VII, pp. 136–47; Marimoutou, C., *L'île écriture* (1982)

MARIE-RENÉE CORNU

SÃO TOMÉ AND PRÍNCIPE LITERATURE

Around the year 1471 Portuguese navigators chanced on two small, uninhabited islands in the Gulf of Guinea. The larger of the equatorial islands was called, with the proper religious zeal, São Tomé (Saint Thomas) and the smaller was called, with all due devotion to the Portuguese royal family, Príncipe (prince). Over the centuries cultural and not a little biological mixing among African slaves and their descendants and Portuguese landowners, administrators, and convicts resulted in a creolization akin to that which occurred on the Cape Verde archipelago. Unlike this process in Cape Verde, however, creolization in São Tomé and Príncipe was undercut by a flourishing plantation economy nurtured by an abusive system of contract labor that for decades after the abolition of slavery brought thousands of black workers from the African continent and Cape Verde.

Despite the lack of a comparable base for the formation of an intellectual elite, by the late 19th c. São Tomé and Príncipe, like Cape Verde, did boast a small black and mestizo (mixed-race) landowning class. From the ranks of this group emerged a tiny number of writers, the first noteworthy one being Caetano da Costa Alegre (1864–1890). Born into a relatively well-to-do black family, he was sent as a boy to study in Portugal, where he lived most of his short life and where he wrote the ninety-six love poems, some of them racially self-conscious, posthumously published by friends in the volume *Versos* (1916; verses).

Nearly a half century would elapse after Alegre's death before another writer of high caliber would appear on the scene; and again the scene was Portugal. Francisco José Tenreiro (1921–1963), the son of a black mother and a white father, also spent most of his life in Portugal, where he rose to prominence as a professor, a geographer, a deputy to the Portuguese National Assembly, and a poet. Together with the Angolan writer Mário de Andrade (b. 1928), Tenreiro compiled the first anthology of black poetry in Portuguese, published in 1953. And although Tenreiro came to be recognized as the foremost poet of Portuguese-language Negritude (q.v.), he also wrote nostalgic and implicitly anticolonialist verse about the island of his birth.

The literature of São Tomé and Príncipe was, in effect, born in Portugal. But Alda Espírito Santo (b. 1926) became the central figure in what can be termed the beginnings of a home-grown literature. Except for a brief period in Lisbon, she has spent most of her life teaching grammar school on her native island of São Tomé. Her forceful, declamatory poems, brought together in *E' nosso o solo sagrado da terra* (1978; the sacred soil of the land is ours), lay defiant claim to the obscure, long exploited, but beautiful and potentially bountiful islands.

When independence was won in 1975, Alda Espírito Santo became the Minister of Education and Culture of the Democratic Republic of São Tomé e Príncipe, and, not surprisingly, her writing virtually came to a halt under the pressure of official duties. Nevertheless, her works, like those of Tenreiro, Tomás Medeiros (b. 1931), and, from Príncipe, Marcelo Veiga (1892–1976) and Maria Manuela Margarido (b. 1925), serve as models for a literature to come.

BIBLIOGRAPHY: Moser, G. M., "The Social and Regional Diversity of African Literature in the Portuguese Language," *Essays in Portuguese-African Literature* (1969), pp. 15–29; Preto-Rodas, R., *Negritude as a Theme in the Poetry of the Portuguese-Speaking World* (1970), pp. 32–54; Ortega, N., "The Motherland in the Modern Poetry of São Tomé e Príncipe" *WLT,* 53 (1979), 53–56

RUSSELL G. HAMILTON

SENEGALESE LITERATURE

There are literatures in the various African languages spoken in Senegal, notably Wolof, Tukolor, Peul, Serere, and Malinké. Since these literatures have been mostly oral, we have little evidence of their history save what can be surmised from songs and chronicles transcribed in Arabic or European script, and from those traces of tradition that remain in the oral African-language literatures today or in Francophone writing based on traditional forms, such as the poems and stories of Birago Diop (q.v.).

In the 19th c. there was an Islamic revival led by al-Hajj Umar ibn Saïd Tall (1794–1864), which led to considerable composition in Arabic, with most of the texts of a theological or philosophical nature and some of them composed in verse. At this time, Islam spread dramatically in Senegal and elsewhere in West Africa and became interfused with the traditional culture. The African and Francophone literatures alike to this day show the Islamic influence. In addition, secular writings in Arabic as well as in native languages have often sung the praise of folk heroes like Lat-Dior.

Today there is a revitalized interest in the oral literatures, and television and other media are helping to disseminate and preserve these art forms. Some contemporary writers have also produced written work in autochthonous languages as well as in French. For example, Cheikh A. Ndao's (b. 1940) first book of verse, *Kaïrée* (1962; Kaïrée), contains poems in French, English, and Wolof; and Assane Diallo (b. c. 1940), who has written poems in French, has also published a book of poems in his native Peul, *Leyd'am* (1967; my land).

Internationally, and in the narrowest sense of what is meant by "literature," the most significant writing in 20th-c. Senegal is in French. The country enjoys a special position in the Francophone community because of its historical links with France and the special status its people were granted under new policies adopted after the French Revolution of 1789. Educational, economic, and cultural ties with France have remained very strong.

Senegalese writing, as well as politics, has been dominated by one person—Léopold Sédar Senghor (q.v.). As a founding father of the nation, a major poet, and perhaps the leading African intellectual of the last thirty years, Senghor has inspired several generations of African writers and thinkers. His stance in behalf of black culture—crystallized in Negritude (q.v.), of which he was a prime mover—has given rise to much debate but has seldom been disregarded. His romantic ethnomystical image of the black man and his defense of an even-handed dialogue with Europe have drawn both praise and criticism; some hail his role as a decolonizer, while others take him to task for being too narrowly restricted to the African, ignoring oppressed peoples of other colors. Whatever one's views on Senghor's philosophy and politics, he looms as an intellectual and political giant in Senegalese and African culture.

Fiction

African fiction is often autobiographical or else closely based on the oral tradition of the tale and its component, the proverb. A link between traditional African-language literature and the young but vital Francophone literature is found in the work of Birago Diop. In his two important collections, *Les contes d'Amadou Koumba* (1947; tales of Amadou Koumba) and *Les nouveaux contes d'Amadou Koumba* (1958; new tales of Amadou Koumba), Diop combines faithfully retold versions of fables he had heard as a youth from the *griot*, or wise-man storyteller, with personal creations based on the old models.

Early novels include *Les trois volontés de Malic* (1920; the three wishes of Malic) by Ahmadou Mapaté Diagne (c. 1890–19??), which may be the first novel written in French by a black African; *Le reprouvé: Roman d'une Sénégalaise* (1925; the outcast: a novel about a Senegalese girl) by Birago Diop's brother Massyla Diop (c. 1886–1932); *Force-bonté* (1926; good will) by Bakary Diallo (1892–1978); and Ousmane Socé Diop's (b. 1911) novel *Karim: Roman sénégalais* (1935; Karim: a Senegalese novel).

The foremost contemporary novelist is Ousmane Sembène (q.v.), whose films—often based on his novels and stories—have brought him international recognition. Unlike most African novelists, who base their styles and subject matter on traditional and proverbial forms, Sembène has adopted a technique not unlike André Malraux's, one in which social commentary and psychological portrayal of characters prevail. Furthermore, whereas most African novels tend to be episodic, Sembène's have a larger sweep one tends to associate with European novels. The best of them—for example, *Les bouts de bois de Dieu* (1960; *God's Bits of Wood*, 1962) and *L'harmattan* (1964; the harmattan [a wind from the desert])—address themselves to crucial issues, specifically the 1947 strike on the Dakar-Niger railroad and the historic 1958 French Federation referendum.

Although he has written only one book, Cheikh Hamidou Kane (b. 1928) managed, with *L'aventure ambiguë* (1961; *Ambiguous Adventure*, 1963), to address in a most concise manner the fundamental problems of colonization and decolonization. This novel has been translated into many languages and has been the focus of much critical analysis. Although discursive and slim of plot, it brilliantly presents the dilemma facing the young protagonist and his community: to struggle to preserve traditional African and Islamic values, or to embrace the new ways imported by colonialism.

Another novel of note, *La plaie* (1967; *The Wound*, 1973) by the poet Malick Fall (1920–1978), is a sardonic tale of a man with a wound that will not heal whose quest for relief and a permanent cure from his ills, paralleled as it is by a search for moral fulfillment, invites manifold and mythic interpretation.

Two woman novelists—a relative rarity in Francophone Africa—have recently attracted considerable critical scrutiny, as much for the social problems they highlight as for their intrinsic literary merit. Mariama Bâ (1929–1981) was awarded the 1980 Noma Prize for her novel *Une si longue lettre* (1979; such a long letter), which focuses on the role women are called upon to play in a changing African society. Aminata Sow Fall (b. 1941) has published several novels. Her *La grève des Bàttu; ou, Les déchets humains* (1979; *The Beggars' Strike; or, The Dregs of Society*, 1981) tells of a beggars' strike after an official has tried to restrict downtown begging. This strike wreaks havoc with the almsgiving that is required by local custom.

There is, on the part of many African fiction writers, as well as dramatists, a penchant for satirical treatment of the constraints on today's citizens and the corruption they encounter. The African sense of humor, linked as it often is to a moral lesson, often expresses itself in caricature and lampoon, as in the traditional trickster tales and such modern political satires as Sembène's *Xala* (1973; *Xala*, 1976) and *Le mandat* (1965; *The Money-Order*, 1972).

Poetry

Léopold Sédar Senghor and David Diop (1927–1960) have dominated Senegalese poetry in French. Senghor has produced a significant corpus of poetry despite the many obligations of his high office. His work tends to the long line, or biblical *verset,* and he has acknowledged his debt to Paul Claudel, Saint-John Perse, and Walt Whitman. However, Senghor has brought to the long line two elements with which he has enriched its imagery: a rhythm based on African metrical conventions, and images of such Senegalese landscapes as the coast south of Dakar. His poems are humanistic, optimistic, and enthusiastic. For example, "Congo" (1956; "Congo," 1964) sings the poet's love of Africa and his vision of a dawning era of hope and fulfillment: "But the canoe will be born anew in the slackwater lilies/And will glide over the sweetness of the bamboo in the transparent morning of the world." Such poems as "Nuit de Sine" (1945; "Night of Sine," 1963), "Femme noire" (1945; "Black Woman," 1964), and "Prière aux masques" (1945; "Prayer to Masks," 1963) are often cited as typifying in literature the spirit of Senghor's rhapsodic version of Negritude.

David Diop was born in Bordeaux to a Senegalese father and a Cameroonian mother, but his fate has been intimately linked with Senegal, which he came to consider his homeland and off whose coast he died in a plane crash. The work he left behind is limited in quantity (twenty-two poems) and not outstanding in execution (he was not yet an experienced writer), but Diop has achieved almost legendary status in the eyes of those who consider him to be the poetic standard-bearer of African nationalism and liberation of oppressed classes. He published only one slim collection of poems, *Coups de pilon* (1956; *Hammer Blows,* 1973), but he had already acquired a following based on five poems published by Senghor in the latter's important *Anthologie de la nouvelle poésie nègre et malgache de langue française* (1948; anthology of the new black and Malagasy poetry in French). Diop's work celebrates the natural beauties of Africa and Africans, while it scathingly condemns the arrogance of colonialism.

Several other poets warrant mention as exponents, in one way or another, of Negritude. Birago Diop's beautiful "animistic" poems in *Leurres et lueurs* (1960; lures and glimmers) are poetic counterparts to his tales. Lamine Diakhaté (b. 1928) reveals in his poetry, for example, *Primordial du sixième jour* (1963; prime order of the sixth day), the same political concerns he expresses in his fiction, as in the novel *Chalys d'Harlem* (1978; Chalys of Harlem). Ousmane Socé Diop's *Rythmes du khalam* (1962; rhythms of the khalam [a guitarlike instrument]) and Lamine Niang's (dates n.a.) *Négristique* (1968; negristics) are lyrical paeans to, and veritable rediscoveries of, African history.

Drama

Drama in the European sense of staged performances of original works designed for the theater has been slow to develop and is rather limited in scope, as in the rest of black Africa. It is not surprising that such should be the case, since African "dramas" in the form of traditional dances, choral song fests, tales told aloud, and mime have wide popularity and consequently render formal staging somewhat alien to the African spirit. Senegal is no exception, and a typical evening's fare at the Daniel Sorano Theater in Dakar consists of a staged adaptation of a tale by Birago Diop and a formalized version of a village *khawaré* (variety show). Even when there is a play proper, it is often poetic in nature, choral in structure. It is difficult to determine, for example, if Senghor's *Chaka* (1956; *Chaka,* 1964) is a poem or play, and many of the epic-historical plays, such as *L'exil d'Albouri* (1967; Albouri's exile) and *Le fils d'Almamy* (1973; Almamy's son) by Cheikh A. Ndao, and *Les Amazoulous* (1972; the Amazulus) by the poet Abdou Anta Ka (dates n.a.), are just as suited to dramatic reading as to full-scale staging.

The Essay

The historical studies of Cheikh Anta Diop (b. 1923), whose thesis posits a preponderant African input in modern world civilization through the intermediary of ancient Sudanese-Nilotic cultures, have brought their author considerable fame, especially in the U.S., where his books are often required reading in courses on African history and culture.

Alioune Diop (1910–1980) made his mark on African cultural affairs as a thinker and as a founder and editor of *Présence africaine,* the pioneering journal and publishing enterprise founded in Paris in 1947.

The Senegalese essay, like poetry, is dominated by Senghor. His academic and presidential speeches, reviews, commemorations, articles, prefaces, and interviews fill many books, the most pertinent to literary and aesthetic theory being collected in *Liberté I: Négritude et humanisme* (1964; liberty I: negritude and humanism) and *Liberté III: Négritude et civilisation de l'universel* (1977; liberty III: negritude and the civilization of the universal).

Senghor's broad knowledge—which spans African literature and philology, Greek philosophy, modern European literature, and many other domains—abetted by his self-discipline and tremendous stamina, has permitted him to continue to write on the humanities while producing an equally impressive body of political essays, notably those collected in *Liberté II: Nation et voie africaine du socialisme* (1971; liberty II: nationhood and African socialism), in which he explains and defends his party's particular brand of socialism as applied to African needs and hopes.

For years, critics spoke of such entities as West African literature, lumping writers from Senegal with those from other Francophone countries in the region. Indeed, the presence in Dakar of exiled Guinean novelist Camara Laye (q.v.) during the last fifteen years of his life had an undeniable impact on Senegalese culture. However, a growing critical acumen among African critics has recently pointed toward a rejection of regional generalization and toward a higher valuation of both national and individual identities. This is true, of course, of all African countries. As in other countries, indicators suggest an ongoing Senegalese Francophone literature for years to come, even as expression continues to be encouraged in African languages and writers lean more and more to such traditional literary components as the proverb and the aphorism.

BIBLIOGRAPHY: Pageard, R., *Littérature négro-africaine* (1966), passim; Jahn, J., *Neo-African Literature: A History of Black Writing* (1968), passim; Michelman, F., "The Beginnings of French-African Fiction," *RAL*, 2, 1 (1971), 5–17; Kesteloot, L., *Black Writers in French: A Literary History of Negritude* (1974), passim; Blair, D. S., *African Literature in French* (1976), passim; Case, F. I., "The Socio-Cultural Functions of Women in the Senegalese Novel," *Cultures et développement*, 9 (1977), 601–29; Dorsinville, R., "Littérature sénégalaise d'expression française," *Éthiopiques*, 15 (1978), 41–51; Wauthier, C., *The Literature and Thought of Modern Africa*, 2nd rev. ed. (1979), passim; Gérard, A. S., and Laurent, J., "Sembène's Progeny: A New Trend in the Senegalese Novel," *StTCL*, 4, 1 (1980), 133–45; Sahel, A.-P., "Calliope au Sénégal," *Éthiopiques*, 22 (1980), 65–80; Gérard, A. S., *African Language Literatures* (1981), pp. 40–45, 57–58, 71–74; "Literature and Civilization of Black Francophone Africa," special issue, *FR*, 55, 6 (1982)

ERIC SELLIN

DIOP, Birago

Senegalese short-story writer and poet (writing in French), b. 11 Dec. 1906, Dakar

D. grew up in a tradition-bound African family. In 1920 he left Dakar to study on a scholarship in Saint Louis, Senegal. After completing college and a year of military service, he left for France to study veterinary medicine at the University of Toulouse. D. then went to Paris to complete his studies.

It was in Paris that he met many African, black American, and Caribbean students, including his compatriot Léopold Sédar Senghor (q.v.) and the Caribbean writers Léon-Gontran Damas (1912–1978) and Aimé Césaire (b. 1913). The concept of Negritude (q.v.), a term coined by Césaire, was gaining importance, and these young students in Paris spoke and wrote about the need to affirm black cultural values in a world in transition.

During this period of enthusiasm for African tradition, D. began to work with the African folktale. His aim was to make the oral tradition accessible to the French reading public, who had no previous contact with it, and to those Africans who, like himself, were living abroad. These tales are collected in *Les contes d'Amadou Koumba* (1947; tales of Amadou Koumba), *Les nouveaux contes d'Amadou Koumba* (1958; new tales of Amadou Koumba), and *Contes et lavanes* (1963; tales and commentaries).

D.'s tales are drawn from the Wolof tradition of Senegal, to which he is intimately bound, and from the traditions he learned about on his travels through Africa as a veterinarian. Men, animals, and supernatural beings are the protagonists. D. draws upon the cycle indigenous to one region of West Africa, that of Leuk, the hare, and Bouki, the hyena. Each animal is portrayed with a stereotyped personality. Leuk and Bouki are locked in eternal combat; the cunning Leuk usually outwits Bouki, who is voracious and dull-witted.

Within the African oral tradition, the *griot* (storyteller) recreates his tales of mystery and enchantment only during the eeriness of the night. D. adheres to the tradition of the *griot* by telling his readers that these tales come by way of Amadou Koumba, a *griot* well acquainted with D.'s family. D. recreates the *griot's* style, one of anecdotes, puns, repetitions, digressions, and the humorous use of daily expressions.

The charm of D.'s work is to be attributed to the poetry, which is interspersed throughout. By alternating prose with poetry and songs, D.

introduces an authentic rhythmic element as well as a heightening of the poetic effect of the work. Within the framework of the written folktale, the songs allow the reader to share more fully in the poetic fantasy of the writer.

Although D. has made stylistic changes and innovations in the tales, his social and moral code and his philosophical commitment remain welded to tradition. In his works we find first a basic conservatism; one must submit to nature and live within its bounds. Second, the supernatural, which is present everywhere, must be respected. Finally, the individual is expected to subordinate himself to the community. Anyone who is at odds with the community is doomed to a tragic fate. The work of D. provides a perspective on African culture that is informative and sensitive.

FURTHER WORKS: *Leurres et lueurs* (1960); *La plume raboutée* (1978).
FURTHER VOLUME IN ENGLISH: *Tales of Amadou Koumba* (1966)

BIBLIOGRAPHY: Senghor, L. S., Preface to *Les nouveaux contes d'Amadou Koumba* (1958), pp. 7–23; Maunick, E., "L'Afrique sans masque: B. D.," *NL,* 16 July 1964, 6; Mercier, R., and Battestini, M. and S., *B. D., écrivain sénégalais* (1964); Kennedy, E. C., Introduction to Kesteloot, L:, *Négritude Is Born: Black Writers in French* (1974), pp. 13–29; Kane, M., *"Les contes d'Amadou Koumba": Du conte traditionnel au conte moderne d'expression française* (1968); Mercier, R., "Un conteur d'Afrique noire: B. D.," *EF,* No. 4 (1968), 119–49

MILDRED MORTIMER

SEMBÈNE, Ousmane

Senegalese novelist and filmmaker (writing in French), b. 8 Jan. 1923, Ziguinchor

S. never received a formal education. At the age of fifteen he enlisted in the French army and fought in Italy and Germany in World War II. He returned to Senegal in 1947 and participated in the Dakar-Niger railroad-workers' strike. He then spent ten years in Marseille, where he became the leader of the longshoremen's union.

S.'s first novel, *Le docker noir* (1956; the black dock worker), depicts the betrayal suffered by an African writer whose novel is published under false pretenses, as well as the betrayal suffered by African workers who lead a wretched existence in Marseille. His second novel, the lyrical *Oh pays, mon beau peuple* (1957; oh country, my beautiful people), presents as its hero an enlightened self-made man who seeks to liberate his countrymen much in the manner of Manuel, the self-sacrificing hero of the Haitian writer Jacques Roumain's (1907–1944) masterpiece *Masters of the Dew*.

S.'s style continued to improve, and his third novel, *Les bouts de bois de Dieu* (1960; *God's Bits of Wood*, 1962), was well received by the critics. A sprawling fresco dealing with the Dakar-Niger railroad strike in 1947, *Les bouts de bois de Dieu* is set in three main towns along the railroad: Dakar, Thiès, and Bamako. In each town S. focuses on a particular family's hardships arising from the strike. In each case the workers and their loved ones must choose between continued struggle and surrender.

The structure of *Les bouts de bois de Dieu* has been compared with that of *Man's Fate* by André Malraux. Indeed, Tiémoko, the leader of the unit in charge of punishing strikebreakers, studies the Malraux novel to learn how to deal with those who desert the workers' cause. The two novels differ, however, in that S. favors nonviolent resistance over violence. This novel, unlike the works of Léopold Sédar Senghor (q.v.) and the Guinean writer Camara Laye (q.v.), was not written for the African elite; S. speaks to the workers as one of them.

S.'s desire to touch the common people in Senegal, who can neither read nor write, and who speak Wolof, not French, led him to turn to film making in the early 1960s. His heart-breaking film *La noire de...* (1966; the black girl of...), adapted from his story of the same name in the collection *Voltaïque* (1962; *Tribal Scars, and Other Stories,* 1975), was based on an actual event reported in the newspaper *Nice-matin* in 1958: the suicide of a young Senegalese servant who, while vacationing with her boss's family on the Riviera, suffered from homesickness and from the insensitivity of her European masters.

When S. turned his short novel *Le mandat (The Money-Order)*— published in *Véhi-Ciosane ou Blanche-Genèse, suivi du Mandat* (1965; *The Money-Order, with White Genesis,* 1972)—into a film in 1969, he produced two versions, one in French for European audiences, and one in Wolof. Thus, both French and Senegalese were able to appreciate the comedy and the pathos of this film, depicting the frustrations encountered by a poor, unemployed African who tries desperately to cash a money order sent to him by his nephew in Paris.

In recent years, S.'s works have become increasingly bitter and exclusively African-oriented. The novel *Xala* (1973; *Xala,* 1976), which S. adapted into a film of the same name (1974), starts in a humorous, almost farcical vein when the pompous protagonist El Hadji Beye is mysteriously afflicted with a curse of impotence (or *xala*) on the night of his wedding to a third bride. *Xala* is a parable of a wealthy, conceited, and basically foolish businessman's downfall. Here, as in his earlier story "Ses trois jours" (her three days) from the collection *Voltaïque,* S. attacks polygamy, vividly depicting the plight of older wives whose husbands acquire younger, more desirable brides. Yet the tone in *Xala* becomes unexpectedly harsh and distressing, as punishments are heaped upon El Hadji, whose manhood can only be restored after he has lost all material possessions, including his bride, and after he has been publicly humiliated for having exploited his fellow Africans in earlier selfish business dealings.

The "father of the African film," S. now devotes his talents to film making. *Ceddo* (1977; common people), which presents the taboo subject of African cooperation in supplying slaves to be sent to the western hemisphere in the 17th c., was banned in Senegal. S.'s open hostility and bitterness toward foreigners, religious leaders, and the African bourgeoisie pitted him against then president Senghor. Deeply committed to spreading socialism and trade unionism in Africa, S. shows in his films and his novels that excessive reverence for authority, whether bureaucratic or traditional, can only impede the progress necessary to build a modern and totally independent Africa.

FURTHER WORKS: *L'harmattan* (1964); *Le dernier de l'empire* (2 vols., 1981; *The Last of the Empire,* 1983)

BIBLIOGRAPHY: Beier, U., on *O pays, mon beau peuple, BO,* Nov. 1959, 56–57; Brench, A. C., *The Novelists' Inheritance in French Africa* (1967), pp. 109–19; Ortava, J., "Les femmes dans l'oeuvre littéraire d'O. S.," *PA,* No. 3 (1969), 69–77; Vieyra, P. S., *S. O. cinéaste* (1973); Achiriga, J. J., *La révolte des romanciers noirs de langue française* (1973), pp. 142–51; Minyono-Nkondo, M.-F., *Comprendre "Les bouts de bois de Dieu" de S.O.* (1979); Bestman, M. T., *S. O. et l'esthétique du roman négro-africain* (1981)

DEBRA POPKIN

SENGHOR, Léopold Sédar

Senegalese poet and essayist (writing in French), b. 9 Oct. 1906, Joal

After receiving his early education in Senegal, S. went to Paris in 1928, where he attended the Lycée Louis-le-Grand and the Sorbonne. During his time in France, S. met other black students from Africa and the Caribbean, and together they began to formulate the principles of Negritude (q.v.). After World War II, having spent about sixteen years in France, S. returned to Senegal to begin a distinguished and influential career as a writer and politician, which was to bring him international recognition. He very quickly assumed the political leadership of Senegal and played a major role in the decolonization of the French African colonies. In 1960 he became the first president of independent Senegal; he held this position without interruption until his retirement in 1980.

S.'s first volume of poetry, *Chants d'ombre* (1945; songs of shadow) revealed the style and themes that were to remain characteristic of his work: the long, biblical line and the celebration of the African past and cultural values. While it is obvious that at least some of these first poems were written before the war, the majority, if not all, of the poems in his next volume, *Hosties noires* (1948; black victims) were inspired by S.'s experience of the war in Europe, particularly as a conscripted soldier in the French army and then as a prisoner-of-war in Germany. He notes with perception but entirely without bitterness the racism to which the black conscripts were subjected by the white soldiers. In the same year, S. published his *Anthologie de la nouvelle poésie nègre et malgache de langue française* (1948; anthology of the new black and Malagasy poetry in French), which, with its famous preface by Jean-Paul Sartre, has acquired a historical importance in the development of modern black writing in French.

Éthiopiques (1956; Ethiopics) is probably S.'s most significant collection and contains some of his best-known poems. Written at the height of his powers as a poet and at a time when his political career was at its most successful, the poetry in this volume has a striking quality of self-assurance, celebrating not only the well-established themes of Negritude but also the poet's own very personal preoccupation with leadership.

Although his subsequent collections have received less attention than these early ones, they show no diminution in the poet's command of his medium. *Nocturnes* (1961; *Nocturnes*, 1969) incorporates a number of love poems previously published in *Chants pour Naëtt* (1949; songs for Naëtt) and a series of new elegies, somewhat reminiscent of Paul Claudel's odes, on the subject of poetry and the creative imagination. He later returned to the love poem with *Lettres d'hivernage* (1972; letters from the wet season), and then to the elegy, with *Élégies majeures* (1979; major elegies).

The themes of S.'s poetry derive very largely from his belief in the importance of justifying African culture in the face of colonialism. As he has felt the success of his enterprise becoming more and more evident, he has increasingly emphasized the need for reconciliation and the fact of interdependence. Indeed, S.'s poetry gains its vitality not so much from the themes based on intellectual principles as from those themes that are important to him personally at a deep emotional level. Reconciliation is one of these, and it expresses itself in much of his poetry as a tension between his love of Africa and his love of Europe. S. is a man of considerable breadth of culture; he therefore finds it extremely difficult to make absolute choices in this area.

Alongside his poetry, S. has published a considerable number of both shorter and book-length works on literary, cultural, and political subjects. The majority of these have been collected in three volumes under the general title of *Liberté*, numbered from I to III (1964, 1971, 1977; liberty). More recently, he has published a survey of his whole career in the form of a series of interviews with a journalist, under the title *La poésie de l'action* (1980; the poetry of action).

Although his style has had virtually no imitators, and although Negritude, which romanticized Africa, is often strongly criticized by the younger generation of black intellectuals, S.'s influence as a poet and thinker, particularly in the period from the late 1940s until 1960, has been very great indeed. In spite of a certain artificiality in the deliberately cultivated rhetoric of his poetry, which many readers now find unattractive, there can be no denying the rich and perceptive imagination that has generated the powerful, often sensuous, imagery and rhythms of his poetry, or his skillful command of the French language as a creative medium.

FURTHER WORKS: *Nation et voie africaine du socialisme* (1961; *On African Socialism*, 1964); *Pierre Teilhard de Chardin et la politique africaine* (1962); *Poèmes* (1964; enlarged ed., 1973); *Les fondements de l'africanité; ou, Négritude et arabité* (1967; *The Foundations of "Africanité"; or, "Négritude" and "Arabité,"* 1971); *Élégie des alizés* (1968); *La parole chez Paul Claudel et chez les négro-africains* (1973); *Paroles* (1975). FURTHER VOLUMES IN ENGLISH: *Selected Poems* (1964); *Prose and Poetry* (1965)

BIBLIOGRAPHY: Markovitz, I., *S. and the Politics of Negritude* (1969); Hymans, J., *L. S. S.: An Intellectual Biography* (1971); Bâ, S., *The Concept of Negritude in the Poetry of L. S. S.* (1973); Mezu, S., *The Poetry of L. S. S.* (1973); Reed, J., "L. S. S.," in King, B., and Ogungbesan, K., eds., *A Celebration of Black and African Writing* (1975), pp. 102–11; *Hommage à L. S. S.: Homme de culture* (1976); Irele, A., Introduction to L. S. S., *Selected Poems* (1977), pp. 1–37; Peters, J., *A Dance of Masks: S., Achebe, Soyinka* (1978), pp. 15–89; Little, R., " 'Je danse, donc je suis': The Rhythm of L. S. S.'s Two Cultures," in Bishop, M., ed., *The Language of Poetry: Crisis and Solution* (1980), pp. 161–76; Moore, G., *Twelve African Writers* (1980), pp. 16–38

CLIVE WAKE

SIERRA LEONEAN LITERATURE

Sierra Leone, a British colony from 1808 to 1961, was used to resettle freed slaves. The political writings, mainly pamphlets, of James Africanus Horton (1835–1883), a local doctor, is the only literary work from the 19th c. that remains of interest today. He vigorously argued for self-government in Africa. After Horton there was a period of nearly a hundred years before a vigorous Sierra Leonean literature developed. Political circumstances were not advantageous but cannot totally explain this puzzling gap.

Contemporary literature began in the late 1950s, with the publication of several competent, if somewhat unimaginative, books written by professional men during their leisure hours. Robert Cole's (b. 1907) autobiographical novel *Kossah Town Boy* (1960), was admired for its enthusiastic and innocent portrayal of village life, but it is little read now. The Gambian-born William Conton (b. 1925) lived long enough in Sierra Leone for his pioneering novel *The African* (1960) to be considered part of the new literature of his adopted country. John Akar's (b. 1927) *Valley without Echo* (1954) was the first African play to be produced in Britain. Dr. Raymond Sarif Easmon (b. 1913) wrote two somewhat formal, artificial plays: the domestic comedy *Dear Parent and Ogre* (1964), and the more satirical *The New Patriots* (1965). Although the characters are African, the general tone and spirit of the plays seems redolent of typically British popular fare.

Dr. Davidson Nicol (b. 1924) wrote one volume of short stories, *The Truly Married Woman* (1965). He is best remembered for a regularly anthologized poem, "The Meaning of Africa" (1959), which received both sympathetic and antagonistic responses, because of its expression of the mixed feelings of the elite toward African culture. An unquestioning acceptance of British values and styles was typical of much writing in the 1960s.

For ten years following this lively beginning there was little publication. Probably because of increasingly restrictive government policies, writers had to leave the country; it is significant that the three most promising younger Sierra Leonean writers composed their main works abroad. Lemuel Johnson's (b. 1940) *Highlife for Caliban* (1975) and Syl Cheney-Coker's (b. 1945) *Concerto for an Exile* (1973), both collections of poetry, were written in the U.S. These two writers share a highly sophisticated and experimental language that owes much to their knowledge of poetic techniques in the rest of the English-speaking world. In theme, they share an angry, embittered disillusion with present-day conditions in Africa—the heavy pressures of external economic forces and the oppressive internal policies of various governments. Their difference is primarily in tone. Johnson uses sardonic wit and penetrating sarcasm. Cheyney-Coker writes with a far more direct anger; dismay burns in his lines.

Yulisa Amadu Maddy (b. 1936) has produced a variety of works. His first volume of verse was published in Denmark and his plays, published in *Obasai, and Other Plays* (1971), were broadcast over European radio services. His first novel indicates much by its very title: *No Past No Present No Future* (1973), although the disintegration suffered by the main characters actually occurs after they arrive in Britain.

Censorship imposed by the government is likely to inhibit the development of Sierra Leonean literature at home, at least as concerns writing in English by the sophisticated elite. But Creole English (Krio), widely spoken in Sierra Leone, is the language of the vigorous, popular street-theater groups and is also printed. Thomas Decker's (b. 1916) Krio poetry is widely known, and he has translated Shakespeare's *Julius Caesar* into Krio (1964). There is a great local vitality in such work, and its potential cannot yet be measured.

BIBLIOGRAPHY: Fyfe, C., and Jones, E., eds., *Freetown: A Symposium* (1968); Cartey, W., *Whispers from a Continent* (1969), pp. 20–23; Olney, J., *Tell Me Africa* (1973), pp. 37–55; Dathorne, O. R., *The Black Mind* (1974), passim; Palmer, E., "The Development of Sierra Leone Writing," in King, B., and Ogungbesan, K., eds., *A Celebration of Black and African Writing* (1975), pp. 245–57; Gérard, A. S., *African Language Literatures* (1981), pp. 243–46, 259–60

JOHN POVEY

SOMALI LITERATURE

Although an official orthography for the Somali language was not introduced until 1972, various private systems of writing had been devised, and were in limited use, in the hundred years or so before this date; from 1940 they were applied to the recording of oral poetry and prose. The poetry, alliterative in form and rich in literary sophistication and reflective thought, is preserved verbatim in the memories of its auditors and passed on faithfully by reciters, with the name of the poet always quoted, as if by an oral copyright law.

Although firmly rooted in the past, Somali oral poetry adapted itself to modern life. Since World War II a new genre called *heello* has developed; it is used extensively in radio broadcasting, in the theater, and in recordings. Its main themes are either love or topical matters concerning politics and public life, and it is usually recited with musical accompaniment. Authors embarking on literature in its written form have taken upon themselves three main tasks: to continue carefully to record and annotate this oral heritage, to incorporate it into modern written genres, and finally to introduce entirely new elements not previously found in Somali culture.

Three important collections of oral prose are *Hikmad Soomaali* (1956; Somali wisdom) by Muuse Haaji Ismaa'iil Galaal (also spelled Muuse Xaaji Ismaaciil Galaal; 1920–1980), *Murti iyo sheekooyin* (1973; traditional wisdom and stories) by Cabdulqaadir F. Bootaan (b. 1949), and *Sheekooyin Soomaaliyeed* (1973; Somali stories) by Muuse Cumar Islaam (b. 1937). Both oral prose and poetry are found in *Gabayo, maahmaah, iyo sheekooyin yaryar* (1965; poems, proverbs, and short stories) by Shire Jaamac Achmed (also spelled Axmed; b. 1934) and in articles in the journal *Iftiinka aqoonta* (1966–67), which also contain materials on Somali history.

Three of the greatest poets have volumes containing their collected poems together with their biographies. In *Diiwaanka gabayadii Sayid Maxamed Cabdulle Xasan* (1974; a collection of the poems of Sayid Maxamed Cabdulle Xasan [1856–1921]) Jaamac Cumar Ciise (b. 1932) has annotated a corpus of oral poems of the national hero and Muslim religious leader, who with his Dervish army waged war on the colonial occupiers until his death. The oral poems of Ismaaciil Mire (1862–1951), one of his generals and chief of intelligence in the Dervish army, are published in *Ismaaciil Mire* (1974; Ismaaciil Mire) by Axmed Faarax Cali "Idaajaa" (b. 1947). And in *Ma dhabba jacayl waa loo dhintaa?* (1975; is it true that people die of love?) Rashiid Maxamed Shabeele (b. 1950) writes of Cilmi Bowndheri (?–1941), an oral poet who is said to have died of unrequited love.

An example of oral poetry incorporated unchanged into original modern work is the play *Dabkuu shiday Darwiishkii* (1975; the fire that the Dervish lit) by Axmed Faarax Cali "Idaajaa" and Cabdulqaadir Xirsi "Yamyam" (b. 1946): the principal characters are Sayid Maxamed Cabdulle Xasan and Ismaaciil Mire, and the authors give to the two national heroes dialogue containing quotations from their poems. Faarax Maxamed Jaamac Cawl (b. 1937), in two historical novels, *Aqoondarro waa u nacab jacayl* (1974; *Ignorance Is the Enemy of Love*, 1982) and *Garbaduubkii gumeysiga* (1978; the shackles of colonialism), similarly weaves into his narratives poems that were composed at the time of the events he describes.

The scansion patterns and alliteration of oral poetry have been carried over intact into written poetry, even when it is concerned with current, mainly political, topics. Typical of such poetry is *Geeddiga wadaay* (1973; lead the trek) by Cabdi Muxumud Aamin (b. 1935), praising the ideals of the Somali revolution of 1969. A complete break with oral poetry and prose is found in those short stories and novels based on European models; the subjects and themes, however, are drawn from modern Somali life. The earliest example is the short story "Qawdhan iyo Qoran" (1967; Qawdhan and Qoran), by Axmed Cartan Xaange (b. 1936), which appeared in the literary journal *Horseed*. It is a love story ending in an elopement to save the heroine from being forced by her family to marry a man she does not want. Two short novels by Shire Jaamac Axmed, *Rooxaan* (1973; the spirits) and *Halgankii nolosha* (1973; life struggle), are, respectively, a bitter satire on the practice of spirit divination, and the story of a young boy's unhappy life as an unwanted stepchild. Much new fiction is serialized in the literary pages of the national daily newspaper; typical of this work are *Waa inoo berrito* (1977; we shall see each other tomorrow) by Axmed Faarax Cali "Idaajaa," about a civil servant engaged in illegal currency deals, and *Wacdaraha jacaylka* (1977; the vicissitudes of love) by Yuusuf Axmed "Hero" (dates n.a.), a love story reflecting the modern feminist trend in Somali society.

A number of works have been produced in languages other than Somali. Somalis writing in Arabic are concerned mainly with religious themes, such as the lives of Muslim saints. In English, Nuruddin Farah (q.v.) has published four novels of life in modern Somalia, which show great psychological depth and poetic vision: *From a Crooked Rib* (1970), which is particularly interesting as a male writer's insight into a Somali woman's experiences; *A Naked Needle* (1976); *Sweet and Sour Milk* (1979); and *Sardines* (1982). William J. F. Syad (b. 1930) writes lyrical and political poems in French and has published four volumes: *Khamsin* (1969; the khamsin wind), *Harmoniques* (1976; harmonics), *Cantiques* (1976; canticles), and *Naufragés du destin* (1978; destiny's shipwreck victims). Mohamed Said Samantar (b. 1928) writes poetry in both French and Italian, and in the bilingual *La pioggia è caduta/Il a plu* (1973; rain has fallen) he is concerned with the problems of Somalia and with pan-Africanism.

Although Somali written literature is of such recent origin, it has already reached a standard of excellence that gives hope for a bright future. Contemporary writers, creative, imaginative, and self-confident, share with the oral poets and narrators a high degree of awareness of the potentialities of language as a medium of artistic expression. In 20th-c. world literature Somalia presents an example of the coexistence of innovative trends with filial piety toward the cultural past.

BIBLIOGRAPHY: Andrzejewski, B. W., and Lewis, I. M., eds., Introduction to *Somali Poetry: An Introduction* (1964), pp. 3–60; Johnson, J. W., *Heellooy Heelleellooy: The Development of the Genre Heello in Modern Somali Poetry* (1974); Andrzejewski, B. W., "The Veneration of Sufi Saints and Its Impact on the Oral Literature of the Somali People and Their Literature in Arabic," *AfrLS*, 15 (1974), 15–53; Andrzejewski, B. W., "The Rise of Written Somali Literature," *ARD*, Nos. 8–9 (1975), 7–14; Andrzejewski, B. W., "Modern and Traditional Aspects of Somali Drama," in Dorson, R. M., ed., *Folklore in the Modern World* (1978), pp. 87–101; Beer, D. F., "Somali Literature in European Languages," *Horn of Africa*, 2, 4 (1979), 27–35; Gérard, A., *African Language Literatures* (1981), pp. 155–70; Andrzejewski, B. W., "The Survival of the National Culture in Somalia during and after the Colonial Era: The Contribution of Poets, Playwrights and Collectors of Oral Literature," *N. E.A.: Journal of Research on North East Africa*, 1, 1 (1981), 3–15; Andrzejewski, B. W., "Alliteration and Scansion in Somali Oral Poetry and Their Cultural Correlates," *JASO*, 13, 1 (1982), 68–83

B. W. ANDRZEJEWSKI

FARAH, Nuruddin

Somali novelist (writing in English and Somali), b. 24 Nov. 1945, Baidoa

Although F. came to English as a fourth language, his reputation as a writer rests on the novels he has written in English. After studying literature in India at the University of Chandigarh, F. returned to Somalia and taught in Mogadisho, then lived in England for a time; he now resides in Rome. Besides his English-language work, he has also written a novel, plays, and short stories in Somali, and has translated children's stories from Arabic, Italian, French, and English into Somali.

F.'s novels are set in 20th-c. Somalia, with most of the action occurring in the capital, Mogadisho. In *From a Crooked Rib* (1970) Mogadisho becomes the home of Ebla, a nomad girl who flees her family's camp because she has been promised in marriage to an old man. Her pilgrimage from desert to small town and eventually on to the capital teaches her to exploit men as they exploit her. Ebla is inquiring and analytical; in rejecting the traditional role of the Somali woman, she becomes her own person, with a thoroughly existential attitude. The book is a sociological novel and a novel of character, and realistically portrays some grim realities of Somali life.

A Naked Needle (1976) possesses more breadth and depth, is more cosmopolitan, and is also technically more complex. Written in the present tense, its tone is reminiscent of the Nigerian writer Wole Soyinka's (q.v.) *The Interpreters,* the favorite novel of F.'s protagonist, Koschin. Koschin, a Mogadisho teacher, while studying overseas had promised to marry an English girl who now, two years later, arrives in Somalia expecting him to keep his promise. A potential situation comedy becomes in F.'s hands an unsettling novel on the sordidness of mid-1970s Somalia. Koschin, like Ebla, is a complex character who reveals himself as he filters his experiences through his consciousness and internally expresses his attitudes toward them.

F.'s most recent novel, *Sweet and Sour Milk* (1979), received the English-Speaking Union Literary Award. The book explores even further the almost unrelieved grimness of Somali life. This time the all-powerful state's license to arrest, imprison without trial, and torture are sharply focused upon. Loyaan's search for the facts behind the sudden death of his twin brother Soyaan, an economic adviser to Somalia's president, is undertaken in an aura of sheer political terror mitigated only by F.'s constraint and his skillful use of interior monologue—a skill already developed in *A Naked Needle.*

F. has a keen eye for physical and psychological details. His use of English is mature, possessing a colloquial flavor that happily blends with an increasingly cosmopolitan stance that retains its authentically Somali subject matter. He is not a self-consciously African writer, but makes the novel form his own, creating an effective bond between mythic and local references and those aspects of his message that have far-reaching human significance.

BIBLIOGRAPHY: Beer, D., "Somali Literature in European Languages," *Horn of Africa,* 2, 4 (1979), 27–35; Cochrane, J., "The Theme of Sacrifice in the Novels of N. F.," *WLWE,* 18 (1979), 69–77; Okomilo, I., on *Sweet and Sour Milk, Africa,* No. 101 (1980), 72–73; Imfeld, A., and Meuer, G., "N. F.: A Modern Nomad," *Afrika* (Munich), 21, 9 (1980), 23–25

DAVID F. BEER

SOUTH AFRICAN LITERATURE

In Afrikaans

Afrikaans literature belongs almost totally to the 20th c., since the written language achieved recognition and acceptance only around the turn of the century. The language of the first European colonizers of the southern tip of Africa (beginning in 1652) was Dutch, from which Afrikaans developed, as a result of the intermingling of different cultures and eventually because of political forces.

After the discovery of diamonds and gold (1870–86), the impact of British imperialism on the Afrikaners had tragic consequences, culminating in the second Anglo-Boer War (1899–1902). Literature early in the century was dominated by this event, and the poetry of C. Louis Leipoldt (1880–1947) is considered the most impressive poetic document of that suffering and the most powerful protest against the physical and spiritual effects of war. Leipoldt and J. F. W. Grosskopf (1885–1948) were the founders of Afrikaans drama. But the most important writers at the beginning of the century were poets. The major ones, in addition to Leipoldt, were Jan F. E. Celliers (1865–1940), Totius (pseud. of Jacob Daniel du Toit, 1877–1953), and Eugène Marais (1871–1936). It was a time that demanded the immediacy of poetry; and when the poets sought respite from the atrocities of war, they worshiped nature, although the best work of A. G. Visser (1878–1929) was his lyrical love poetry.

The economic disruption after the war—poverty, land dispossession, urbanization, and the beginnings of the proletarianization of the Afrikaners—became a persistent theme in the fiction of the 1920s and 1930s. Novels glorifying the idyll of farm life and the work ethic and extolling the superiority of country over city were produced by D. F. Malherbe (1881–1969) and C. M. van den Heever (1902–1957), whose *Somer* (1935; *Harvest Home,* 1945) is typical of the treatment of this theme. The poetry of Toon van den Heever (1894–1956) also reflects the problems and conflicts facing the Afrikaner during this period. The sharpest realist—almost a naturalist—was Jochem van Bruggen (1881–1957), who portrayed the helplessness of a people being forced unwillingly into proletarianization, the destruction of the feudal system, and the poverty of tenant farmers. Mikro (pseud. of C. H. Kühn, 1903–1968), on the other hand, wrote comic novels and sketches of life in the Cape Province.

Projects by newly formed organizations working for the economic rehabilitation of the Afrikaners and the strengthening of nationalism during the 1930s did not have a direct influence on the literature of the time. But the attempts to liberate the Afrikaners economically and politically did bring with them a cultural uplifting, of which a sophisticated literature was part.

The most important figure of the group that came to prominence during the 1930s (known as the Dertigers) was N. P. van Wyk Louw (1906–1970), primarily a poet, but also a playwright and literary essayist. He educated his people about the nature of literature and criticism, about the aesthetics of poetry, and politically about the necessity of a "liberal" nationalism. His early poetry is individualistic and at times nihilistic; in his second phase, with the narrative poem *Raka* (1941; *Raka,* 1941), he turned to folk themes and styles; his third period is again personal, but with a sense of affirmation. His best play is the verse drama *Germanicus* (1956; Germanicus). A selection of his poetry is available in the bilingual collection *Oh, Wide and Sad Land* (1975). Other important poets of the same generation are Elisabeth Eybers (b. 1915), W. E. G. Louw (b. 1913), and Uys Krige (b. 1910), all writers of lyric verse.

During the 1930s poetry became an aristocratic ideal, a sublime trade—the word being man's sole instrument for the attainment of high truths of human existence. Ever since, Afrikaans poetry has retained this isolation of aestheticism, and those who in later decades have attempted to move toward social or political verse still meet severe criticism from some quarters.

The poets of the 1940s, particularly Ernst van Heerden (b. 1916), furthered the quest for the aesthetic word and image. Van Heerden employed complex metaphorical structures. But D. J. Opperman (b. 1914), also a playwright and critic, took images from everyday modern life. His metaphors and his themes show a consciousness of Africa and of the South African social and political realities, of urbanization, and of the Afrikaners' growing nationalism. The degree of political commitment that did enter Afrikaans poetry, despite efforts to oppose it, can be traced to Opperman.

In 1948 the Afrikaner Nationalist Party came to power in South Africa. The Afrikaners' rise to political control culminated in the declaration of the Republic in 1960. There was a shift in fiction, which had been relatively uncontroversial since the 1920s and had dealt with themes such as urbanization, poverty, the Boer War, and racial differences—often didactically, as in the work of G. H. Franz (1896–1956), M. E. R. (pseud. of Mimie E. Rothman, 1875–1975), and Johannes van Melle (1887–1953). Now there was protest writing, directed at the authoritarian power structure, apartheid, and the inherent discrimination at the core of this ideology. Much of this writing came from the Sestigers, those who began their careers in the 1960s.

These innovative young writers of fiction, poetry, and drama had precursors in Van Wyk Louw in his later poetry, the cynical and satiric poet Peter Blum (b. 1925), the dramatist Bartho Smit (b. 1924), the polemicist, novelist, and short-story writer Jan Rabie (b. 1920), and the novelist Étienne Leroux (pseud. of Stephanus Petrus Daniel Le Roux, b. 1922). The first short stories of Rabie, published in the early 1950s, influenced by European surrealism and symbolism, showed the way.

The influence of Europe was strong on the Sestigers. Many of them went to Europe and lived there for considerable periods of time. Their experiments in technique and theme therefore to a great extent represented a transference to Afrikaans literature of the more recent literary movements in Europe. The increasing political consciousness of the younger writers, however, led to a greater involvement in the affairs of the country.

Leroux is the most distinguished novelist of the Sestiger group, best known for the Welgevonden trilogy—*Sewe dae by die Silbersteins* (1962; *Seven Days at the Silbersteins*, 1964), *Een vir Azazel* (1964; *One for the Devil*, 1969), and *Die derde oog* (1966; *The Third Eye*, 1969)—in which, using experimental techniques and Carl Jung's concept of archetypes, he explores the psychology of the Afrikaner. He comments on the loss of myths and satirizes some aspects of South African society.

André P. Brink (b. 1935) is the most popular contemporary Afrikaans novelist, and his novels are also the most politically committed, protesting against the injustices of apartheid, the falseness of the new Afrikaner capitalism, the power of the police, and the heritage of slavery. His books have frequently been banned. Brink is bilingual and writes the English versions of his novels himself; these include *Kennis van die aand* (1973; *Looking on Darkness*, 1975), *'n Oomblik in die wind* (1977; *An Instant in the Wind*, 1977), *Gerugte van reën* (1978; *Rumours of Rain*, 1978), *'n Droë wit seisoen* (1979; *A Dry White Season*, 1980), and *Houd-den-bek* (1982; *A Chain of Voices*, 1982).

The short story became an important genre in the 1960s. Rabie's influence cannot be underestimated in the often poetic, highly concentrated and daring ventures into the darker side of the human psyche by Abraham H. de Vries (b. 1937), Hennie Aucamp (b. 1934), Chris Barnard (b. 1939), and John Miles (b. 1938), developing eventually into the portrayal of violence by later writers, as in the work of P. J. Haasbroek (b. 1943).

Of the poets of the 1960s, Ingrid Jonker (1933-1965), who committed suicide, was undoubtedly the most significant. Her disturbing personal poetry has been likened to that of Sylvia Plath. Adam Small (b. 1936), a Cape Coloured, is a politically committed poet and playwright who began writing in Afrikaans, although he now writes in English.

In drama, Chris Barnard and André P. Brink attempted a transposition of the Theater of the Absurd into Afrikaans. But the plays of Bartho Smit, as well as the later works of Brink, epitomize the 1960s: an awareness of the techniques of playwriting, combined with the presentation of relevant political themes.

Politically and aesthetically the most significant Sestiger writer is the poet and painter Breyten Breytenbach (b. 1939), who considered Paris as his home after his political self-exile because of his opposition to apartheid laws. The Zen Buddhist and Tantric aspects of his poetry stunned his traditional Calvinist readers; his opposition to the Afrikaners' ideology angered them. Returning to South Africa in 1975 in disguise, he was arrested and sentenced to nine years' imprisonment on a charge of "terrorism" (he was released in 1983 and returned to Paris). Even while in prison he managed to publish a number of volumes of his brilliant, innovative poetry. Two bilingual collections of his poetry, *And Death White as Words: An Anthology of the Poems of Breyten Breytenbach* (1978) and *In Africa Even the Flies Are Happy: Selected Poems, 1964-1977* (1978) offer a representative selection. His *'n Seisoen in Paradys* (1976; *A Season in Paradise,* 1980) is a half-real, half-imaginary travelogue in poetic prose that is, ultimately, a meditation on South Africa. His imprisonment left Afrikaans literature—where there has always been the "guiding force" of a single strong creative personality—in a desert between commitment on the one hand and ivory-tower aestheticism and private obsessions on the other. Breytenbach may well have been a watershed in Afrikaans literature.

In addition to Breytenbach, leading poets of the 1970s were Wilma Stockenström (b. 1933) and Sheila Cussons (b. 1922). They, however, both write in the tradition of poetic refinement started by the Dertigers.

The most meaningful recent developments have been in fiction, specifically the "political" novel initiated and continued by Brink. There has been an attempt at the documentary novel, by Elsa Joubert (b. 1922) in *Die swerfjare van Poppie Nongena* (1978; *The Long Journey of Poppie Nongena*, 1980), the actual life story of a woman suppressed by apartheid. John Miles and Karel Schoeman (b. 1939) have explored various possible South African political scenarios: their fictional visions are bleak.

The principal forum for literary discussion, criticism, and scholarship today is the journal *Standpunte*. Creative writing continues under difficult circumstances. There is uncertainty about the political future of South Africa, and there are debates about the future of Afrikaans as a language. Strict censorship and the banning of many books have taken their toll, and some dissident Afrikaans writers have ceased writing, have switched to writing in English in order to be published outside the country, or have gone into exile. Hence the present lull in significant literary production in Afrikaans.

BIBLIOGRAPHY: Bosman, H. C., "Aspects of South African Literature" (1948), *EinA*, 7, 1 (1980), 36–39; Grové, A. P., and Harvey, C. J. D., eds., Introduction to *Afrikaans Poems with English Translations* (1962), pp. xiii–xviii; Antonissen, R., "Facets of Contemporary Afrikaans Literature," *ESA*, 13, 1 (1970), 191–206; Brink, A., "Afrikaans Theatre: The Contemporary Scene," *TheatreQ*, 28 (1977–78), 71–76; Bullier, A. J., "The Position of the Black Man in Afrikaans Literature," *PA*, 114 (1980), 27–52; February, V., *Mind Your Colour: The "Coloured" Stereotype in South African Literature* (1981); Lelyveld, J., "Breakup of a Community," *NYTBR*, 17 May 1981, 3, 29–30; Cope, J., *The Adversary Within: Dissident Writers in Afrikaans* (1982)

A. J. COETZEE

In English

English South African culture is a composite culture; based originally on the British model and mediated to the indigenous population through mission education, it now is the mother tongue and literary medium of a heterogenous population, its vocabulary sufficiently different from that of British English to have occasioned a *Dictionary of South African English* (1978). Its literature is at present in a state of flux: works are being rediscovered, writers reassessed; critics are beginning to attend properly to problems of canon and periodization, and to discuss the relation of South African literature in English to literature in Afrikaans and the vernaculars and thus to South African literature as a whole. Moreover, the increasing viability of local publishing during the last decade has given many writers a sense of a real audience at home; South African literature is no longer only a literature for export. Yet the social divisions created by apartheid still inform the literature and its criticism: the censors' recent decision to condone literature of "merit" addressed to a "literary" audience simply means that much writing by black writers is banned, while most writing by whites is accessible.

The white literary tradition is generally liberal, primarily rooted in realism in fiction and drama and in romanticism and symbolism in poetry. Olive Schreiner (q.v.), whose work spans the turn of the century, departed from the 19th-c. colonial romance because of her interest in milieu and psychology as determinants of character and because of her concern with the inequalities of race, class, and gender. Sarah Gertrude Millin (q.v.) represents a fuller move into realism, but her obsession with "miscegenation" vitiates her social analysis. The fiction of Pauline Smith (q.v.) explores various kinds of oppression that marked the lives of 19th-c. rural Afrikaners. Her indebtedness to the Afrikaner storytelling tradition and her use of Afrikaans speech patterns foreshadow the short stories of Herman Charles Bosman (1905–1951), whose mingling of ironic and romantic modes provides a complex comment on racial attitudes. His novels, poems, autobiographical prose, and essays also attest to his creative energy and skill, although his humorous manner sometimes dissolves into spurious pastoralism.

Whereas Smith used biblical language to characterize the Afrikaners' self-image as "the chosen people," Alan Paton (q.v.) uses similar language to present his own Christian world view. His *Cry, the Beloved Country* (1948), subtitled "A Story of Comfort in Desolation," marks the apex of liberal humanism in South African literature.

Dan Jacobson (b. 1929), also concerned with the social disintegration imposed by whites on Africa, stresses their moral decay; his stance toward liberalism is critical, whereas Paton's liberalism is confident. The bitterness and disgust in his early fiction, of which *The Trap* (1955) and *A Dance in the Sun* (1956) are the best-known examples, finally give way to disengagement: in his more recent novels he turns away from the South Africa he in fact left as a young man, and only in *The Confessions of Josef Baisz* (1977), a satire that makes subtle links between Russian and South African totalitarianism, is there any return to his South African experience. Nadine Gordimer (q.v.) in her fiction started from a position of liberalism and then moved beyond it into an exposure of the malaise and, indeed, the irrelevance of liberal and colonial values in Southern Africa. The theme of exploitation has been most brilliantly explored by J. M. Coetzee (b. 1940), whose novels *Dusklands* (1974), *In the Heart of the Country* (1977), and *Waiting for the Barbarians* (1980) represent the first break with realism in South African English fiction, a break anticipated in the hesitant experimentalism of *Turbott Wolfe* by William Plomer (q.v.) in 1925.

In drama and poetry by whites, as in fiction, the major concerns have been dissociation from Europe and from white bourgeois values and a hankering for rootedness to counteract displacement, insecurity, and guilt. The most outstanding poets of the first part of the century were Roy Campbell (q.v.) and William Plomer; the major representatives of the next generations are Guy Butler (b. 1918), Sydney Clouts (1926–1982), and Douglas Livingstone (b. 1932).

While earlier poets such as Thomas Pringle (1789–1834) and, later, Francis Carey Slater (1876–1958) tried to present Africa within romantic conventions, Campbell and Plomer employed the language of symbolism. Both had a gift for satire; they debunked, for instance, romantic notions of the veld and ridiculed local political and social institutions. Campbell's style is flamboyant, energetic, heroic; Plomer's is more restrained. In his verse, as in his plays, Butler strives to legitimize and give significance to the English presence in South Africa. Clouts is more reflective and metaphysical, and is especially impressive for his visionary concentration on particularity. Livingstone is probably the most powerful of the present generation: his six volumes to date trace the development of a major poet.

Although the early satirical drama of Stephen Black (1880–1931) is noteworthy, Athol Fugard (q.v.) is the only internationally renowned white South African dramatist. His particular contribution lies in his focus on the victims of apartheid and in his creation of a dramatic mode and language that have as much to do with indigenous expression and polylingualism as with Western theater and standard English.

Black writers (with whom those officially classified as "Coloured" and "Asian" usually identify) have developed an impressive literary tradition, characterized, of course, by different class perspective and subject matter and also by the use of autobiographical modes. *Mhudi* (written c. 1917, pub. 1930), by Sol T. Plaatje (1875–1932), is the first novel written in English by a black South African, and thus is the first inside view in English of a traditional society in transition. By the time *Mhudi* was published there was a growing body of writing in African languages as well as the long-established tradition of oral literature. Plaatje's career as a creative writer-cum-journalist—he is acclaimed particularly for his attack on land and labor legislation in *Native Life in South Africa* (1916)—is typical of black South African writers. H. I. E. Dhlomo (1903–1956) had a similar career: he published only two books in his lifetime but wrote several plays, numerous poems, and some short stories, employing a range of voices from the lyrical and nostalgic to the overtly political. Much of his work violated the norms of "mission literature" demanded by white publishers.

Of the various writer-journalists to combine the genres of novel and autobiography, two are particularly outstanding: Peter Abrahams and Ezekiel Mphahlele (qq.v.). Both Abrahams's *Tell Freedom* (1954) and Mphahlele's *Down Second Avenue* (1959) chart the pains of deprived and frustrated boyhood only partially resolved by exile; Mphahlele's *The Wanderers* (1971) contrasts newfound freedom with loneliness, anonymity, and rootlessness. These writers, along with other writer-journalists who worked or wrote for *Drum* magazine and *The Classic,* such as Can Themba (1924–1968), Lewis Nkosi (b. 1936), Nat Nakasa (1937–1965), Bloke Modisane (b. 1923), and Richard Rive (b. 1931), brought into South African literature a vibrant township language, its tones hilarious and brash, sharply satiric of the social inequalities they were subjected to, with just occasional glimpses of despair under the swaggering manner. They looked to American writers for literary models: to naturalism and "hard-boiled" detective fiction, as well as to black American literary expression, already echoed by Abrahams in his poetry of the 1930s. Most of these writers went into exile during the 1950s and 1960s in response to apartheid. Almost all of them were sooner or later banned under the Suppression of Communism Act. A few, notably the poets Dennis Brutus (q.v.) and Arthur Nortje (1942–1970), established themselves as voices of exile; others, like Alex La Guma (q.v.), seem to have lost abroad the sense of specific time and place so necessary to social realism.

The next wave of protest writing by black writers in the country started in the late 1960s and began initially in poetry (there has been a very recent swing to fiction). The new black poetry, whose audience was at first predominantly white liberals, concentrated primarily on township life, using stark imagery, blunt language, and free forms; its tones were those of nostalgia and betrayal, plaintive rather than aggressive. By the mid-1970s the influence of the Black Consciousness movement had brought a new militancy; poets abandoned the romantic-symbolist conventions of the earlier writers and employed the traditional techniques of oral poetry—repetition, parallelism, naming, ideophones (sounds that communicate meaning)—in combination with their aggressively nonliterary street language. The poetry of Oswald Mbuyiseni Mtshali (b. 1940), from *Sounds of a Cowhide Drum* (1971) to *Fireflames* (1980), maps this development. Other major poets are Mongane Wally Serote (b. 1944), Sydney Sipho Sepamla (b. 1932), and Mafika Pascal Gwala (b. 1946).

A comparable shift has occurred in drama. Aside from recent plays that reinforce myths about the tribal, rural nature of blacks or the difficulties of adapting traditional values to urban living, township theater is aggressively urban and political, frequently unscripted and without props, often group-authored. Of those that have been published, Zakes Mda's (b. 1948) are particularly powerful.

A divided literature is simply one manifestation of a deeply divided society; it is unlikely that South African literature will bridge its rifts before South African society does. Whether because of or despite these rifts, there is a great deal of energy in South African literature and criticism in English, as evidenced by such periodicals as *Staffrider* (Johannesburg) and *English in Africa* (Grahamstown), by the frequency of literary conferences and the numerous writers' workshops throughout the country, and by the volume of new writing and criticism published by the three major South African publishers.

BIBLIOGRAPHY: Miller, G., and Sergeant, H., *A Critical Survey of South African Poetry in English* (1957); Mphahlele, E., *The African Image* (1962; rev. ed., 1974); Gordimer, N., "Literature and Politics in South Africa," *SoRA,* 7 (1974), 205–27; Wilhelm, P., and Polley, J., eds., *Poetry South Africa: Papers from Poetry '74* (1976); Visser, N., "South Africa: The Renaissance That Failed," *JCL,* 11 (1976), 42–57; Heywood, C., ed., *Aspects of South African Literature* (1976); Gorman, G., *The South African Novel in English since 1950: An Information and Resource Guide* (1978); Parker, K., ed., *The South African Novel in English: Essays in Criticism and Society* (1978); Gray, S., *Southern African Literature: An Introduction* (1979); Sole, K., "Class, Continuity and Change in Black South African Literature 1948–1960," in Bozzoli, B., ed., *Labour, Townships and Protest: Studies in the Social History of the Witwatersrand* (1979), pp. 143–82; Christie, S., et al., *Perspectives on South African Fiction* (1980); Chapman, M., ed., *Soweto Poetry* (1982)

DOROTHY DRIVER

In Pedi

Although the Pedi (Northern Sotho) written alphabet goes back to 1861, the first literary works were not published until the 20th c. One of the early publications was Mampšhe Phala's (dates n.a.) *Kxomo 'a tshwa* (1935; the cow spits), a collection of traditional praise poems. This work served as an example for many later poets, who, even though they composed original poems, kept close to the practices of oral poetry.

While the praise poem is still held in high esteem, some changes have taken place. Poetry has become subjective and emotional, and the works of Phorohlo Mamogobo (b. 1926), Thipakgolo Maditsi (b. 1937), and Matome Fela (b. 1918) contain some of the most moving and dramatic passages in Pedi literature. Changes in tone have paralleled a new outlook on life: themes include man's destiny, social evils, and nationalistic or political topics. Some experiments with rhyme were undertaken but then abandoned. A more recent trend has been verse whose meter is rather loosely knit.

In the 1960s and early 1970s Pedi literature was dominated by Kgadime Matsepe (1932–1974), a master of irony who satirized man's complacency. His oeuvre includes six collections of poetry and nine novels. The complex structure of his novels, which are set against a background of traditional life, is a culmination of a development that can be traced to the early 1950s, with the short stories of Mogagabise Ramaila (1897–1962), which expose the evils of contemporary urban life. Cedric Phatudi (b. 1912), using traditional life as background, contemplates the inexorability of fate in his novels. Maggie Rammala (b. 1924) uses contemporary settings; her principal work is an account of a father's tragic blindness to his favorite son's evil ways. The reflective essays of Lesiba Mahapa (b. 1933) describe several visits to his Lebowa homeland.

By comparison with poetry and fiction, Pedi drama is still underdeveloped. The only exception is Elias Matlala's (b. 1913) tragedy in verse, *Tšhukudu* (1941; rhinoceros); based on the Samson and Delilah story, it is a monumental drama.

BIBLIOGRAPHY: Mokgokong, P. C., "A Brief Survey of Modern Literature in the South African Bantu Languages—Northern Sotho," *Limi*, No. 6 (1968), 60–67; Gérard, A. S., *African Language Literatures* (1981), pp. 220–23

P. S. GROENEWALD

In South Sotho

Linguistically, stylistically, and even thematically, South African writing in South Sotho parallels literature published in that language in Lesotho. It is hard to separate South Sotho writers living in South Africa from those in Lesotho except by checking birthplace and residence. Moreover, major Lesotho writers like Attwell Sidwell Mopeli-Paulus (1913–1960) and Benjamin Leshoai (b. 1920) have lived in South Africa for extended periods.

The earliest published South Sotho writer in South Africa was Zakea Dolphin Mangoaela (1883–1963). He began by producing elementary-school readers and religious tracts, but he also published one work of fiction, a collection of folk tales *Har'a libatana le linyamat'sane* (1912; among the wild animals large and small). In later life he turned primarily to religious subjects and traditional literature, including the first publication of Sotho oral praise poetry in written form, *Lithoko tsa marena a Basotho* (1921; praises of the Sotho chief).

Like Mangoaela, most South Sotho writers took up teaching as the most available career. They first published translations and school texts. When they turned to creative writing, they showed themselves as amateurs by displaying no special affinity for a particular genre. Typical of such writers are James Jantjies Moiloa (b. 1916), who was a lecturer in Bantu languages before publishing volumes of poetry and short stories, a play, and a novel. A. C. J. Ramathe (1907–1958) was a supervisor of Bantu schools before publishing a novel, *Tsepo* (1957; hope). Jacob Russell Saoli (b. 1914), while a school principal, published a collection of songs, *Meloli ea tumelo* (1951; songs of faith).

The most able of South African writers in South Sotho was Sophonia Machabe Mofokeng (1923–1957), a linguist who earned his doctorate with a dissertation on Sotho literature. His creative work includes *Senkatana* (1952; Senkatana), a play dealing with the legend of a many-headed monster Kgodumodumo, who is killed by the heroic young Senkatana; the collection *Leetong* (1954; on the road), which was the first real attempt in South Sotho to produce modern short stories; and a collection of essays, *Pelong ya ka* (1961; in my heart).

Samson Mbizo Guma (b. c. 1923) turned to history for his two novels: *Morena Mohlomi, mor'a Monyane* (1960; Chief Mohlomi, son of Monyane) about the conflict between traditional and modern custom regarding the killing of twins; and *Tshehlana tseo tsa Basia* (1962; the light-colored Basia girls), about a crisis in a tribe following a chief's death. Samson Rasebilu Machaka (b. 1932), after years of teaching, published *Meholdi ya polelo* (1962; the flavor of the language) and several more collections of verse.

In a more modern vein, Dyke Sentso (b. 1924) wrote several short stories and a volume of verse, *Matlakala* (1948; bits of grass), and contributed to the pioneering anthology *African Voices* (1959), edited by Peggy Rutherford. J. G. Mocoancoeng's (c. 1914–?) play *Tseleng ea bophelo* (1947; the path of life), set in an African township in the Orange Free State, deals with the contemporary problem of a husband who is led astray by city temptations and becomes a drunkard.

The most prolific recent writer is Ephraim Alfred Lesoro (b. 1929), with several radio plays, numerous books of poetry and, most notably, two novels, *Leshala le tswala molara* (c. 1960; charcoals make ashes) and *Pere ntsho Blackmore* (1968; Blackmore, the black horse), both edifying tales suitable for the moral education of the young.

The emphasis on education in the mother tongue, advocated, ironically, with equal intensity and diametrically opposed motivation in both South Africa and Lesotho, seems likely to maintain both market and audience for a continuing modern literature in the South Sotho language.

BIBLIOGRAPHY: Beuchat, P.-D., *Do the Bantus Have a Literature?* (1963); Guma, S. M., *The Form, Content and Technique of Traditional Literature in Southern Sotho* (1967); Gérard, A. S., "Southern Sotho Literature Today," *African Digest,* No. 15 (1968), 25–29; Lenake, J. M., "A Brief Survey of Modern Literature in the South African Bantu Languages: Southern Sotho," *Limi,* No. 6 (1968), 75–81; Moloi, A. J., "The Germination of Southern Sotho Poetry," *Limi,* No. 8 (1969), 28–59; Gérard, A. S., *Four African Literatures* (1971), pp. 101–81; Gérard, A. S., *African Language Literatures* (1981), pp. 190–223

JOHN POVEY

In Tsonga

Swiss missionaries in South Africa started working among the Tsonga people in 1875 and soon thereafter translated the Bible into Tsonga, thereby creating a written language.

Daniel Cornel Marivate (b. 1897) wrote the first Tsonga novel, *Sa-

savona (1938; Sasavona), whose central theme is the condemnation of irresponsibility and recklessness, which Marivate seems to attribute to lack of education and refusal to adopt the Christian faith. Although Marivate dealt with social problems, the religious orientation prevailed in Tsonga fiction through the 1950s. For example, Samuel Jonas Baloyi's (1918–1980) novelette *Murhandziwani* (1949; Murhandziwani) depicts the evil effects of city life on young rural converts. H. W. E. Ntsanwisi's (b. 1922?) *Masungi* (1954; Masungi) was an attempt to depart from the moralistic and religious tendency: he described the clash between traditional Tsonga culture and Western innovations.

In the early 1960s socioeconomic themes emerged. Love, as well as the clash of old and new, also began to receive more attention. B. K. M. Mtombeni's (1926–1976) novel *Mibya ya nyekanyeka* (1967; the straps of the baby sling are loose) shows that each individual must lead his own life, but it also demonstrates that nobody, including pastors, is immune to temptation. His novel *Ndzi tshikeni* (1973; leave me alone) depicts a man who dies as a result of avenging the murders of his wife and son.

Another noteworthy writer of fiction is F. A. Thuketana (b. 1933), whose novel *Xisomisana* (1968; Xisomisana) asserts that Christianity brings salvation. His other novel, *N'waningininigi ma ka tindleve* (1978; N'waningininigi does not listen), shows that disregarding parental advice leads to disaster.

Tsonga drama emerged only in 1960, but has developed considerably during the last decade. *Xaka* (1960; Chaka), by Samuel Jonas Baloyi, the first published Tsonga play, is a historical drama portraying the great Zulu king. Most Tsonga plays have social themes. For example, *Ririmi i madlayisani* (1964; the tongue gets you killed) by H. A. Mangwane (b. 1932) illustrates marital difficulties when one partner, especially the woman, is better educated than the other. *Gija wanuna wa matimbu* (1965; Gija, the strong man), by H. S. V. Muzwayine (b. 1923) and Bill T. Mageza (b. 1926), depicts family problems caused by migratory labor. B. K. M. Mtombeni's *Malangavi ya mbilu* (1966; flames of the heart) artfully portrays the futility of deceit in love affairs. P. M. Makgoana's (b. 1948) *Vugima-musi* (1975; the horizon) criticizes parents who interfere in their child's choice of a marriage partner.

Eric Mashangu Nkondo's (b. 1930) play *Muhlupheki Ngwanazi* (1974; Muhlupheki Ngwanazi) has a political subject: the attempts of Tsongas to free themselves from white oppression. E. G. W. Mbhombi's (b 1940) *Madumelani* (1976; Madumelani) uses a plot reminiscent of *Macbeth*, adapted to a Tsonga rural community.

E. P. Ndhambi's (b. 1913) pioneering collection of poetry *Swiphato* (1949; praises) uses the traditional praise-poem style. P. E. Ntsanwisi (b. 1923), in *Vuluva bya switlhokovetselo* (1957; flowers of praises), followed Ndhambi's style. The poetry of this period was descriptive and objective.

Since 1965 poets have tended to write subjectively about socioeconomic problems in a changing world; B. J. Masebenza's (b. 1933) *Chochela-mandleni* (1965; fuchsia bush) was a trailblazing collection in this mode.The approach was developed by the Nkondo brothers, whose poetry reveals depth of insight and concentration on spiritual content. Eric Mashangu Nkondo's poetry treats a variety of themes, including the black man's frustrations and aspirations in South Africa. Even more profound is Winston Zinjiva Nkondo (b. 1941?), as revealed in his *Mbita ya vulombe* (1969; pot of honey). Another poet of great insight is M. M. Marhanele (b. 1950?).

BIBLIOGRAPHY: Marivate, C. T. D., "Publications to End of 1965 (Tsonga)," *Limi*, No. 2 (1966), 36–39; Marivate, C. T. D., "Publications to End of 1966 (Tsonga)," *Limi*, No. 4 (1967), 18–19; Marivate, C. T. D., "A Brief Survey of Modern Literature in South African Bantu Languages (Tsonga)," *Limi*, No. 6 (1968), 36–44; Marivate, C. T. D., "Tsonga Publications, 1970–1972," *Limi*, 3, 2 (1975), 71–73; Marivate, C. T. D., "Book Reviews (Tsonga)," *Limi*, 7, 1–2 (1979), 80–83; Marivate, C. T. D., "Tsonga Book Reviews," *Limi*, 8, 1–2 (1980), 61–72; Gérard, A. S., *African Language Literatures* (1981), pp. 203–4, 218–20

C. T. D. MARIVATE

In Tswana

Until toward the end of the first quarter of the 20th c., publication in Tswana consisted mainly of translations of the Bible and other religious material by white missionaries endeavoring to convert the Tswana to Christianity.

A pioneer in creative writing was Sol T. Plaatje (1875–1932), although his novel *Mhudi* (1930) was published in English, presumably because he wanted to reach a wider readership. He did, however, translate some of Shakespeare's plays into Tswana, and his translations show considerable command of his native language.

The man considered the father of Tswana literature is D. P. Moloto

(b. 1910). In his first novel, *Mokwena* (1940; Mokwena), he describes the customs of the Bakwena, a Tswana subgroup, and depicts in a matter-of-fact style the upbringing of a chief's son. This novel shows the influence of traditional Tswana storytelling. In his second novel, *Motimedi* (1953; the lost person), he focuses on the plight of the Tswana and other African groups living in urban areas; they have discarded their old ways of life and have thus lost some of their moral fiber.

Didactic Christian themes mark the work of several Tswana writers. Foremost among them is S. A. Moroke (b. 1912), an ordained Methodist minister whose main subject in his novels, short stories, plays, and poems is sin and redemption. His novel *Sephaphati* (1959; Sephaphati) is based on the biblical story of the prodigal son. In his play *Lobisa Radipitse* (1962; Lobisa Radipitse) the chief character dies because of excessive drinking. Moroke moralizes to such an extent that his works are more like sermons than literature.

The most influential writer, in both his use of the Tswana language and his themes, has been D. P. Semakaleng Monyaise (b. 1921). A truly creative writer with a distinctive and interesting conversational style, he is primarily concerned with man's helplessness against the forces of evil, as in the novels *Marara* (1961; confusion) and *Go ša baori* (1970; those who sit by the fire get burned).

Monyaise sees life as inherently cruel, while J. M. Ntsime (b. 1930) is deeply concerned with man's relationship with God. He juxtaposes Christianity, which he sees as bringing saving grace, with witchcraft, which in his view leads to destruction. These opposing forces come into conflict in his plays *Kobo e ntsho* (1968; the black robe) and *Pelo e ntsho* (1972; the black heart), with Christianity offering happiness and redemption.

Two important recent writers have focused on the problems of the young. Masego T. Mmileng (b. 1951), in his novels *Mangomo* (1975; despair) and *Lehudu* (1980; hollow place used for stamping corn), is concerned with the consequences of a harmful upbringing. R. M. Malope (b. 1944) shows how ignorance hampers young people. His style is so learned that his fiction, such as the novel *Matlhoko, matlhoko* (1980; sorrows, sorrows) and the short-story collection *Mmualebe* (1982; Mmualebe), is rather artificial.

Although Tswana literature has advanced steadily, most writers have focused on social and religious issues, disregarding politics and economics. There is good reason to hope, however, as evidenced by the work of Monyaise, that Tswana creative writing will develop further.

BIBLIOGRAPHY: Malepe, A. T., "A Brief Survey of Modern Literature in Tswana," *Limi*, No. 6 (1968), 68–75; Gérard, A. S., *African Language Literatures* (1981), pp. 194–95, 202–3, 217–18

A. T. MALEPE

See also Botswana Literature

In Venda

Since earliest times the Venda people, who live in northeastern Transvaal, have had an oral literature. Only with the coming of Lutheran missionaries, however, did written Venda literature come into being. The first printed work was a school reader published in 1899. In 1913 the missionary Theodor Schwellnus (?–1923) collected Venda folk-tales and fables in *Ndede ya luambo lwa Tshivenda* (a guide to the Venda language). A complete Venda Bible, translated by Paul Erdmann Schwellnus (?-1946) appeared in 1937; it set the standard for written Venda. P. E. Schwellnus may be called the father of Venda literature, since he also tried various imaginative genres, with a fair amount of success.

A modern Venda literature began in the mid-1950s with the publication of several works of fiction. The first Venda "novel" was *Elelwani* (1954; remember), really a novella, by Titus N. Maumela (b. 1924), about tribal marriage customs. Maumela published several more short novels, dealing primarily with the clash between tradition and new ideas. E. S. Madima (b. 1922) depicted the evils of city life in his first short novel *A si ene* (1955; it is not he). Later, in *Maduvha ha fani* (1971; the days are not the same), he wrote about success in the city. M. E. R. Mathivha (b. 1921), in the long short story *Tsha ri vhone* (1956; let us see), focused on the conflict of generations. And in *Nungo nzi mulomoni* (1958; strength is in the mouth), by Paul Selaelo Mosehle Masekela (b. 1925), the hero is a young teacher born in the city who goes to live among his own people.

Maumela was also the founder of Venda drama. His *Tshililo* (1957; Tshililo), like his first novel, deals with tribal marriage customs. Other playwrights are M. E. R. Mathivha, whose *Mabalanganye* (1963; Mabalanganye) is about a prince who tries to gain power by foul methods, and Elias S. Netshilema (b. 1928), author of *Vha Musanda VhoDzegere* (c. 1957; Lord Dzegere).

The pioneer in modern Venda poetry was P. H. Nenzhelele (b. 1908), who published his first collection, *Zwirendo na zwimbo* (praises and songs), in 1958. The natural beauty of Vendaland inspired the poems of

R. R. Matshili (b. 1933) in *Zwiala zwa Venda* (1967; medals of Vendaland). The publication of the collection *Tsiko-tshiphiri* (1971; secret creation) by W. M. R. Sigwavhulimu (b. 1937) heralded a new type of Venda poetry, which deals with nontraditional themes. Other poets of note are D. M. Ngwana (b. 1933), Michael N. Neumukovhani (b. 1945), and Paul Tshindane Mashuwa (b. 1945). The future of Venda poetry seems to be a blending of traditional themes and forms and modern techniques and subjects, such as urban life and war.

BIBLIOGRAPHY: Dau, R. S., "A Brief Survey of Modern Literature in the South African Bantu Languages: Venda," *Limi,* No. 6 (1968), 44–60; Mathivha, M. E. R., *History of Venda Literature* (1970); Mathivha, M. E. R., *An Outline History of the Development of Venda as a Written Language* (1973); Gérard, A. S., *African Language Literatures* (1981), pp. 223–25

M. E. R. MATHIVHA

In Xhosa

Spoken by some five and a half million people in the Republic of South Africa and the "homelands" of Transkei and Ciskei, Xhosa is one of the most important Bantu languages of southern Africa. It was also the first to be affected by the literary impact of the West. The earliest work on record is an early-19th-c. Christian hymn composed orally by a preliterate convert named Ntsikana (c. 1783–c. 1820). Until the conquest of Xhosaland was completed in 1877, hymn writing and Bible translation were the main literary activities. During the last quarter of the 19th c., scattered poems in the vernacular journals issued by missionaries testified to increasingly articulate doubts about the benefits to be derived from the white man's presence.

The first major Xhosa author was Samuel Edward Krune Mqhayi (1875–1945), a highly esteemed oral poet as well as a prolific writer. After *Ityala lamawele* (1914; *The Case of the Twins,* 1966), a tale in defense of traditional law, his most ambitious published work was a utopian novel, *U-Don Jadu* (1929; Don Jadu), which projects his vision of a multiracial Africa.

Xhosa literature came into its own between the two world wars. Mqhayi's less gifted followers produced moralizing popular novelettes such as *U-Nomalizo* (1918; *Nomalizo,* 1928) by Enoch S. Guma (1896–1918), but Guybon B. Sinxo (1902–1962) wrote several realistic novels describing the misery and moral degradation of native slum life in the emergent industrial cities; his *Imfene kaDebeza* (1925; Debeza's baboon) was the first play in Xhosa. But serious drama did not appear until James J. R. Jolobe (1902–1976) published *Amathunzi obomi* (1958; the shadows of life), which focuses on the traumas of urban experience. Jolobe, a Protestant minister, is better known, however, as a lyric poet. His famed *Umyezo* (1936; *Poems of an African,* 1946), a collection of deeply Christian poems, introduced descriptive motifs unknown to the oral tradition of praise poetry; while some of the poems focus on important events in the past of the Xhosa, others contain oblique criticism of white racism.

The best Xhosa novel is *Ingqumbo yaminyanya* (1940; *The Wrath of the Ancestors,* 1980), the only imaginative work of Archibald C. Jordan (1906–1968). A breathtaking story of social and cultural upheaval in a Xhosa chiefdom, it is a perceptive and genuinely tragic treatment of two major themes in modern African literature: the conflict between tradition and the need for modernization; and the rejection of clan authority by the literate young in favor of individual choice in matters of love and marriage.

The Bantu Education Act of 1953 had highly ambiguous consequences for Xhosa as for the other vernacular literatures of South Africa. On the one hand, the enforced development of vernacular education suddenly created a vast potential audience of younger readers and thus an unexpected market for writers. On the other hand, because of the predominance of an immature readership and the hardening of censorship, there was no corresponding improvement in literary quality. The new market made it possible for older writers to reach print: R. M. Tshaka (b. 1904) had his first collection of poetry published in 1953. The only novel of Godfrey Malunga Mzamane (1909–1977) *Izinto zodidi* (1959; things of value) is just a sample of much edifying prose fiction that followed in the wake of Sinxo's prewar stories. This trite vein was also exploited by Witness K. Tamsanqa (b. 1928), one of the most prolific and popular Xhosa writers, who is more notable for his contribution to the growth of drama, especially radio plays. The most promising writer who emerged in the 1970s was Zitobile Sunshine Qangule (1934–1982): the intellectual content of his collection of poetry *Intshuntshe* (1970; a spear) and the sense of personal tragedy in his novel *Izagweba* (1972; fighting sticks) held out a promise of renewal that was unfortunately thwarted by his untimely death.

BIBLIOGRAPHY: Qangule, S. Z., "A Brief Survey of Modern Literature in the South African Bantu Languages: Xhosa," *Limi,* No. 6. (1968), 14–28; Gérard, A. S., *Four African Literatures* (1971), pp. 21–100; Jordan, A. C., *Towards an African Literature: The Emergence of Literary Form in Xhosa* (1973); Mahlasela, B. E. N., *A General Survey of Xhosa Literature from Its Early Beginings in the 1800s to the Present* (1973); special Xhosa section, *South African Outlook,* No. 103 (1973), 93–137; Opland, J., "Imbongi Nezibongo: The Xhosa Tribal Poet and the Contemporary Poetic Tradition," *PMLA,* 90 (1975), 185–208; Gérard, A. S., *African Language Literatures* (1981), pp. 186–201, 211–14

ALBERT S. GÉRARD

In Zulu

Apart from their "homeland," Kwazulu, the Zulu people, about five and a half million in number, make up much of the population of the province of Natal, South Africa. They were not fully brought under colonial rule until the beginning of this century. Literacy, therefore, lagged; and, unlike the Xhosa and Sotho peoples, the Zulus did not start creating a written literature until the early 1920s, when some one-act plays, dramatizing folk-tales, were published in the Natal *Native Teachers' Journal.*

The first Zulu writer of note was John L. Dube (1871–1946). Although he belonged to the same generation as the Sotho novelist Thomas Mofolo (q.v.) and the Xhosa writer S. E. K. Mqhayi (1875–1945), he did not embark on imaginative writing until 1933, when he published the first Zulu novel, *Insila kaTshaka (Jeqe, the Body-Servant of King Shaka,* 1951), a lively story dealing with Shaka, an early-19th-c. Zulu conqueror. Dube's earlier *U-Shembe* (1930; Shembe) was a biography of Shembe (c. 1865–1935), the founder of a dissident African church. A distinguishing feature of Zulu literature is that much of it consists of more or less fictionalized biographies of the nation's leaders.

Whereas Dube was the only author of his own generation, a number of gifted and ambitious younger writers came to the fore in the 1930s. R. R. R. Dhlomo (1901–1971) began his literary career with a novella in English, *An African Tragedy* (1928), which presented a somber picture of native life in city slums but also offered some cogent criticism of such customs as the bride-price. The true founder of Zulu literature in English, however, was his younger brother Herbert I. E. Dhlomo (1905–1956), author of *The Girl Who Killed to Save* (1936), *The Valley of a Thousand Hills* (1951), and many other works as yet unpublished.

Meanwhile, R. R. R. Dhlomo turned to writing in Zulu and over the years wrote a number of biographical accounts of 19th-c. chiefs. With *Indlele yababi* (1948; the path of the wicked ones), a novel of Zulu life in the native townships of Johannesburg, he reverted to his early inspiration. E. H. A. Made (1905–1978) initiated the edifying novel with *Indlafa yaseHarrisdale* (1940; the heir of Harrisdale).

Benedict W. Vilakazi (1906–1947), the best Zulu poet, was also a linguist and a student of traditional Zulu poetry. After some experiments with European verse forms, he returned to African forms in two collections: *Inkondlo kaZulu* (1935; Zulu poems) and *Amal'ezulu* (1945; *Zulu Horizons,* 1962). Of his two novels, the better is the posthumously published *Nje nempela* (1955; just how!), which deals with the 1906 Zulu uprising.

The 1950s saw the emergence of C. L. S. Nyembezi (b. 1919), who is usually regarded as the best Zulu novelist. His *Mntanami! Mntanami!* (1950; my child! my child!) is about the snares of city life; the humorous *Inkinsela yaseMgungundlovu* (1961; the tycoon from Pietermaritzburg) satirizes the black bourgeoisie.

In contemporary Zulu writing anecdotes about Zulu kings are popular, and nostalgia for past freedom and traditions is an abundant source of inspiration. Such themes appear in many tales by Kenneth Bhengu (b. 1916), Joice J. Gwayi (b. 1928), and Moses Ngcobo (b. 1928). But following in the wake of Nyembezi's work, many recent novels focus on city life and the clash of cultures; this theme often takes the form of a conflict between generations on matters of love relations and marriage, as in works by Jordan K. Ngubane (b. 1917), E. E. N. T. Mkhize (b. 1931), Z. Kuzwayo (b. 1935), and I. S. Kubheka (b. 1933).

Zulu drama, which was initiated in 1937 by Nimrod Ndebele (b. 1913), was slow to develop. Seldom designed for actual stage production, the plays often focus on episodes in some chieftain's life or anecdotes about the culture clash. The more significant dramatists are Elliot Zondi (b. 1930) and especially D. B. Z. Ntuli (b. 1940), whose radio plays have appeared in book form.

Although about forty anthologies of poetry have been issued since the death of Vilakazi, Zulu poetry lacks distinction. It is hampered by censorship, by the fact that its main outlet is the school audience, and by an unfortunate zeal for imitating European prosody. Among the few worthwhile recent poets are John C. Dlamini (b. 1916), O. E. H. Nxumalo (b. 1938), C. T. Msimang (b. 1938), and D. B. Z. Ntuli.

Several Zulu writers living in exile have turned to English. The most notable are Lewis Nkosi (b. 1936), a critic and playwright; Jordan K. Ngubane, who wrote *Ushaba: The Hurtle to Blood River* (1974), a novel that envisions how South African blacks will begin the process of overcoming their white oppressors; and Mazisi Kunene (b. 1936), author of two impressive Zulu epics, which he translated into English himself: *Emperor Shaka the Great* (1979) and *Anthem of the Decades* (1981).

BIBLIOGRAPHY: Nyembezi, C. L. S., *A Review of Zulu Literature* (1961); Ntuli, D. B. Z., "A Brief Survey of Modern Literature in the South African Bantu Languages: Zulu," *Limi,* No. 6 (1968), 28–36; Gérard, A. S., *Four African Literatures* (1971), pp. 181–270; Gérard, A. S., *African Language Literatures* (1981), pp. 192–201, 214–17

ALBERT S. GÉRARD

ABRAHAMS, Peter

South African novelist (writing in English), b. 19 March 1919, Johannesburg

A. began his education at the age of eleven, attending Diocesan Training College in Grace Dieu and St. Peter's Secondary School in Rosettenville before leaving South Africa in 1939, when he was only nineteen years old. Today he lives in Jamaica, where he works as a broadcaster.

Nonetheless, the racial and political problems of his troubled native land have continued to dominate his imagination. All but one of his seven novels are set entirely or in part in South Africa, and the exception, *This Island Now* (1966), deals with race and politics in a Caribbean island which, like South Africa, has a poor, oppressed black majority and an affluent white minority. A. has also written a volume of short stories, *Dark Testament* (1942), and two autobiographical books, *Return to Goli* (1953) and *Tell Freedom* (1954), both of which focus on his experiences as a mulatto in South Africa.

Influenced by Marxist ideas, A.'s early novels tend to be concerned more with race and economics than with politics. *Song of the City* (1945) and *Mine Boy* (1946) tell of the effects of urbanization and industrialization on the lives of young black workers who move from the country to the city. *Song of the City* takes place at the time of World War II, *Mine Boy* against the backdrop of booming gold mines in Johannesburg. In both novels nonwhites are mistreated and oppressed by whites.

In *The Path of Thunder* (1948) A. turned more fully to the theme of interracial love, exploring its impact on a young Coloured schoolteacher and an Afrikaner girl whose passionate affair ultimately ends in tragedy when the Afrikaner community discovers they are lovers.

Two years later A. moved in yet another direction, this time reconstructing the era of the Afrikaner migration, or "Great Trek," in *Wild Conquest* (1950), a historical novel in which he made an effort to be fair to all the major ethnic groups in South Africa—Bantu, Boer, and Briton.

After these early works A.'s fiction became more overtly political. *A Wreath for Udomo* (1956), published just before Ghana attained its independence, was an attempt to predict what might happen when independent Black African nations were confronted with the choice between the financial advantages of collaborating with the white regimes in southern Africa and the moral imperative of opposing them by actively supporting black liberation movements. *A Night of Their Own* (1965) carried the revolutionary theme further by detailing the adventures of an African underground agent involved in smuggling funds to an Indian resistance organization in South Africa. And *This Island Now* told of racial tensions and internal power struggles in a small, black-ruled Caribbean island-state.

In each successive novel A. has moved further away from a depiction of South African social realities to the construction of hypothetical situations which afforded greater creative liberties. Even *A Night of Their Own*, although set in South Africa, had elements of fantasy and wishful thinking in it. A.'s increased dependence on his imagination in these later novels may reflect how far out of touch he is with contemporary conditions in his native land.

A. has always written in a simple, direct prose style that wavers between superior reporting and maudlin romanticizing. He is at his best when transcribing newsworthy events having a basis in fact; his autobiographical and travel writings, for instance, are superb. But he has a regrettable tendency to sentimentalize personal relationships between men and women, especially if they are of different races, as they so often are in his novels. His accounts of miscegenation are nearly always marred by unconvincing melodrama.

FURTHER WORK: *Jamaica: An Island Mosaic* (1957)

BIBLIOGRAPHY: Senghor, L. S., "P. A.; ou, le classique de la négritude" (1963), in *Liberté I: Négritude et humanisme* (1964), pp. 425–30; Gérard, A., "P. A.," *Black Orpheus*, 2, 5–6 (1971), 15–19; Heywood,

C., "The Novels of P. A.," in Heywood, C., ed., *Perspectives on African Literature* (1971), pp. 157–72; Wade M., *P. A.* (1972); Ogungbesan, K., *The Writings of P. A.* (1979)

BERNTH LINDFORS

BRUTUS, Dennis

South African poet (writing in English), b. 28 Nov. 1924, Salisbury, Zimbabwe (then Southern Rhodesia)

B. was brought up in Port Elizabeth, South Africa, as a "coloured." He took his B.A. at the segregated Fort Hare University College and taught high school. In 1962 he entered Witwatersrand University to study law. Inevitably in South Africa, racial politics intruded and he became active against the regime. For his challenges to government racial policy he was first banned and then arrested and sentenced to serve on the notorious Robben Island prison. Concluding his sentence, he accepted enforced exile and has since lived in England and America, always involved with the anti-apartheid movement and particularly with SANROC (South African Non-Racial Olympic Committee). In 1971 he settled permanently in the U.S. and is now a professor of English at Northwestern University, but he continues to travel widely for political purposes. He is a teacher and a poet, yet his life remains dedicated to challenging the apartheid system.

Given his experiences, it is obvious that B.'s poetry is likely to derive from his own bitter encounter with racial prejudice. Yet the reader is impressed to discern how the activist never destroys the poet. His first collection, *Sirens, Knuckles and Boots* (1963), indicates much of the social context by its very title, yet rarely is B.'s work violent or hectoring, no matter the anger implicit in his lines. In all his writing there remains a palpable tenderness and humanity. His earlier poems have a rich diction employing an almost metaphysical complexity that he was later very consciously to simplify. Throughout this first collection there is the constant theme of love, both for his wife and, more unexpectedly, for his suffering country, for which he still holds the strongest affection. He asserts a tolerant love as a challenge to the insensate racial hatred that dominates South Africa.

Similarly, his poems from prison, designed as a series of epistles to his wife, *Letters to Martha* (1968), describe appalling and horrific abuse suffered at the hands of both guards and other inmates, but they are expressed with an unqualified honesty and acute compassion that never romanticizes or justifies the suffering, but rather regards it with a pained tenderness.

The titles of his later collections, written outside of South Africa, indicate the many countries in which they were written: *Poems from Algiers* (1970), *Thoughts from Abroad* (1970), *China Poems* (1975). His diction has become increasingly spartan and severe. In contrast with the occasional lushness of his earliest poems, his later ones are often almost haiku-brief in their precision and suggestiveness.

There is an obvious tension between the man's commitment to politics and the poet's commitment to his art. Yet B.'s protest verse provides continuing evidence of a poetic skill that is committed to social action and yet does not become aesthetically subservient to that obligation.

FURTHER WORK: *A Simple Lust* (1973)

BIBLIOGRAPHY: Povey, J., "Simply to Stand," in Okpaku, J., ed., *New African Literatures and the Arts* (1970), pp. 105–13; Egudu, R. N., "Pictures in Pain," in Heywood, C., ed., *Aspects of South African Literature* (1976), pp. 131–45; Lindfors, B., "Dialectical Development in the Poetry of D. B.," in Niven, A., ed., *The Commonwealth Writer Overseas: Themes of Exile and Expatriation* (1976), pp. 219–29

JOHN POVEY

CAMPBELL, Roy

South African poet and translator (writing in English), b. 2 Oct. 1901, Durban; d. 23 April 1957, near Setubal, Portugal

Memories of his happy childhood in an influential Durban family deeply affected C. throughout his life. Although he left his subtropical native city in 1919, to return only for short periods, C.'s love of his unfettered outdoor youth shaped many of his later attitudes. His adult life was spent in England, France, Spain, and Portugal. A perpetual outsider, he left English literary circles in disgust in 1928 to live an individualistic, sun-loving life along the Mediterranean coast and in Toledo, Spain, until the civil war forced him to return to the United Kingdom in 1936. A Catholic convert and a fervent right-winger, his support for Franco during the Spanish Civil War further alienated him from British literary coteries. During World War II, however, he served as a volunteer in the ranks of the British army. Following a postwar career in the B.B.C., he spent his last years in Portugal, his persona firmly established as a swashbuckling, down-to-earth man's man.

C.'s best poetry has a lyrical intensity unique among English-language poets of the 20th c. Neither his sensibility nor his models were British. His early enthusiasm for Elizabethan and Jacobean verse does inform his poetry, but the major influences on his work are French: Baudelaire, Rimbaud, and Valéry all served as models for his early and middle poems. A Spanish influence is more pronounced in his later work. The combination of these elements gives his best poems a distinctive, ringing certainty of tone, a vividness of imagery, and an insistent energy.

C. was acclaimed as a major new poetic talent when his first work was published. *The Flaming Terrapin* (1924) is a long poem, dealing with the mythical regeneration of man. In it C. encapsulated his rugged, southern rejection of postwar European demoralization. Strongly reminiscent of Rimbaud's *Bateau ivre,* the poem is a dazzling description of the towing of Noah's ark by the vital and exotic terrapin, which symbolizes masculine strength.

His next volume, *Adamastor* (1930), contains many of his best-known and justly celebrated short poems. They derive from an unhappy return visit to South Africa and C.'s later delight in his new-found Mediterranean home. In each case, natural scenes are evoked with verve and passion. Celebrations of natural beauty and vigor embody a distinctive moral tone in which C.'s own belief in heroic individualism is organic to his descriptions.

Flowering Reeds (1933), a volume of beautifully controlled Mediterranean lyrics, represents the culmination of C.'s early lyrical style. The French influence is at its strongest in these poems, and the control over a still-exotic imagery more marked.

A satirical and argumentative strain had been evident throughout C.'s early career. The *Wayzgoose* (1928) is a broad attack on Natal, his native South African province, and the provincialism C. had encountered there. *The Georgiad* (1931) is a biting personal attack on Harold Nicolson (1886–1968), Vita Sackville-West (1892–1962), and English literary coteries, again deriving from personal experience. This argumentative element became more pronounced in C.'s later work, particularly as he felt the need to defend his conservative views.

Mithraic Emblems (1936) contains many attacks on left-wingers and do-gooders as well as intricate, emblematic poems depicting the curiously ornate elements in C.'s brand of conservative, heroic Catholicism. His long, undisciplined defense of Franco, *Flowering Rifle* (1939), embodies the most extreme of his conservative attitudes and unyielding passions. C.'s last volume of original poems *Talking Bronco* (1946), shows a return to some of the lyrical ease of his earlier work, but repetitive polemical attacks on left-wing groups and enemies spoil its total effect.

In his last years C. devoted much of his time to verse translations. In *Poems of St. John of the Cross* (1951) and *Baudelaire: Poems: A Translation of "Les fleurs du mal"* (1952) he produced vivid and controlled English versions, reflecting his own life-long sympathy with Continental styles and attitudes.

C.'s celebration of the heroic and the vital is distinctive, as is the rich texture of his poetry. He often lacked a sense of proportion, but his best work has an unequaled passion and vigor.

FURTHER WORKS: *Poems* (1930); *Taurine Provence* (1932); *Broken Record* (1934); *Sons of the Mistral* (1941); *Light on a Dark Horse* (1951); *Lorca* (1952); *The Mamba's Precipice* (1953); *Portugal* (1957); *Collected Poems I* (1949), *II* (1957), *III* (1960)

BIBLIOGRAPHY: Gardner, W. H., "Voltage of Delight," *The Month,* Jan. 1958, 5–17; Wright, D., *R. C.* (1961); Bergonzi, B., "R. C.: Outsider on the Right," *JCH,* 2 (1967), 133–47; Smith, R., *Lyric and Polemic: The Literary Personality of R. C.* (1972); Paton, A., "R. C.," in Heywood, C., ed., *Aspects of South African Literature* (1976), pp. 3–23

ROWLAND SMITH

FUGARD, Athol

South African dramatist (writing in English), b. 11 June 1932, Middleburg

F., of mixed Afrikaner and English parentage, grew up in Port Elizabeth. He first became involved in the theater in 1957, when he organized an experimental group in Cape Town. A year later his experience as a clerk in the Native Commissioner's Court in Johannesburg, dealing with "pass law" violations, led him to write plays based on the unhappy circumstances of Africans whom he met in the court. His first works, *No-good*

Friday (perf. 1958, pub. 1974) and *Nogogo* (perf. 1958, pub. 1974), set in Sophia Town, Johannesburg's black "township," were written for a multiracial theater group he organized in 1958. The first is concerned with a black correspondence-school student whose efforts to improve his social condition by his studies are cut short by a confrontation with an extortionist. *Nogogo* is set in a "shebeen" (a cheap African saloon) run by a woman whose past as a miners' whore destroys her hopes for happiness with an enterprising but naïve salesman.

The first works by F. to achieve international recognition were his "Port Elizabeth plays": *The Blood Knot* (perf. 1961, pub. 1963), *Hello and Goodbye* (perf. 1965, pub. 1966), and *Boesman and Lena* (perf. and pub. 1969). *Hello and Goodbye* and *Boesman and Lena* were written for the Serpent Players, a drama group that some hopeful black actors in Port Elizabeth's "township" asked him to organize in 1963. The casts of these plays are small: two or three characters confront each other in tense, painful moments which reveal a humanity that cannot be completely overmastered by an antihuman racial milieu. *The Blood Knot* deals with two half brothers, sons of the same mother, who work to save for a farm where they can be free. Zachariah, the darker brother, learns that the "pen pal" he has discovered in a newspaper advertisement is the sister of a white policeman, and Morris, who is light-skinned enough to "pass" for white, realizes that the dream of the farm is hopeless but that the blood that links him to Zachariah is less of a "knot" than their love. *Hello and Goodbye,* the most despairing of the three plays, concerns a brother and sister waiting for their father to die so that they can claim an inheritance which, in fact, does not exist. *Boesman and Lena* are a "Coloured" husband and wife, homeless because "progress" has bulldozed their shantytown; they camp by a roadside and berate each other until Lena finds a release in her pity for an old African who has been dumped in a field to die.

In 1967, influenced by the theories of the Polish experimental theater director Jerzy Grotowski (b. 1933), F. and his black actors began to experiment with improvisational theater. While F. provided the starting point for the two resulting plays and directed the process by which John Kani and Winston Ntshoni improvised the dialogue, the plays' texture and force emerged from the inner experiences of the actors; F. credited them as fellow "devisers" of the plays, *Sizwe Bansi Is Dead* (perf. 1972, pub. 1974) and *The Island* (perf. 1973, pub. 1974). These works avoid the pitfalls of didacticism, a real danger because of their subject matter (the "pass" law and the political prison on Robben Island, respectively), by transforming the real social ordeal of the doubly real people—the actors *and* their roles—into artistic and therefore meaningful structures.

F.'s most recent work uses more conventional artistic procedures, but *Dimetos* (perf. 1975, pub. 1977) is a daring experiment based on a few lines from the notebooks of Albert Camus. Here F. for the first time abandoned a South African setting. Dimetos, a distinguished engineer, exiles himself to a distant province of an unspecified country, refuses to return to "the city," and permits his emotions to become entangled in incestuous affections for his niece. Her suicide finally causes him to come to terms with his guilt, his irresponsibility, and his existential predicament.

Tsotsi, a powerful short novel written in 1959–60, was published in 1979. It is concerned with a Sophia Town thug who is orphaned as a child, survives by crimes ranging from theft to murder, and, before his violent death, begins to discover his humanity when he happens to find an abandoned baby. The novel is stark in its realism, the social conditions it describes are appalling, and the mastery of fictional techniques makes clear that if F. had not chosen the theater he probably would have had an equally distinguished career as a novelist.

F.'s career reveals a great courage to experiment, a willingness to take artistic risks, a remarkable capacity for avoiding mere didacticism, and profound sympathy for his human subjects. His ability to transform local South African conflicts into universal human predicaments suggests that his future career will continue the steady growth he has already demonstrated.

FURTHER WORKS: *People Are Living There* (1970); *The Coat* (1971); *Statements after an Arrest under the Immorality Act* (1974); *The Guest: An Episode in the Life of Eugene Marais* (1977, with Ross Devenish); *A Lesson from Aloes* (1978)

BIBLIOGRAPHY: Berner, R. L., "A. F. and the Theatre of Improvisation," *BA,* 50 (1976), 81–84; Tucker, A. C., "A. F. Interviewed," *Transatlantic,* Nos. 53–54 (1976), 87–90, Green, R. J., "Politics and Literature in Africa: The Drama of A. F.," in Hayward, C., ed., *Aspects of South African Literature* (1976), pp. 163–73; Benson, M., "Keeping an Appointment with the Future: The Theatre of A. F., *TheatreQ,* 28 (1977–78), 77–83; "F. on Acting: Actors on F.," *TheatreQ,* 28 (1977–78), 83–87; O'Sheel, P., "A. F.'s 'Poor Theatre,' " *JCL,* 12, 3 (1978), 67–77

ROBERT L. BERNER

GORDIMER, Nadine

South African novelist (writing in English), b. 20 Nov. 1923, Springs

G. was educated in the Transvaal and attended the University of the Witwatersrand in Johannesburg. Her home is in Johannesburg, the setting of most of her fiction. Although she has not lived outside South Africa for any extended period, she has traveled extensively in Africa, Europe, and North America, and has made many appearances as a lecturer abroad, particularly in the U.S.

G.'s writing career extends over thirty years of political turbulence in her native country. Her novels and short stories are predominantly concerned with the effects on individual lives and sensibilities of the political situation in southern Africa. "In South Africa, society is the political situation," she stated in an interview with Alan Ross in *London Magazine* (May 1965).

Her fiction reflects the changes in the life of the region since 1949, when her first collection of stories, *Face to Face,* was published. She shows a startling clarity of perception as she chronicles the corrosive effects of life in authoritarian, segregated South Africa, with its taboos, restrictions, and intricate apparatus of police power. The world she knows intimately is that of the white, English-speaking middle class. In describing the strange reality of comfortable, isolated white society she usually links closely observed details with overriding emotional effects: aridity, a sense of fear or powerlessness, distrust, lost spontaneity.

Her short stories have changed as the situation in South Africa has deteriorated. In *The Soft Voice of the Serpent* (1952) and *Six Feet of the Country* (1956) many tales reveal injustices caused by white supremacy. "Decent" and "humane" whites are shown to be themselves emotional casualties of the discriminatory system in which they are involuntarily involved. The later collections, *Not for Publication* (1965) and *Livingstone's Companions* (1971), depict the growing powerlessness of opposition to the tentacular police state. As effective political action from both whites and blacks is crushed, opportunistic political gesturing takes its place. Not all the stories carry political overtones, however. Several are short, closely focused evocations of moods, attitudes, or moments in the emotional lives of their protagonists.

G.'s novels show a similar development. *The Lying Days* (1953) is a *Bildungsroman*. Its protagonist is a young woman who decides to remain in South Africa in spite of her sense of guilt and foreboding after the Afrikaner Nationalists come to power in 1948. The novel has many beautifully observed descriptions of the decorum-ridden mining community in which the heroine grows up. The stresses of life in a segregated society are depicted in both *A World of Strangers* (1958) and *Occasion for Loving* (1963). In the former an Englishman finds himself unable to maintain friendships with both middle-class Johannesburg whites and a black acquaintance from the "townships." In the latter an illicit love affair between a black man and a white woman ends bitterly for all those involved.

Political events themselves inform *The Late Bourgeois World* (1966). The central character is a young white divorcee who is asked for help by a friend in the black underground. Her fear at his request and her memory of the futile sabotage attempts of her ex-husband provide constant tension and menace while she goes about her bland daily round in white Johannesburg.

G. maintains an interest in politics in *A Guest of Honour* (1970). Its setting is not, however, South Africa, but a newly independent African country whose problems are revealed through the experiences of a former English official, returned as a guest of the new government.

Two recent novels are again set in South Africa. *The Conservationist* (1974) has at its center a successful industrialist. His sense of possession is troubled by memories of unsuccessful personal relations and by the obtrusive presence of blacks on his weekend farm. They have a more natural claim on the land and community than he. *Burger's Daughter* (1979) is a poignant account of the unsuccessful attempt by the daughter of a renowned Afrikaans Communist to live an apolitical life after her father's death in prison.

Burger's Daughter, dealing with the Soweto riots of 1976 and black-power rejection of all white assistance and good faith, encapsulates the intractability of the tainted society described by G. with haunting clarity throughout her creative life.

FURTHER WORKS: *Friday's Footprint, and Other Stories* (1960); *The Black Interpreters* (1973); *Selected Stories* (1975); *Some Monday for Sure* (1976); *A Soldier's Embrace* (1980); *July's People* (1981)

BIBLIOGRAPHY: Haugh, R. S., *N. G.* (1974); Hope, C., "Out of the Picture: The Novels of N. G.," *London,* 15, 1 (1975), 49–55; Smith, R., "The Johannesburg Genre," in Smith, R., ed., *Exile and Tradition* (1976), pp. 116–31; Green, R. J., "N. G.: The Politics of Race," *WLWE,* 16 (1977), 256–62; Parker, K., "N. G. and the Pitfalls of

Liberalism," in Parker, K., ed., *The South African Novel in English* (1978), pp. 114–30

ROWLAND SMITH

LA GUMA, Alex

South African novelist and short-story writer (writing in English), b. 20 Feb. 1925, Cape Town

After attending secondary school, L. held a variety of jobs before beginning a career as a journalist. His active opposition to the South African government and its policy of apartheid led to periods of imprisonment, house arrest, and in 1966 exile to England, where he now lives.

L.'s writing frequently stems from personal experience as a black man and reflects his deep opposition to the South African regime. Thus, *A Walk in the Night* (1962), set in the slums of Cape Town, pictures the losing struggle to retain a fundamental humanity in the face of racial oppression. *And a Threefold Cord* (1964) is also based on life in the ghetto, while *The Stone Country* (1967) is inspired by L.'s own imprisonment and is dedicated to "the daily 70,351 prisoners in South African gaols in 1964." L.'s early political activism is reflected in *In the Fog of the Season's End* (1972), a novel based on organizing underground opposition to apartheid.

Thus L.'s literary world grimly mirrors the realities of life for nonwhites in South Africa. Crime and brutality inevitably erupt as people keenly aware of their own powerlessness find themselves in intolerable situations. Little room for sentimentality exists in such a world, yet love and even comedy can occasionally and fleetingly blossom. L. handles his settings concretely and vividly, whether a prison, shantytown, white suburbs, or, as in *Time of the Butcherbird* (1979), a new Bantu homeland to which people have been forcefully removed.

Characters in L.'s fiction are inevitably victims of society. People like Michael Adonis, a "coloured" who unjustly loses his job in *A Walk in the Night,* and Charlie Pauls, who in *And a Threefold Cord* attacks a white policeman, move outside the law because the social structure allows them no other choice. For L., this structure can only produce disease and parasitism, whether in the form of a petty criminal living off shanty people, a tough jailbird off other prisoners, or whites off the rest of the country's population. Given the vicious situation they find themselves in, moral action for L.'s characters becomes defensive, passive, and even perverted, rather than assertive and positive, as might be possible in a freer society.

Since L. is concerned with the enormous direct impact that political and social realities have on the life of his country and its people, it has been argued that his characters become artistically subordinated to the depiction of particular situations. Yet L. cannot be validly accused, as some black South African writers might be, of presenting journalistic fact in the guise of creative literature. Rather, L. comes to his subject with freshness and originality. His description of person and place is graphic, his accurate rendition of various dialects invigorating. He masterfully evokes both mood and atmosphere, and even on occasion finds humor in the midst of pathos; these qualities enable him to make some telling points about the human condition. He is considered by many critics to be one of black South Africa's most significant and successful writers.

FURTHER WORKS: *A Walk in the Night, and Other Stories* (1967); *A Soviet Journey* (1978)

BIBLIOGRAPHY: Rabkin, D., "L. and Reality in South Africa," *JCL*, 8 (1973), 54–61; Wanjala, C. L., "The Face of Injustice: A. L.'s Fiction," in Wanjala, C. L., ed., *Standpoints on African Literature* (1973), pp. 305–22; Asein, S., "The Revolutionary Vision in A. L.'s Novels," *LAAW*, 24–25 (1975), 9–21 (also in *Phylon*, 39 [1978], 74–86); Gakwandi, A., *The Novel and Contemporary Experience in Africa* (1977), pp. 8, 21–26; Wade, M., "Art and Morality in A. L.'s *A Walk in the Night*," in Parker, K., ed., *The South African Novel in English: Essays in Criticism and Society* (1978), pp. 164–91; Scanlon, P. A., "A. L.'s Novels of Protest: The Growth of the Revolutionary," *Okike*, 16 (1979), 85–93; Moore, G., *Twelve African Writers* (1980), pp. 104–20

DAVID F. BEER

MILLIN, Sarah Gertrude

South African novelist, biographer, and diarist (writing in English), b. 3 March 1888, Zagar, Lithuania; d. 16 July 1968, Johannesburg

M.'s Jewish parents emigrated to South Africa when she was five months old. The family settled on alluvial diamond diggings on the Vaal River near Kimberley. M. spent her early years keenly observing the diggers whose lives were to form the major inspiration for her fiction. Her disapproval of the racial mixing she saw on the river developed into a lifelong obsession with miscegenation. In later life she turned her back on the liberal tradition established by her fellow writers in South Africa and became instead a supporter of apartheid and of white supremacy in southern Africa. An interest in the work of her husband, Philip Millin, a barrister and judge, led to her familiarity with the law courts of Johannesburg. She attended trials and based some of her plots on them.

At the end of a long life, M. claimed that she had provided South African literature with "bulk." Apart from fifteen novels and a volume of short stories, *Two Bucks without Hair* (1957), interest in politics and history resulted in a two-volume biography of the famous Boer soldier and statesman Jan Smuts, *General Smuts* (1936), another biography, *Cecil Rhodes* (1933), and an autobiography, *The Night is Long* (1941), which she saw as a prelude to her ambitious 1,600-page *War Diary* (6 vols., 1944-48).

M. chose a dynastic structure for several novels *God's Stepchildren* (1924), *King of the Bastards* (1949), and *The Burning Man* (1952). *God's Stepchildren,* her most popular work, covers four generations of South African life, and the theme of biological destiny is prominent. In the somber, tragic world of her novels miscegenation is the physical manifestation of original sin. Sometimes M.'s characters are disgraced by poor and demanding relations, whose connections with darker people are economic rather than sexual, as in *The Jordans* (1923). The belief in superior or inferior genes, however, is germane to M.'s world view.

M.'s numerous female characters are striking for their emotional strength and their ruthlessness. They will often stop at nothing to indulge an obsession. In *Mary Glenn* (1925) M. describes feminine ambition in a small provincial town. Typically, Mary marries for social advantage and not for love. Many of M.'s women are haunted by the fear of spinsterhood; the dread of remaining sexually unfulfilled poisons their lives.

M. sees money as the driving force in modern society. Her characters come from the deprived classes of South Africa. They are landless, uneducated, temperamentally unstable—social outcasts, poor whites, halfbreeds, or simply "bastards" (that is, people of mixed race). In M.'s fiction, crimes are committed and lives blighted over trifling sums of money. Even if the economic problem is solved, M.'s protagonists are frequently unable to arrive at self-determination. Guilt, fear, or an innate self-destructiveness prevent them from rising above an inferior background.

Despite her color prejudice, incorporated in a deterministic world view, M.'s fiction is of a distinguished caliber. She writes in a tragic mode, achieving real poignancy in a style that is at once plain and forceful. She is a master of dialogue and situation, and her portraits of the poor and degenerate families who eked out a living in a provincial and rural South Africa during the first decades of the 20th c. are both emotionally compelling and authentic.

FURTHER WORKS: *The Dark River* (1919); *Middle-Class* (1921); *Adam's Rest* (1922); *The South Africans* (1926); *An Artist in the Family* (1928); *The Coming of the Lord* (1928); *The Fiddler* (1929); *Men on a Voyage* (1930); *The Sons of Mrs. Aab* (1931); *What Hath a Man?* (1938); *South Africa* (1941); *The Herr Witchdoctor* (1941; Am., *The Dark Gods*); *The People of South Africa* (1951); *The Measure of My Days* (1955); *The Wizard Bird* (1962); *Goodbye, Dear England* (1965); *White Africans Are Also People* (1966)

BIBLIOGRAPHY: Snyman, P. P. L., *The Works of S. G. M.* (1955); Rubin, M., *S. G. M.: A South African Life* (1977); Rabkin, D., "Race and Fiction: *God's Stepchildren* and [William Plomer's] *Turbott Wolfe*," in Parker, K., ed., *The South African Novel in English: Essays in Criticism and Society* (1978), pp. 77–94; Sarvan, C., and Sarvan, L., "*God's Stepchildren* and *Lady Chatterley's Lover:* Failure and Triumph," *JCL*, 14, 1 (1979), 53–57; Coetzee, J. M., "Blood, Flaw, Taint, Degeneration: The Case of S. G. M.," *ESA*, 23 (1980), 41–58

JEAN MARQUARD

MPHAHLELE, Ezekiel (Es'kia)

South African novelist, short-story writer, and essayist (writing in English), b. 17 Dec. 1919, Pretoria

Born in the slums of Pretoria, M. lived as a child on poor farms, then, as a teenager, returned to the urban life of Marabastad, the locale of his autobiography. He obtained a certificate in 1940 to teach English and Afrikaans in Johannesburg. In 1952 he was dismissed from his post because he protested apartheid. After working as a journalist, he left South Africa in 1957 to live in Nigeria. He moved to Nairobi, Kenya, in 1963 to teach English at University College; he also journeyed to England, the U.S., and France. The first draft of M.'s novel *The Wanderers* (1971) served as his dissertation for his degree from the University of

Denver. He then moved to the University of Pennsylvania, where he taught English. He left that post in 1977 to return to his native land and changed his first name from Ezekiel to its corresponding African form, Es'kia. M. now teaches at the Center for African Studies of Witwatersrand University, on its Soweto campus.

M.'s views of human life have remained remarkably consistent. Always concerned about human rights, he has tried to avoid simplistic answers to the enormous racial problems of South Africa. His autobiography, *Down Second Avenue* (1959), exemplifies his wish to see people as human beings, not as "victims of political circumstance."

M.'s autobiographical novel *The Wanderers* is a lyric cry of pain for the many rootless black exiles who wander across the African continent searching for a new home. The protagonist, Timi Tabane, is a journalist forced to flee South Africa because he exposed the activities of a slave farm to which blacks were abducted and where they were beaten and murdered. Timi becomes an exile in more ways than just physically; he feels his alienation in free Nigeria and Kenya and in his job as a high-school teacher in eastern Africa; he even becomes alienated from his wife and children. Only in the tragic death of his son, who had joined an underground movement in South Africa, does a sense of catharsis and new resolution take hold in him.

In his second novel, *Chirundu* (1980), M. portrays an ambitious, self-made politician in a fictional country resembling Zambia. Chirundu, minister of transport and public works, is determined to gain power and wealth. He ends up in jail on a charge of bigamy brought by his first wife. Chirundu's "fall," however, is regarded by him as a boon to come later in the form of support by his tribal people, since bigamy is not recognized as a crime by his tribe. M. uses the bigamy trial to explore questions of modernism and tribalism, and of individualism and communal responsibility.

M. has also published three collections of short stories. *The Living and the Dead* (1961) and *In Corner B* (1967) portray life both in the urban slums and on the estates of wealthy English and Boer families. These stories are more charged with violence and with sexual imagery than M.'s other narrative work.

M.'s first critical study, *The African Image* (1962; rev. ed., 1974), is another attempt to gain perspective on himself and on his role as writer in a land torn by the struggle for political and human rights. In this book he attempts to reconstruct the image of the African as seen by white and black writers.

M.'s study *Voices in the Whirlwind* (1972) is a series of six essays on black culture. He expands his discussion of "African" to include black American and West Indian cultures. He remains conscious of the many differences among black men, just as he had earlier remained unconvinced by Negritude (q.v.). In the "whirlwind" created by the new awareness of black art and literature, M. sees education as the single most important force.

M. is also well known as an editor of many distinguished periodicals. His *African Writing Today* (1967), an anthology, is highly regarded, both for its comprehensiveness and for his illuminating introductions.

FURTHER WORK: *Man Must Live, and Other Stories* (1947)

BIBLIOGRAPHY: Cartey, W., *Whispers from a Continent* (1969), pp. 27–38, 110–22; Duerden, D., and Pieterse, C., eds., *African Writers Talking* (1972), pp. 95–115; Olney, J., *Tell Me, Africa* (1973), pp. 26–79; Barnett, U. A., *E. M.* (1976); Roscoe, A., *Uhuru's Fire: African Literature East to South* (1977), pp. 225–34; Moore, G., *Twelve African Writers* (1980), pp. 40–66; Tucker, M., on *Chirundu, Worldview,* June 1982, 25–26

MARTIN TUCKER

PATON, Alan

South African novelist, short-story writer, essayist, and poet (writing in English), b. 11 Jan. 1903, Pietermaritzburg

P.'s upbringing by deeply religious parents of English stock sensitized him to the moral and ethical principles underlying the racial conflicts in South Africa. He interprets the race struggle as a larger revolt of man against domination—against dominating and being dominated.

This view marked his innovations as principal of Diep Kloof Reformatory near Johannesburg, an experience that provided the material for several short stories and moved him to political action in the antiapartheid Liberal Association, of which he was founder (1953) and president. The poles of his political views and literary themes are the same: the negative, a distrust of institutionalized power; the positive, a belief in the power of love expressed as human brotherhood.

The subject of an early, uncompleted novel—Christ's return to South Africa—anticipates the material of P.'s later fiction. His first published novel, *Cry, the Beloved Country* (1948), the story of Stephen Kumalo, a Zulu minister, and his search for his son in Johannesburg, is about racial tensions, but its primary theme is the brotherhood of man. His second, *Too Late the Phalarope* (1953), is about a white man destroyed because of an affair with a native girl. Again the primary object is to indict the inhumanity of racial separation as institutionalized in such legislation as the Immorality Act, which prohibits sexual relations between black and white. Moving as these novels are, they are open to the charge that P. manipulates characters to conform to his thesis about the political and social situations they dramatize.

The death of P.'s wife in 1967 turned him to a self-searching analysis of domination in the complex structure of marriage in *Kontakion for You Departed* (1969). In this painful, sometimes moving account of the relationship with his wife, P. attempted to define marital communion as the sacramental point of transition from what is at best a flawed *agape* existing within society toward the perfection of the Creator's love.

Critics often overlook this thematic preoccupation when they object that humanitarian zeal sometimes reduces P.'s fiction to the level of propaganda. The charge is in any case more applicable to the volume of short stories *Debbie Go Home* (1961; Am., *Tales from a Troubled Land*) than to the novels.

The appeal of his fiction derives from the language—simple, seemingly unadorned, but modified by the rhythms of African languages and Afrikaans—and from an intricate symbolic interweaving of land, people, and theme.

In 1980 appeared *Towards the Mountain,* an account of P.'s life up to 1948. It deals largely with the public events of his life, as *Kontakion for You Departed* does with the private. The promised second part of the autobiography will likely also deal mainly with public involvements. But these have already been well documented in *The Long View* (1967), a selection of essays on political and social matters originally published in the South African journal *Contact* between 1955 and 1966, which exhibit the insistent reason of his arguments, and in *Knocking at the Door* (1976), a collection of short fiction, poems, and articles on various subjects, including politics and penal reform.

The nonfiction that P. produced in the 1960s and 1970s prepared the way for the novel *Ah, But Your Land Is Beautiful* (1981), a narrative marked by greater stylistic variety than his earlier fiction. He uses a sequence of poison-pen letters and speeches by public figures, which, although they newly dramatize his long-standing advocacy of individual freedom and racial equality, do little for characterization.

P.'s poetry is governed by the qualities so evident in his prose: feeling, reason, and clarity of expression. These qualities, however, work to disadvantage in the poetry, sometimes leaving the didactic element too apparent: The ideal medium for his characteristic intensity of feeling and simplicity of style is provided by *Instrument of Thy Peace* (1968), reflections on a prayer of Saint Francis of Assisi. In this meditative work P. confronts without equivocation the difficulties of the region in which personal and social relationships come into conflict. Wherever the uncertainties of this kind of conflict reach the danger stage, both P.'s personal commitment and his achievements in literature will be consulted as touchstones of courage and integrity.

FURTHER WORKS: *South Africa Today* (1953); *The Land and People of South Africa* (1955; rev. ed., 1972); *South Africa in Transition* (1956, with Dan Weiner); *Hope for South Africa* (1958); *Hofmeyr* (1964; Am., South African Tragedy: The Life and Times of Jan Hofmeyr); *Sponomo* (1965, with Krishna Shah); *Apartheid and the Archbishop: The Life and Times of Geoffrey Clayton, Archbishop of Cape Town* (1973)

BIBLIOGRAPHY: on *Cry, the Beloved Country, TLS,* 23 Oct. 1948, 593; on *Too Late the Phalarope, TLS,* 28 Aug. 1953, 545; Baker, S., "P.'s Beloved Country and the Morality of Geography," *CE,* 19, 2 (1957), 56–61; Callan, E., *A. P.* (1968); Breslin, J. B., "Inside South Africa," *America,* 17 April 1976, 344–46; Sharma, R. C., "A. P.'s *Cry, the Beloved Country:* The Parable of Compassion," *LHY,* 19, 2 (1978), 64–82; Cooke, J., " 'A Hunger of the Soul': *Too Late the Phalarope* Reconsidered," *ESA,* 22 (1979), 37–43

MANLY JOHNSON

PLOMER, William
South African novelist, poet, short-story writer, and librettist (writing in English), b. 10 Dec. 1903, Pietersburg; d. 22 Sept. 1973, London, England

After completing his education in South Africa and England, P. worked on a farm and on a trading station with his father. By the time he was nineteen, he was writing verse and had begun *Turbott Wolfe* (1925), his first novel. His writing brought him into contact with Roy Campbell (q.v.) and Laurens van der Post (b. 1906), with whom he cofounded the significant although short-lived literary magazine *Voorslag.* In 1926 P.

went to Japan, where he lived until 1929. He returned to England, where he was to spend the larger part of his life. In 1963 he was awarded the Queen's Gold Medal for Poetry; he was President of the Poetry Society from 1968 to 1971.

Of P.'s five novels, *Turbott Wolfe* is the most renowned; it has recently received renewed attention from South African and American critics. *Turbott Wolfe* shows an Africa capable of developing within its own civilization, despite the intervention of Western values. Its focus, as the eponymous narrator states, is on the "unavoidable question of colour." It is written with enormous force and descriptive power, but it is structurally uneven: there is an anecdotal quality to the events described, and the ineffectual narrator is incapable of serving as a unifying device. The novel flashes with understated wit, interspersed with a coarse humor, like the coarseness of the world he describes.

P. was a prolific poet; like his short stories, his verse is a reflection of personal experience. The strength of his poetry lies in its descriptive power, its economy of detail, and its symbolic imagery. He wrote of Africa from the colonial perspective, and in his poems written in Japan and Europe the point of view is that of a concerned foreigner. The phrase "Ballads Abroad," the title P. gave to a section of his *Collected Poems* (1960; expanded ed., 1973), suggests the position with which he was most comfortable, that of the tolerant outsider, generally observing with detached humor and ironic wit. He had a great love of landscape and used natural detail to capture impressions of local atmosphere. In two poems written in Japan, "The Aburaya" and "Hotel Magnificent," collectively labeled "Two Hotels" in the *Collected Poems,* a sense of nostalgia is expressed for a delicate and transient culture, contrasted with the hollowness of a "tradition" ready-made for foreigners.

A poem that expresses many of P.'s central concerns is "The Scorpion," one of the "African Poems" in the *Collected Poems*. It speaks of the drowning of an African culture: both the traditional domestic and magical elements have been swept away. The poem focuses on two images, the corpse of a black woman and a scorpion, which P. uses to convey the demise of an Africa that was dangerous, sensuous, and noble.

P. also worked as a librettist with Benjamin Britten: their collaborations include the opera *Gloriana* (1953) for the coronation of Queen Elizabeth II. P.'s autobiography *Double Lives* (1943) describes with wit and detachment the early part of his life, in South Africa.

P. can be regarded as representing the beginnings of the "protest novel" in South Africa; however, critics now generally see him as a writer whose outlook was shaped by his world view as a liberal humanist in the tradition of Joseph Conrad. In his writings about Africa there is a sense of his alienation from the country he lived in and loved but never fully possessed.

FURTHER WORKS: *I Speak of Africa* (1927); *Notes for Poems* (1927); *The Family Tree* (1929); *Paper Houses* (1929); *Sado* (1931; Am., *They Never Came Back*); *The Fivefold Screen* (1932); *The Case Is Altered* (1932); *The Child of Queen Victoria* (1933); *Cecil Rhodes* (1933); *The Invaders* (1934); *Visiting the Caves* (1936); *Ali the Lion* (1936; rpt. as *The Diamond of Jannina: Ali Pasha 1741–1822*, 1970); *Selected Poems* (1940); *The Dorking Thigh, and Other Satires* (1945); *Curious Relations* (1945, under pseud. William D'Arfey); *Four Countries* (1949); *Museum Pieces* (1952); *A Shot in the Park* (1955); *Borderline Ballads* (1955); *At Home* (1958); *Curlew River* (libretto, 1965); *The Burning Fiery Furnace* (libretto, 1966); *Taste and Remember* (1966); *The Prodigal Son* (libretto, 1968); *Celebrations* (1972); *The Butterfly Ball and the Grasshopper Feast* (1973); *The Autobiography of W. P.* (1975); *Electric Delights* (1977)

BIBLIOGRAPHY: Margery, K., "The South African Novel and Race," *SoRA*, 1 (1963), 27–46; Doyle, J. R., Jr., *W. P.* (1969); Rabkin, D., "Race and Fiction: [Sarah Gertrude Milin's] *God's Stepchildren* and *Turbott Wolfe*," in Parker, K., ed., *The South African Novel in English* (1978), pp. 77–94; Marquard, J., Introduction to *A Century of South African Short Stories* (1978), pp. 22–31; Hallet, R., "The Importance of *Voorslag:* Roy Campbell, W. P., and the Development of South African Literature," *Theoria*, 50 (1978), 29–39; Herbert, M., "The Early Writings of W. P.: Some New Material," *ESA*, 22 (1979), 13–26; Gray, S., ed., *W. P., Turbott Wolfe*, with background pieces by Laurens van der Post, Roy Campbell, Michael Herbert, Nadine Gordimer, Peter Wilhelm, David Brown, and Stephen Gray (1980)

GILLIAN L. G. NOERO

SCHREINER, Olive

South African novelist (writing in English), b. 24 March 1855, Wittebergen; d. 10 Dec. 1920, Wynberg

The daughter of missionary parents, S. spent her early years on isolated mission stations, receiving no formal education. She became a governess on Eastern Cape farms (1871–80), where she read the works of Charles Darwin, Herbert Spencer, John Stuart Mill, and Ralph Waldo Emerson. They confirmed her instinctive tendency to reject formalized Christianity for an intuitive perception of spiritual truth, an adherence to individual rights, and a belief in evolutionary progress. From 1881 to 1889 S. lived in England, meeting members of early socialist groups such as Edward Carpenter (1844–1929) and sexologist Havelock Ellis (1859–1939), and traveling in Europe. After her return to South Africa her energies were taken up mainly in polemical journalism and other nonfiction writing, crusading against Cecil Rhodes and British expansionism in Africa, expressing the South African outlook during the Boer War (1899–1902), and developing her view of women's problems and rights. Although she married a liberal South African farmer, S. C. Cronwright, in 1894, she spent the last seven years of her life alone in England before returning to South Africa to die.

S.'s main achievement as a novelist is *The Story of an African Farm* (1883), first published under the pseudonym Ralph Iron. It is a landmark work in South African fiction because of its powerful imaginative use of the landscape of the Great Karoo, an arid interior plateau of South Africa sparsely populated by farmers, and its exploration of spiritual conflict in its young protagonists, Lyndall and Waldo. The novel aroused controversy in England because of Lyndall's championship of women's rights and rejection of conventional marriage, and also because of Waldo's rejection of orthodox Christian belief. S.'s second published novel, *Trooper Peter Halket of Mashonaland* (1897), directed at Rhodes and his policies, is a satirical allegory in which a young trooper is confronted by Jesus Christ as a nighttime visitant. Her most ambitious work, the posthumously published *From Man to Man* (1926), never completed, focuses on the contrasted lives of two sisters who struggle in different ways against social norms and sexual hypocrisy. *Undine* (1929) is a posthumously published juvenile work, combining realistic scenes of the Kimberley diamond fields with a fairytale English setting.

Shorter fictions by S. include allegories in the form of dream visions, a few short tales for children, and autobiographical stories exalting the need for the renunciation of possessive sexual love. "Eighteen-Ninety-nine" (pub. 1923), generally considered her best short story, is a celebration of Afrikaner endurance that links the Afrikaner with the cyclical fertility of the land.

All of S.'s fiction is concerned with the centrality of childhood experience in shaping later life and with the difficulty of maintaining ideals or individual integrity in a corrupt or hostile environment. Her vision is one of suffering and of struggle toward a glimpse of universal harmony. The 19th-c. belief in progress is tempered by her early experience of hardship, by the asthmatic illness that troubled her from adolescence onward, and by an awareness of painful conflict in sexual relationships. Her fiction speaks didactically to contemporary issues, such as socialism, feminism, imperialism, and racism; but, in a carefully structured blend of realism and allegory, it situates these causes in a cosmic framework. She spans concrete local detail and dream landscapes, social protest and philosophical meditation, with enormous confidence and power.

S.'s belief in individual rights remained a central tenet of her polemical writing. Her political pamphlets included *Closer Union* (1909), which advocates a form of federal government to protect the individual features of the provinces as South Africa moved toward unification. Her concern with women's rights resulted in an influential and ardent work, *Woman and Labour* (1911), which proclaimed a woman's need to escape parasitic dependence and her right to choose any occupation. *Thoughts on South Africa* (1923) is a lucid study of the country's features and problems, revealing a strong grasp of their historical and geographical causes.

Despite S.'s belief in the organic unity of art, she always stressed that art should be of assistance to others. She believed in a shared human nature and condition, and felt that the passionate exploration of basic problems, especially discord in male-female relationships, would show other women that they were not suffering alone. She is honored by later generations of South African writers for making the local landscape vivid and viable in *The Story of an African Farm*. Many of her statements on the South African "race problem" are now seen as prophetic and ahead of her time. Her compassion and eloquence in speaking out for women have made her a symbolic founding mother of the feminist movement of recent decades.

FURTHER WORKS: *Dreams* (1890); *Dream Life and Real Life* (1893); *The Political Situation* (1895, with S. C. Cronwright-Schreiner); *An English-South African's View of the Situation* (1899); *Stories, Dreams and Allegories* (1923); *The Letters of O. S.* (1924)

BIBLIOGRAPHY: Lessing, D., Afterword to *The Story of an African Farm* (1968), pp. 273–90; Jacobson, D., "O. S.: A South African Writer," *London*, Feb. 1971, 5–21; Berkman, J. A., *O. S.: Feminism on the Frontier* (1979); Gray, S., *Southern African Literature: An Introduction* (1979), pp. 133–59; First, R., and Scott, A., *O. S.* (1980); Clayton, C., ed., *O. S.* (1983)

CHERRY CLAYTON

SMITH, Pauline

South African short-story writer and novelist (writing in English), b. 2 April 1882, Oudtshoorn; d. 29 Jan. 1959, Broadstone, England

S. spent her childhood in the Little Karoo region, just south of Olive Schreiner's (q.v.) Great Karoo. She completed her formal education in England and spent the rest of her life quietly in Dorset, returning on several occasions to South Africa to gather material for her fiction.

During her adolescence and twenties S. began the stories about her childhood that later became the children's stories *Platkops Children* (1935). She also published in Aberdeen newspapers a set of sketches and poems about Scottish life. The period of her friendship with Arnold Bennett from 1909 to 1931 coincided with her major literary activity, in which she published twelve short stories (a thirteenth, undated, was published posthumously), several sketches based on her South African journals, a one-act play, and a novel called *The Beadle* (1926). That she was unable to finish the novel she worked on for the rest of her life was probably due to growing despair at the political climate in Europe and South Africa and to chronic ill health, which worsened during the war years.

The stories collected in *The Little Karoo* (1925; expanded ed., 1930) deal with relations between rich and poor, God and man, farmer and *bywoner* (sharecropper), man and woman; the atmosphere of poverty and dependency is partially alleviated by love and forgiveness, generally embodied in women. The comment is often harsh: in "The Sisters" a young girl's sacrifice to a rich farmer to pay off her father's mortgage is represented by the image of blood flowing in the place of water through her father's lands.

S. was the first South African English writer to focus on the Afrikaner rural proletariat. The sympathetic attitude taken in *The Little Karoo*, which constituted a significant revision of the predominant British anti-

Boer attitude, is balanced by a depreciation of patriarchy: men, victims of drought, poverty, and encroaching industrialism, in turn victimize their dependents. In *The Beadle,* however, S. presents the community as feudal, in tones more nostalgic than corrective. While she provides a critique of the destructive tendencies that fester in this isolated, suspicious, and intensely religious community, her celebration of innocence, embodied both in the heroine and in the organic community, places the novel in the idyllic mode and softens her polemic.

While S.'s reputation will depend partly on the evaluation of her liberal perspective, her technical achievements secure her a prominent place in South African literature: she is distinguished particularly for her thematically significant blending of the rhythms of Afrikaans speech and Old Testament prose, her control of narrative distance, the use of structural features that recall the classic folktale, and the balance and limpidity of her prose. She will be remembered above all as South Africa's first successful regional writer, who depicted a community and a landscape in such a way that they appear at once familiar and strange.

FURTHER WORKS: *A. B. "... a minor marginal note"* (1933); *South African Journal, 1913–1914* (1983); *Stories, Diaries and Other Unpublished or Out-of-Print Work* (1983)

BIBLIOGRAPHY: Haresnape, G., *P. S.* (1969); Beeton, R., "P. S. and South African Literature in English," *UES,* 11, 1 (1973), 35–50; Ravenscroft, A., "P. S.," in Parker, K., ed., *The South African Novel in English* (1978), pp. 46–56; Christie, S., et al., *Perspectives on South African Fiction* (1980), pp. 57–69; Marquard, J., "P. S. and Her Beadle: Chosen or Fallen?" *English Academy Review* (1981), 16–25; Driver, D., ed., *P. S.* (1983); Gardiner, M., "Critical Responses and the Fiction of P. S.," *Theoria,* 60 (1983), 1–12

DOROTHY DRIVER

SUDANESE LITERATURE

The rise of the Mahdist state in the Sudan in the late 19th c. provided Sudanese writers, particularly poets, with new themes. The poetry of this period, mainly epic in form, primarily sought to glorify the Mahdī and his followers. Despite this new subject, the cliché-ridden traditional style of Arabic poetry prevailed, except for a few poems. The most prominent poets were 'Abd al-Ghanī al-Salawī (1822–?), al-Shaykh Husayn al-Zahrā' (1833–1894), and Muhammad 'Umar al-Banna (1848–1919).

Most prose writing of the period consisted of religious or linguistic treatises. The only exceptions were the manifestos and letters of the Mahdi himself.

Poetry

The most characteristic genre in Sudanese literature remains poetry. The major currents since the beginning of this century have been neoclassicism, romanticism, and realism. One should be cautioned, however, that these three terms do not have the same meanings as in European literature.

Important representatives of the neoclassical current were 'Abdallāh al-Banna (b. 1890) and 'Abdallāh 'Abd al-Rahmān (1891–1964), and especially Muhammad Sa'īd al-'Abbāssī (1880–1963). Their poetry is characterized by carefully chosen diction, clarity of style, and enchanting musicality. The poets of this period, following World War I, were influenced by the Egyptian poets who had forged a renascence in Arabic literature. Although many were later affected by the romanticism of the 1930s, others remained faithful to classical style. Among later writers, 'Abdallah al-Tayyib (b. 1921) is a good representative of the neoclassicists, who looked for models in Arabic poetry of the golden age. They rejected Western civilization and conceived of nationalism not as confined to the modern Sudan but as embracing the whole Arab and Muslim world. Their clinging to the classical style was in itself a rejection of Westernization.

Al-Amīn 'Alī Madanī (b. 1910) was the first to attack neoclassical poetry. Hamza Tambal (1893–1960) rejected all traditional verse and called for a new, "genuine" poetry. Along with Tambal, the most prominent romantic poets were Tījānī Yūsuf Bashīr (1910–1936), Idrīs Jammā'

(1922–1980), and Muhammad Ahmad Mahjūb (1910–1976). Both Tambal and Mahjūb insisted on the value of local color, then a new element. Some romantic poets were influenced by Arab poets living in America, such as Kahlil Gibran (Khalīl Jubrān, 1883–1931); others, by the English romantic poets Shelley, Keats, and Wordsworth. Unlike the neoclassicists, the romantics were receptive to Western influences in both form and content. Many of their works had a somewhat morbid tone.

With the shattering disillusionment of World War II, the romantic tide started to ebb, giving way to realistic expression. The forerunner of this trend was Husayn Mansūr (b. 1915), author of *Al-Shāti' al-sakhrī* (n.d.; the stony beach), a collection of poems. Muhammad al-Mahdī al-Majdhūb (b. 1919), author of the poetry collection *Nār al-Majādhīb* (1973; the fire of Majādhīb), and Ismā'īl Hasan (?–1982) are considered the best representatives of realism. These poets sometimes used free forms. Al-Majdhūb, however, wonderfully blended all three currents: neoclassicism, romanticism, and realism.

Poetry with a socialist purpose is an offshoot of the realistic trend. The major leftist poets are Salāh Ahmad Ibrāhīm (b. 1933), Tāj al-Hasan (b. 1929), Jaylī 'Abd al-Rahmān (b. 1930), and Muhyī al-dīn Fāris (b. 1936). Most outstanding is Salāh Ahmad Ibrāhīm, with his volumes *Ghābat al-Abanus* (1963; the wood of Abanus) and *Ghabdat al-Hababai* (1965; anger of Hababai). His style is subtle and sophisticated yet spontaneous, and his poetry is solidly intellectual and humane. These socialist poets tend to generalize from their personal experiences, to embrace people in similar situations. They also favor specifically African imagery and have introduced new vocabulary and narrative forms.

The Essay

At the turn of the century prose writing in the Sudan was a weak imitation of classical Arabic works. It was characterized by a flowery style that treated language as an object in itself. The first real newspaper, *Al-Hadara,* founded in 1919, became the training ground for Sudanese essayists and journalists. The influence of Egyptian and Syrian writers was particularly strong on journalists. The two major literary periodicals of the 1930s were *Al-Nahda* and *Al-Fajr.*

The most distinguished essayists of the 1930s were Muhammad Ahmad Mahjūb, Muhammad 'Ashrī al-Siddīq (1908–1972), and Mu'awiya Nūr (1919–1942). Mahjūb's style combines the clarity of classical Arabic with the fluency of the English language. He was influenced by British essayists in both approach and style, as was al-Siddīq. Nūr, however, emulated Egyptian writers (he lived most of his life in Egypt). The romanticism that dominated Sudanese literature during the 1930s appeared first in criticism and only later in poetry. Most essayistic writing of this period discussed social problems or literature, since political writings were forbidden under colonial rule.

Since independence in 1956, politics and the autonomy of Sudanese culture have become popular topics. A leading critic of pan-Arabist orientation is 'Abdallah al-Tayyib.

Fiction

Sudanese fiction first appeared in the journals *Al-Nahda* and *Al-Fajr*. The short story, born during the height of romanticism, had as its principal early theme the obstacles that stand between lovers in a closed society.

The foremost short-story writers are 'Uthmān 'Alī Nūr (b. 1923) and Mu'awiya Nūr. The stories of 'Uthmān 'Alī Nūr—collected in *Ghādat al-qarya* (1953; the village beauty), *Al-Bayt al-maskūn* (1955; the haunted house), and *Al-Hubb al-kabīr* (1958; the great love)—deal with social problems in the style of folktales. The simplicity of his technique made his stories widely popular.

Although Abū Bakr Khālid (1934–1976) evokes Sudanese customs and landscapes, he seems to direct his stories to readers in the Arab world in general rather than to a specifically Sudanese audience. Country life is a prominent subject in his stories, and his style is a mixture of classical Arabic and colloquial Sudanese, particularly so in dialogue. Often his stories end with a moral drawn from the events narrated.

Romanticism gradually gave way to the realism that dominated the literary scene in the 1950s and 1960s. The three leading writers of fiction in this mode are al-Tayyib Zarūq (b. 1935), Salāh Ahmad Ibrāhīm, and 'Alī al-Mak (b. 1937). Zarūq's two collections, *Hayāt saghīra* (1957; a small life) and *Al-Ard al-safrā'* (1961; the yellow land), are marked by simple, straightforward realism. Both Ibrāhīm and al-Mak, the coauthors of the short-story collection *Al-Būrjwaziyya al-saghīra* (1958; the petite bourgeoisie), are representative of Socialist Realism. They criticized the new bourgeois class that ruled after the British left.

The major literary figure, not belonging to any trend or school is al-Tayyib Sālih (b. 1929). The masterpiece of Sudanese fiction is his novel *Mawsim al-hijra ilā al-shimāl* (1966; *Season of Migration to the North*,

1969), whose main theme is the encounter of Afro-Arab and European cultures, an encounter represented by the behavior of the principal character, Muṣṭafā Sa'īd, who as a Sudanese is a mixture of Africa and Arabia. The African side appears in the color of his skin, his Arabism in his Islamic background. He both hates and respects European culture. This conflict results in a kind of split personality. Since neither complete integration in nor total rejection of European culture is possible or desirable, the question confronting him is what to take of it and what to leave—the dilemma, indeed, of all African Arab intellectuals who have to deal with European civilization. Although in Sālih's other novels and in his short stories he is at times rather provincial, his works are always rich in symbol and metaphor, and he has achieved an international reputation.

At present there is a host of young short-story writers and novelists; the short story in particular is experiencing a great vogue.

Sudanese literature in the 20th c. has had a development similar to that of other Arab countries, but it has its own distinctive features. The influence of both Egyptian and English writers has been especially strong. Although it was very imitative of both at the beginning of this century, it has now established itself as an independent literature. In all genres except the drama, which has not yet taken hold, much writing of high quality is being produced.

BIBLIOGRAPHY: Jayyusi, S. K., *Trends and Movements in Modern Arabic Poetry* (1977), Vol. II, pp. 452–64; Marchand, B., "Écrivains soudanais," *Maghreb-Machrek,* No. 76 (1977), 67–69; Ahmed, O. H., ed., Introduction to *Sixteen Sudanese Short Stories* (1981), pp. 1–5; Abdul-Hai, M., *Tradition and English and American Influences in Arabic Romantic Poetry* (1982), passim

IBRAHIM AL-HARDALLO

TANZANIAN LITERATURE

Until recently scholars erroneously regarded Tanzania—a nation born in 1964 of the union of Zanzibar and other islands with mainland Tanganyika, which had won independence from Great Britain in 1961—as the driest patch in a supposed East African literary desert.

Tanzania's "socialist" path, outlined by President Julius Nyerere in the Arusha Declaration of 1967, has drawn the world's attention to all spheres of Tanzania's life as a social laboratory. Its literature, and a body of scholarship that nurtures it, are conscious parts of the Tanzanian experiment. Since the Arusha Declaration the country has been developing a distinct national literature out of three preindependence currents: (1) traditional Swahili literature; (2) writing in the English language; (3) the oral literatures of over 120 linguistically distinct ethnic groups.

In Swahili

Swahili did not obtain the designation of the Tanzanian national language until 1966, yet the oldest continuous tradition of written literature in Africa is the Swahili epic poetry of the East African coast, dating back several hundred years. Extant pre-19th-c. examples deal mainly with Islamic religious themes in an esoteric language. Recent scholarship, much of it coming from the Institute of Kiswahili Research at the University of Dar es Salaam, has begun to demolish earlier assertions generated by European scholars, and is now showing that most likely Swahili literature has not all derived from and imitated Arabic culture. Its African basis is now being established and explored.

Among the writing that prepared the way for the emerging Tanzanian national literature in the Swahili language are a number of *tenzis* (roughly, "epics") chronicling resistance struggles against foreign occupiers. Around 1905 Hemed Abdallah (dates n.a.) wrote *Vita vya Wadachi kutamalaki mrima* (war between the Germans and the coastal people), describing the Abushiri war from a united African-Arab point of view. The Maji Maji war of resistance against German colonialism, led by Kinjeketile Ngwale from 1905 to 1907, was told from the vantage point of the valiant oppressed and from a national, nonethnic perspective in *Vita vya Maji Maji* (written c. 1912; the Maji Maji war) by Abdul Karim (dates n.a.).

Following suppression of the Maji Maji uprising, nationalist sentiment disappeared from poetry, and a vacuum of apathy was filled with religious and escapist verse until the rise of the nationalist movement in the late 1940s. This new flowering saw the emergence of East Africa's "Shakespeare," Shaaban Robert (q.v.). In 1934 he began writing Swahili verse in a conservative vein, but he soon adopted progressive nationalist themes.

In the epic tradition, other harbingers of a national poetry were Amri Abedi (c. 1906–1965), Saadan Kandoro (dates n.a.), and Akilimali (dates n.a.). A great boost was given to this cultural awakening in 1954 with the publication of Amri Abedi's *Sheria za kutunga mashairi na diwani ya Amri* (Amri's rules and advice for composing poetry), which for the first time put the rules of Swahili versification into print.

In the postindependence period the *tenzi* survives in Tanzania as a living, now national, tradition of commemoration. Recent examples are *Karume* (1966; Karume), a chronicle of the life and achievements of Karume, the leader of the Zanzibar revolution in 1964, by Z. H. Mohammed (dates n.a.); *Jamhuri ya Tanzania* (1968; the Republic of Tanzania) by R. Mwaruka (dates n.a.); and *Zinduko la ujamaa* (1972; the awakening of socialism) by Z. H. Lesso (dates n.a.).

Second in stature as a poet only to Shaaban Robert was Mathias E. Mnyampala (c. 1919–1969), who wrote an epic on the life of Christ, *Utenzi wa Injili* (c. 1960; epic of the Holy Gospel) and who revived another traditional form, the *ngonjera,* a kind of poetic debate. Answering President Nyerere's 1968 call for poets and writers to become propaganda mouthpieces for the Arusha Declaration's principles of "socialism," Mnyampala produced two volumes of *ngonjera* in the last year of his life.

While Mnyampala's example was lauded and his verse was of very high quality, it was composed in a style too arcane to catch on with a mass audience. Nevertheless, the Arusha Declaration has spawned many volumes of popular poetry.

The founder of a major new trend in Swahili poetry, Euphrase Kezilahabi (b. 1944), has broken not only with traditional themes but, more importantly, with traditional forms. His collection *Kichomi* (1974; heartburn) has inspired many other poets to abandon the ancient rigid conventions for composing Swahili verse and to explore the expressive capacities of free verse. The grip of the coastal tradition and its conventions broken, Swahili poetry in Tanzania is now a national poetry. Politics, and not religious moralizing, is the main theme. Unlike Swahili verse in other countries, in Tanzania it has become a force of social mobilization instead of maintaining the status quo. Poetry remains the most important literary genre. The "novels" of Shaaban Robert reflect this fact, for they are in conventional Swahili verse.

The first "modern" Swahili novel is James Mbotela's (dates n.a.) *Uhuru wa watumwa* (1934; freedom of the slaves). It praises the British for having "freed" African slaves from Arab chains. Having a very small audience until only very recently, Swahili prose literature in Tanzania before 1970 was primarily confined to simple stories of crime and passion.

The main focus of the more sophisticated contemporary Tanzanian Swahili prose writers is also social. Primarily themes are wars of liberation, village versus city life, and the building of socialism. Among the better known novels are F. Nkwera's (dates n.a.) *Mzishi wa Baba Ana Radhi* (1967; Baba Ana Radhi's undertaker), a utopian view of village life that resembles the Guinean novelist Camara Laye's (q.v.) seminal *The Dark Child;* J. M. Simbamwene's (dates n.a.) love-and-intrigue works *Mwisho wa mapenzi* (1971; the end of love) and *Kwa sababu ya pesa* (1972; because of money), the latter a condemnation of city life as the root of all evils; M. S. Abdulla's (dates n.a.) detective novels *Kisimi cha Giningi* (1968; Giningi's fountain [or, well]), *Siri ya sifuri* (1974; secret of zero), and *Duniani kuna watu* (1974; it takes all kinds), nonsocialist works in which the worthy propertied people are protected from the rabble by shrewd sleuths; E. A. Musiba's (dates n.a.) *Kufa na kupona* (1974; life and death), in which detective work supports the liberation struggle; C. K. Omari's (dates n.a.) *Mwenda kwao* (1976; return of the prodigal), the chronicle of the breakdown of a marriage between a Tanzanian and his American wife; J. K. Kiimbila's (dates n.a.) *Ubeberu utashindwa* (1971; imperialism will be vanquished), set in Mozambique; N. Balisidya's (dates n.a.) *Shida* (1975; hardship), a female *Bildungsroman* on the town-versus-country theme; and F. E. M. K. Senkoro's (dates n.a.) *Mzalendo* (1977; the patriot), a novelistic demonstration that the victory of the masses is inevitable. Two recent works frequently pointed to as establishing a new trend in which oppression of Africans by Africans is defeated by class struggle are *Nyota ya Rehema* (1976; Rehema's star) by M. S. Mohamed (dates n.a.) and *Asali chungu* (1977; bitter honey) by S. A. Mohamed (dates n.a.).

Tanzania's major novelist is Euphrase Kezilahabi. His best-known work is *Rosa mistika* (1971; mystic rose), about a girl's odyssey from purity to whoredom to death and a dialogue with God. Stigmatized by some compatriot critics as an existentialist because of his pessimistic tendencies and his emphasis on anxiety, loneliness, and absurdity, Kezilahabi has responded by gradually increased militancy. Critics are now discovering the subtlety of even his early works, seeing that his present preoccupations with the theme of corruption in the ruling class and of its gulling of the people with pseudorevolutionary posturing were latent from the outset of his career in fiction.

Activity in drama has not been significant in Tanzania. Only one playwright, Ebrahim Hussein (dates n.a.), has had international exposure, largely due to a translation into English of his *Kinjeketile* (1969; *Kinjeketile,* 1970), a powerful dramatization of inter-ethnic unity in the Maji Maji war. Tanzania's only other important dramatist is Penina Muhando (dates n.a.). Although unknown abroad, she has had greater domestic impact than Hussein because her concerns are closer to those of the masses. In her often controversial plays she has dealt with political themes and with the oppression of women.

As a way of disarming detractors of Swahili who said it could not be the vehicle of science and high culture, and who were opposed to its adoption as a national language, President Nyerere translated Shakespeare's *Merchant of Venice* and *Julius Caesar* into Swahili in the 1960s, thus assisting the meteoric rise of literature in Swahili to its stature as a national literature today, and cautiously asserting that some things in the former colonialist's culture might be of value in the formation of Tanzanian national culture.

In English

Tanzanian literature in English gives a distorted image of the country, but it too has taken on a distinct national flavor. It began with Martin Kayamba's (1891–1940) posthumously published *An African in Europe* (1948) and *African Problems* (1948), accounts of his travels to England beginning in 1931, and of his British-tutored notions of how to "civilize" Africa.

The brief period from independence in 1961 to the Arusha Declaration in 1967 saw English-language literary activity centered at the University of Dar es Salaam, with many works from this time being published in the literary magazine *Darlite* (1966–70). Most of this apprentice work stiffly aped British romantics. By 1970, soon after the Arusha Declaration, when *Umma* (masses) replaced *Darlite,* the rootless cosmopolitanism of "commonwealth" writing gave way to distinctly national, socially committed writing.

No major figures have yet emerged in English, and several who began in that language in *Darlite* and *Umma* have gone on to establish themselves in Swahili. It is only from novels in English, however, that a Western audience can gain any accurate insight into Tanzanian literature. Peter Palangyo's (dates n.a.) *Dying in the Sun* (1968) was first to appear; its main themes are generation conflict, alienation, and love. Gabriel Ruhumbika's (dates n.a.) *Village in Uhuru* (1969) focuses on difficulties in breaking tribal and regional identities in order to build a nation. Barnabas Katigula's (dates n.a.) *Groping in the Dark* (1974), an excellent novelette, grapples with individual problems understood as social problems from the nonrevolutionary, reformist point of view of *ujamaa* (socialism). Ismail Mbise's (dates n.a.) *Blood on Our Land* (1974) blends fiction with documentary more skillfully than Ruhumbika's novel. Although a gripping account of the events leading up to the expulsion of the Wameru people from their ancestral lands by the British in 1951, it fails in its attempt at allegorical evocation of the neocolonial situation of most of contemporary Africa, including Tanzania. W. E. Mkufya's (dates n.a.) *The Wicked Walk* (1977) is about the corruption of city-based bureaucrats in Dar es Salaam. It is the first fully urban Tanzanian novel in English, and in it an ideological convergence of the Tanzanian literatures in English and Swahili can definitely be seen.

Oral Traditions

Government policies have clearly given shape to trends that distinguish Tanzanian literature from those of its East African neighbors. Currently a tremendous amount of oral material from more than one hundred ethnic groups is being gathered under government sponsorship, and the results of this campaign will definitely further enrich the hybrid culture being forged.

Since about 1975 a serious group of critics based in Tanzania has been establishing a necessary, salutary, symbiotic relationship with the country's writers. The locally topical nature of the national literature is now being brought to maturity by aesthetic as well as ideological scrutiny, and soon translations will reveal to the world what a ripening, dynamic literature has developed in a very short time.

BIBLIOGRAPHY: Mulokozi, M., "Revolution and Reaction in Swahili Poetry," *Umma*, 4 (1974), 118–38; Knappert, J., *Four Centuries of Swahili Verse: A Literary History and Anthology* (1979), pp. 264–310 and passim; Parker, C., "What Is Swahili Literature?: More Questions than Answers," *The Gar,* No. 33 (1979), 28; Arnold, S. H., "Popular Literature in Tanzania: Its Background and Relation to 'East African' Literature," in Parker, C., et al., eds., *When the Drumbeat Changes* (1981), pp. 88–118; Gérard, A. S., *African Language Literatures* (1981), pp. 93–153; Senkoro, F. E. M. K., "Ngombe Akivundika Guu...: Preliminary Remarks on the Proverb-Story in Written Swahili Literature," in Dorsey, D., et al., eds., *Design and Intent in African Literature* (1982), pp. 59–69; Arnold, S. H., "A History of Tanzanian Literature in English," in Gérard, A. S., ed., *History of African Literatures in European Languages* (1983), pp. 1877–1902

STEPHEN H. ARNOLD

ROBERT, Shaaban

Tanzanian poet, novelist, and essayist (writing in Swahili), b. 1 Jan. 1909, Vibambani; d. 20 June 1962, Tanga

Since his death from tuberculosis a year after Tanganyika gained its independence from Great Britain, R. has become known as the "Shakespeare of East Africa." He had only four years of formal education (during the colonial era a Muslim child was not allowed to go beyond grade five unless he converted to Christianity). R. worked as a minor government clerk, never learning more than a smattering of English, and devoted himself to the twofold task of rescuing Swahili literature from the decline colonialism had brought to it and of developing the potential of the Swahili language as a unifier and lingua franca of a vast African population by bringing modern ideas and popular language into a formerly esoteric, elitist written literature.

In 1934 R. began writing Swahili verse in a conservative vein, but his third-class position beneath Europeans and Asians brought him rapidly around to progressive writing, often on nationalist themes. In order to promote his own work, he started a publishing house in Tanga. It failed, and most of his works were not published until after his death, since the British would tolerate no criticism, even in abstruse fairy tales.

R. was more than the first national poet in Swahili; in his works he looked beyond the borders of his country to the rest of Africa and the world, anticipating in his ethical vision of work as a source of salvation and in his antipathy to money some of the basic principles of the 1967 "Arusha Declaration," in which Tanzania's aspirations for "socialism," were outlined. His *Utenzi wa vita vya uhuru, 1939 hata 1945* (1967; the epic of the war for freedom, 1939–1945), a global epic about World War II, shows how vast a change in scope he brought to a literature previously preoccupied with local and metaphysical issues. He even introduced the "insha" (essay) form into Swahili. However, he also continued the nonreligious tradition of Swahili verse in homiletic poems such as "Adili" (c. 1947; good conduct), a didactic poem for his son on the value of hard work, good manners, obedience to parents, God, government, and so forth, and in "Hati" (c. 1947; document), a similar poem for his daughter that enumerates the virtues she should embody.

R.'s most enduring works will probably be his anticolonial verse novels like *Kufikirika* (1946; Kufikirika), *Kusadikika* (1951; Kusadikika)—both are names of imaginary countries—and *Utubora mkulima* (1968; Utubora the farmer), and his utopian works such as the verse novel *Siku ya watenzi wote* (1968; the day of all workers), which looks beyond independence to an ideal state whose description often resembles the programmatic dreams of Tanzania's President Julius Nyerere.

R.'s love for his nonethnic language is largely responsible for Swahili's status as his country's national language today.

FURTHER WORKS: *Adili na nduguguze* (1952); *Marudi mema* (1952); *Tenzi za marudi mema, na Omar Khayyam* (1952); *Kielezo cha insha* (1954); *Insha na mashairi* (1959); *Diwani ya Shaaban* (14 vols. to date, 1959 ff.); *Koja la lugha* (1969); *Pambo la lugha* (1969)

BIBLIOGRAPHY: Allen, J., "The Complete Works of the Late S. R., MBE," *Kiswahili*, 33, 2 (1963), 128–42; Mgeni, A., "Recipe for a Utopia," *Kiswahili*, 41, 2 (1971), 91–94; Mulokozi, M., "Two Utopias: A Comparative Examination of William Morris' *News from Nowhere* and S. R.'s *Siku ya watenzi wote*," *Umma*, 5, 2 (1975), 134–58; Arnold, R., *Afrikanische Literatur und nationale Befreiung: Menschbild und Gesellschaftskonzeption im Prosawerk S. R.s* (1977); Knappert, J., *Four Centuries of Swahili Verse* (1979), pp. 266–75; Senkoro, F. E. M. K., "Ngombe Akivundika Guu...: Preliminary Remarks on the Proverb-Story in Written Swahili Literature," in Dorsey, D., et al., eds., *Design and Intent in African Literature* (1982), pp. 59–69

STEPHEN H. ARNOLD

TOGOLESE LITERATURE

The German colony of Togoland was occupied by Britain and France at the beginning of World War I, and was divided between the two countries by the League of Nations after the war. What became British Togoland—the western part—was administered by the Gold Coast (now Ghana) and merged with it in 1956. French Togo, the larger and poorer eastern area, became the independent republic of Togo in 1960.

During their thirty-year stay, the Germans had done intensive linguistic research and encouraged the Togolese to write and study their own languages. It was therefore not surprising that a western Togolese, Kwasi Fiawoo (1891–1969), became the first West African to write and publish a play in an African language, Ewe: *Toko atolia* (1937; *The Fifth Landing Stage*, 1943). This was the first of a long series of dramatic and novelistic works in Ewe, a noteworthy example being Sam Obianim's (b. 1920) novel *Amegbetoa: alo, Agbezuge fe nutinya* (1949; humanity; or, the struggles of Agbezuge).

Writing and publishing in Ewe was rather widespread in British Togoland and continues today in Ghana. In French Togo, where the colonial language was encouraged, it took several decades for a French-speaking intelligentsia to emerge. The rise of Togolese nationalism after World War II led to the development of an active press, which, thanks to the United Nations trusteeship, was kept alive and fighting against French colonialism. The first Togolese novel written in French was not, however, an anticolonial tract but a Church-inspired ethnographic novel, *Le fils du fétiche* (1955; the son of the fetish), by a schoolteacher, David Ananou (b. 1917).

After independence, Editogo, the national publishing house, issued its first novel, *Les secrets d'Éléonore* (1963; Éléonore's secrets), by Benin-born Félix Couchoro (1900–1968). The only daily newspaper, *Togo-Presse*, published serially nineteen novels by Couchoro. A tradition of journalistic novelettes was born; Victor Aladji's (b. 1941) *L'équilibriste* (1972; the tightrope walker) is typical of the genre.

Poetry in French is mainly written by students and schoolteachers and very seldom finds its way into print; an interesting and fairly representative selection has been made by Yves-Emmanuel Dogbe (b. 1939), himself a poet, in *Anthologie de la poésie togolaise* (1980; anthology of Togolese poetry).

Dramatic writing in Ewe, especially religious plays and musical comedies (called *kantatas*) influenced playwriting in French. Senouvo Nestor Zinsou's (b. 1946) *On joue la comédie* (1972; let's act) is certainly one of the most brilliantly written plays to have come out of French-speaking Africa. It has also been very successful on the stage.

BIBLIOGRAPHY: Amegbleame, S. A., *Le livre ewe: Essai de bibliographie* (1975); Baratte-Eno Belinga, T., et al., *Bibliographie des auteurs africains de langue française,* 4th ed. (1979), pp. 164–68; Amegbleame, S. A., "La fiction narrative dans la production littérature ewe: La nouvelle et le roman," *AfricaL,* 50 (1980), 24–36

ALAIN RICARD

UGANDAN LITERATURE

The republic of Uganda resulted from the unification by the British of several nations speaking different languages. The most powerful of these was the kingdom of Buganda, whose language was given written form in the 1880s; the Ganda Bible (1896) was soon followed by the first books of native authorship; these were the work of the kingdom's *katikiro* (prime minister), Apolo (later Sir Apolo) Kagwa (1865–1927), and of his secretary, Ham Mukasa (1871–1956); they dealt with the history of the Ganda kings and the customs of the Ganda people, as did the memoirs that the *kabaka* (king) himself, Sir Daudi Chwa (1897–1939), published between the two world wars.

Although vernacular imaginative writing received some encouragement through the International African Institute competitions, it did not get a real start until the foundation of the East African Literature Bureau soon after World War II. Much of the Bureau's publications consisted of prose fiction designed for juvenile readers, such as *Muddu awulira* (1953; the obedient servant) by Michael Bazze Nsimbi (b. 1910). During the ensuing years creative writing in Ganda gradually diversified with such novels as *Zinunula omunaka* (1954; they buy a poor man) by Edward E. N. Kawere (dates n.a.) and the poetry of *Ennyimba ezimu* (1958; some songs) by Y. B. Lubambula (dates n.a.). By the time independence came in 1962, the foundations had thus been laid for a written art in Ganda.

The East African Literature Bureau was also concerned with literacy in other languages, especially Luo (which is also spoken in Kenya). The first literary publication in Luo was a novel in the Acholi dialect, *Lak tar miyo kinyero wi lobo* (1953; are your teeth white? then laugh) by Okot p'Bitek (q.v.), whose next work, a long satirical poem, was to become famous in English as *Song of Lawino: A Lament* (1966) before the vernacular original, *War pa Lawino* (1968), could reach print. Several other Luo writers were prompted to use English, although J. P. Ocitti (dates n.a.) continued to write fiction in Luo, publishing *Lacan ma kwo pe kinyero* (1960; every dog has its day), a collection of tales, and other works.

One admittedly minor aspect of Uganda's first prime minister Milton Obote's determination to abolish Ganda supremacy was the spreading of literacy in yet other Ugandan languages. Even as early as 1955, the East

African Literature Bureau had published an account of traditional history in Runyankore, *Abagabe b'Ankole* (the kings of Ankole), by A. G. Katate (dates n.a.) and L. Kamugungunu (dates n.a.). After independence Timothy B. Bazarrabusa (1912–1966) inaugurated modern fiction in Nyoro-Toro with *Ha munwa gw'ekituuro* (1963; the point of death), and E. J. Lyavala-Lwanga (dates n.a.) produced the first collection of folk stories in Soga, *Endheso dh'Abasoga* (1967; tales of the Basoga).

While such developments took place throughout British Africa, it is Uganda's peculiar distinction that it was where East African creative writing in English originated in the late 1950s. This development was due in part to the role played by David Cook of the English department of Makerere College, an interterritorial institution set up near Kampala in 1939 to serve the whole of British East Africa. The magazine *Penpoint* (founded 1958) was the launching pad for a number of budding writers, the majority of whom, admittedly, were Kenyans. At the Kampala conference of 1962 Anglophone writers from West and South Africa gave further encouragement to their young East African colleagues, and an anthology of *Penpoint* contributions, *Origin East Africa,* edited by David Cook, was published in 1965.

Ugandan creative writing in English began in earnest in the mid-1960s with *Kalasanda* (1965) and *Kalasanda Revisited* (1966), rather conventional tales of peaceful Ganda village life by Barbara Kimenye (b. 1939), and with Okot p'Bitek's *Song of Lawino*. The latter's immediate success encouraged several younger writers to experiment with loose forms mixing narrative and soliloquy, prose and verse. Okello Oculi (b. 1942) described his blank-verse story "Orphan" (1968) as a "village opera"; in his novel *Prostitute* (1968) the narrative is interspersed with verse passages. *The Abandoned Hut* (1969) by Joseph Buruga (b. 1942) is a long poem denouncing the erosion of African values under Western influence. As for p'Bitek himself, after his initial plea for tradition, he somewhat hastily and feebly tried to show the other side of the coin in *Song of Ocol* (1970); but his *Two Songs* (1971) demonstrated the flexibility of a genre whose plain diction had proved capable of the most subtle irony: the desultory ribaldry of "Song of Malaya" is balanced by the committed concern of "Song of Prisoner," a poem inspired by the assassination of Tom Mboya.

Other writers, however, found the Western-type novel a more appropriate medium for the literature of a modern country. In *Return to the Shadows* (1969) Robert Serumaga (b. 1939) prophetically sets the story in a nation ridden by military coups; his play *The Elephants* (1971) deals with the predicament of an intellectual in a world of political violence. *The Experience* (1970) by Eneriko Seruma (pseud. of Henry Kimbugwe, b. 1944) provides a bitter image of the confusion and alienation of the Westernized African.

As a result of Idi Amin Dada's coup in 1971, the 1970s were particularly marked by the growth of a Ugandan literature in exile. A majority of writers found it advisable to leave their country for less lethal parts of the world, especially Kenya, where most Ugandan works were henceforth published. Although this situation contributed to restoring a sort of interterritorial mood among East African authors in Nairobi, Ugandan writing maintained its specific individuality.

While the poet Richard Ntiru (b. 1946) in *Tensions* (1971) rejected p'Bitek's example in favor of a more personal and more intellectual type of lyricism, nearer the examples of T. S. Eliot and W. B. Yeats, the novel remained the most popular genre, exploring a wide range of themes.

Arcadian vignettes of village life figure prominently in novels by Ganda authors writing in English, like *The Outcasts* (1971) by Bonnie Lubega (b. 1930) and *A Son of Kabira* (1972) by Davis Sebukima (b. 1943), as well as in the fiction of non-Ganda novelists, such as Tumusiime-Rushedge's (dates n.a.) *The Bull's Horn* (1972), and *Pulse of the Woods* (1974) and other early works by Uganda's most prolific popular writer, Godfrey Kalimugogo (dates n.a.).

There is a stark contrast between these and the many novels that, in Uganda as in most successor states of British Africa, focus on the theme of political violence. This obsessive trend, initiated by Robert Serumaga and emphasized in his play *Majangwa* (1972), was taken up by John Ruganda (b. 1941) in the play *The Burdens* (1972) and by Davis Sebukima in the darkly satirical novel *The Half Brothers* (1970).

Race relations—a major subject in a polyethnic country with a tradition of tribal rivalries and an economically important Asian (Indian) minority, and especially in the literary circles, where European expatriates used to be very visible—had been first explored in Eneriko Seruma's *The Experience*. His stories, collected in *The Heart Seller* (1971), concentrate on their sexual implications, as does *The People's Bachelor* (1971) by Austin S. Bukenya (b. 1944). Interracial sex is also central to a number of novels and plays by such Ugandans of Asian origin as Bahadur Tejani (dates n.a.) in *Days after Tomorrow* (1971) and Laban Erapu (b. 1955) and Jagjit Singh (b. 1949) in their popular radio plays. More prominence is given to the political problems that national independence raises for Asians in an important novel, *In a Brown Mantle* (1972), by Peter Nazareth (b. 1940), a well-known creative writer and critic of Goan origin. By the mid-1970s greater explicitness in sexual matters and the example of Kenyan writers had given rise to a popular literature with an undisguised pornographic bent, as represented by *The Sobbing Sounds* (1975) by an as yet unidentified English-language Ganda writer who signs himself Omunjakko Nakibimbiri.

Along with Okot p'Bitek, who died in 1982, the most impressive writer Uganda has produced so far is Taban lo Liyong (b. 1938), whose family had migrated from the Sudan. By the late 1970s, when he left Uganda to acquire Sudanese citizenship and teach in Juba, he had published about a dozen books—essays and short-story collections, poetry, and recordings of oral art—including *The Last Word* (1969), a collection of essays; *Ballads of Underdevelopment* (1976); and *The Popular Culture of East Africa* (1979). Contrary to his fellow Acholi p'Bitek, and despite the eccentricity built into his outlook and literary style, Taban lo Liyong is all in favor of modernization. In his anger and bitterness at the ruptured condition of black Africa after two decades of independence, he proclaimed his conviction that "what we can write legitimately are fragments.... Never a story. Nor a tragedy."

As the 1970s came to a close with the collapse of the Idi Amin regime, there was some hope that Uganda might heal its wounds and once more offer its writers the shelter and the congenial atmosphere of a peaceful home. Continued disorder, however, has prevented such expectations from materializing during the ensuing years.

BIBLIOGRAPHY: Roscoe, A., *Uhuru's Fire: African Literature East and South* (1977), pp. 32–87, 107–34, 260–65; Horn, A., "Uhuru to Amin: The Golden Decade of Theatre in Uganda," *LHY,* 19, 1 (1978), 22–49; Gérard, A. S., *African Language Literatures* (1981), pp. 299–307

ALBERT S. GÉRARD

P'BITEK, Okot

Ugandan poet, anthropologist, and social critic (writing in English and Luo), b. 1931, Gulu; d. 20 July 1982, Kampala

Bursting onto the literary scene in the mid-1960s, p'B. drew to East Africa the attention and acclaim for literature in English that West Africa had long enjoyed. It was a fitting effect, for p'B. had all his life displayed an "unabashed commitment" to his native culture and to African standards and values.

Under the influence of his mother, a gifted singer and composer and a leader in her clan, p'B. early absorbed the rich songs, proverbs, and customs of the Luo people. He was also exposed to missionary training early, and after completing his secondary education in Gulu, attended King's College, Budo. He went abroad as a member of the Uganda national soccer team, and stayed in Britain to take a diploma in education in Bristol, a degree in law at Aberystwyth, and a further degree in social anthropology at Oxford. He returned home as lecturer at University College in Makerere, founded the Festival of African Arts in Gulu, and went on to serve as director of the National Cultural Center in Kampala. As a result of trenchant criticisms he uttered in Zambia, he made himself persona non grata to the Uganda government then in power and elected to move to Kenya. In 1971 he took up the post of senior research fellow at the Institute of African Studies in Nairobi.

As an administrator, p'B. showed an intense practical involvement in the sociocultural life of East Africa, shifting the emphasis in song, dance, theater, and art from the dominant British to the basic African style. He also emerged as an important champion of African values, in a somewhat polemical mode. He corrected long-standing misapprehensions and created an enhanced view of African culture in such works as *African Religions and Western Scholarship* (1970), *Religion of the Central Luo* (1971), *Africa's Cultural Revolution* (1973), and the critical anthology of poetry and prose, *The Horn of My Love* (1974).

By his own testimony p'B. was less concerned with fixed "ontological definitions" than with "dynamic function," and he was at his most arresting and incisive in creative embodiments and complex dramatizations of the culture-conscious East African scene. His youthful novel in the Acholi dialect of Luo, *Lak tar miyo kinyero wi lobo* (1953; are your teeth white? then laugh), has perhaps been put into the shade by the rich suites of Songs: *Song of Lawino: A Lament* (1966), *Song of Ocol* (1970), *Song of (a) Prisoner* (1971), and *Two Songs: Song of Prisoner; Song of Malaya* (1971), which reprints the earlier title along with the new song. The first of these was composed in Acholi, and p'B. himself made the English translation that brought him international fame.

That fame was not untouched by controversy. British observers have felt that the Songs convey animosity toward their ways and influence, while African observers have contended that African personalities and ways are exposed to satirical barbs. Access to the poems is simplified as soon as we realize they are dramatic monologues, that is, emotionally and intellectually partial utterances by characters who have silent interlocutors and who are in situations more complex than the characters directly apprehend. The reader must look through their eyes, but also into their minds—between the lines of overt statement—for the full values of the poems.

It helps further to recognize two facts: (1) that the acute social anthropologist in p'B. is not stifled in the poetry, for the main characters are really representative figures, distillations of major features of African experience in the aspiring and dislocating postindependence world; and (2) that the characters operate poetically in a kind of allegory of naïveté, where all impressions are curiously pursued by a mind too sensitive to withstand them and too fresh to organize them in a stable system.

The four Songs constitute veritable compass points of African experience. *Song of Lawino* is the plangent, minutely detailed utterance of resentment and grief by a traditional wife abandoned by her newfangled husband for a modernized woman and the new urban prosperity. *Song of Ocol* is the husband's overemphatic counterstatement, the last lines revealing his true character, one of selfish weakness and hidden anguish. *Song of a Prisoner* shows, in what appears to be a composite character, the ugly machinations and specious hopes of the new politics. And *Song of Malaya* sets forth the alternately harsh and tender world view of the new woman of pleasure in the new African town *(malaya* means "prostitute").

Song of Lawino and *Song of a Prisoner* are poems of defense; *Song of Ocol* and *Song of Malaya* are poems of attack. All are poems of seething desperation, representing points of transition and crisis not only for the individuals speaking but also for their very culture. If we want to know what p'B. thought, we may turn to his polemical anthropological writing. But if we want to know what he apprehended and what he aspired to, then we must turn to the poetry.

BIBLIOGRAPHY: Lo Liyong, T., *The Last Word* (1969), pp. 135–56; Blishen, E., Introduction to *Song of Prisoner* (1971), pp. 1–40; Cooke, M., on *Song of a Prisoner, Parnassus,* 1, 2 (1973), 115, 117–19; Heron, G., *The Poetry of O. p'B.* (1976); Asein, S. O., "O. p'B.: Literature and the Cultural Revolution in East Africa," *WLWE,* 16 (1977), 7–24; Heron, G., "O. p'B. and the Elite in African Writing," *LHY,* 19, 1 (1978), 66–93; Moore, G., *Twelve African Writers* (1980), pp. 170–90; Heywood,

A., "Modes of Freedom: The Songs of O. p'B.," *JCL,* 15, 1 (1980), 65–83

MICHAEL G. COOKE

UPPER VOLTA LITERATURE

The West African country of Upper Volta had an intermittent separate identity during French colonial rule; it was, however, partitioned between the Ivory Coast and Mali (French Sudan) from 1932 to 1947. After independence, in 1960, a civilian regime lasted six years until the military came into power to stay, but not to impose any kind of censorship. Political and cultural life in Upper Volta has been remarkably active.

Nazi Boni (1912–1969), a former deputy in the French parliament, wrote the first Upper Volta novel, *Crépuscule des temps anciens* (1962; twilight of the old times). It deals with three centuries of the old Bwamu empire, which lasted until the French conquest and is still revered in present-day Upper Volta. This chronicle-novel was written in a colorful and expressive style that surprised many Francophone purists. Another important Upper Volta novel is *Les dieux délinquants* (1974; delinquent gods) by the well-known journalist Augustin Sondé Coulibaly (b. 1933). It deals with the attempt and failure of Titenga, a mythical detribalized hero, to re-create idealized communal living with an urban context.

Storytelling on the radio has been a very popular form of expression during the last two decades. Several volumes based on the radio broadcasts of Tiendrebeogo Yamba (b. 1907), a tribal chief, have been published in Upper Volta's capital, Ouagadougou: *Contes du Larhalle* (1963; tales from the Larhalle) and *O Mogo: Terre d'Afrique* (1976; oh, Mogo: land of Africa).

Economic circumstances in Upper Volta have led people in recent decades to look for work in the Ivory Coast; this experience is the background of Kollin Noaga's (b. 1944) novels about the social and emotional consequences of emigration, such as *Dawa à Abidjan* (1975; Dawa in Abidjan).

A very active sociopolitical life has been congenial to the development of the drama, especially among students; hundreds of schools perform plays. Pierre Dabire's (b. 1935) *Sansoa* (1970; Sansoa) is representative; it vividly portrays forced labor, reminding audiences of the hardships of colonial times, when Upper Volta was a large purveyor of manpower.

Upper Volta has also produced one of Africa's foremost historians, Professor Joseph Ki-Zerbo (b. 1922), editor of UNESCO's *Histoire de l'Afrique* (1970; history of Africa).

BIBLIOGRAPHY: Baratte-Eno Belinga, T., et al., *Bibliographie des auteurs africains de langue française,* 4th ed. (1970), pp. 103–6

ALAIN RICARD

ZAIRIAN LITERATURE

The region along the estuary of the Zaire River was probably the first part of sub-Saharan Africa where there was writing in a European language: as early as the 16th c. the rulers of the Kongo kingdom exchanged written messages in Portuguese with royalty and officials in Lisbon. The whole area thereafter became a happy hunting ground for the slave trade and for the supply of cheap manpower to overseas plantations. When the Congo became the personal empire of Leopold II, King of the Belgians, in 1885, African muscle was used locally, for feeding the ivory and rubber trades. Although these circumstances were not conducive to a high level of education, Protestant missionaries managed to establish a few stations and schools where the Kikongo language was used in writing for the propagation of Scripture. The need for reading material led to the translation of Bunyan's *The Pilgrim's Progress* in 1912; converts were encouraged to help in the translation and in the composition of the four hundred hymns that were printed in *Minkunga miayenge* (1887; songs of peace).

For several decades, Kikongo literature consisted mostly of Protestant hymns. A new trend emerged after World War I, when the disciples of the syncretic religious leader Simon Kimbangu (1889–1951) started composing hymns reflecting their own creed. During the 1930s a Swedish missionary, John Patterson (dates n.a.), produced a didactic novel in the language, *Nsamu a Mpanzu* (3 vols., 1935–38; the life of Mpanzu), and his example was followed by the first genuine Kongo novelists: Émile Disengomoka (1915–1965) with *Kwenkwenda* (c. 1943; Kwenkwenda), and Jacques N. Bahele (b. 1911) with *Kinzonzi ye ntekelo andi Makundu* (1948; Kinzoni and his grandson Makundu). These two main trends—hymn writing and edifying prose fiction—remained dominant in Kikongo literature in the writing of André Massaki (b. 1923) and Noé Diawaky (b. 1932), even though the Protestant clergyman Homère-Antoine Wantwadi's (b. 1921) novel *Niklisto mu Kongo dia kimpwanza* (1965; the Christian in independent Congo) contained a belated indictment of colonial rule, and Fikiau Kia Bunseki (b. 1934) devoted most of his attention to the traditional, pre-Christian Kongo world view, especially in the poems collected in *Dingo-dingo* (1966; life cycle).

The other main vernaculars of Zaire have not been used for written art, and it was not until World War II that writing in French began to emerge in the country. The tardiness was due to several factors: once Leopold II had bequeathed his empire to his country as its only African colony, the school system that was created was entrusted to Catholic missionaries; its purpose was to spread a minimal degree of literacy so as to provide inexpensive but comparatively competent help to the colonizer: primary-school teachers, junior clerks, medical assistants, and the like. Only by studying for the priesthood was it possible for a Congolese to acquire a modicum of higher education. No African in the Belgian Congo was in a position to enter a university.

It was only in the aftermath of World War II that a process of liberalization was initiated. *La voix du Congolais,* a magazine launched in 1945, offered educated Congolese an opportunity for airing some of their views under the colonial administration's sponsorship and paternalistic control; its editor, Antoine-Roger Bolamba (b. 1913), later gained some repute with *Esanzo: Chants pour mon pays* (1955; esanzo [a musical instrument]: songs for my country), the first Zairian literary work to be printed in Paris. Paul Lomami-Tshibamba (b. 1914) won a Belgian literary prize for his novel *Ngando* (1948; the crocodile), which was subsequently published in Brussels. In the mid-1950s two universities were established, and scholarships became available for study abroad. At long last a favorable climate was created, which prepared for the growth of creative writing in French after independence (1960).

During the chaotic years that followed independence a number of poetry clubs such as the Pléiade du Congo (1964–66) were formed by young intellectuals headed by Clémentine Nzuji (b. 1944), who is also well known for her linguistic and folkloric research. Their work was printed locally, as was *Somme première* (1968; first sum), a poetry collection by Philippe Masegabio (b. 1944). Other talented poets of this generation are Matala Mukadi Tshiakatumba (b. 1942); the very prolific Elebe Lisembe (b. 1937), also a playwright; and Dr. Mukala Kadima-Nzuji (b. 1947), who is also a critic and a historian of Zairian literature.

Although there is intense theatrical activity in Zaire, few plays have actually reached print. It can be said that the founders of literary drama were Mobyem M. K. Mikanza (b. 1944), whose *La bataille de Kamanyola* (1975; the battle of Kamanyola) celebrates the Mobutu regime, and P. Ngandu Nkashama (b. 1946), whose *La délivrance d'Ilunga* (1977; the freeing of Ilunga) extols the values of freedom.

An analogous split characterizes the Zairian novel. On the one hand, several writers, led by Zamenga Batukezanga (b. 1933), comply with the demands of "Zairian concretism," a phrase coined in 1972 by the poet

Tito Yisuku Gafudzi (b. 1941) to denote a realistic, down-to-earth portrayal of present-day Zairian society. On the other hand, although this kind of realism is by far the most popular trend among local readers, the best novelist to have emerged in the country is V. Y. Mudimbe (b. 1941), whose *Entre les eaux* (1973; between the waters), *Le bel immonde* (1976; the handsome filthy one), and *L'écart* (1979; the gap) concentrate on the psychological and ethical problems deriving from the extraordinary outburst of despotism and corruption that has afflicted many newly independent African states.

As the 1970s came to a close, the literary output of Zaire was by no means negligible. It is different from that of other French-speaking countries in notable ways. For one thing, the influence of the Catholic missionaries resulted in an exceptionally intense preoccupation with the role of religion and the Church in the new Zairian society. More specifically, since Zaire had never been under French rule, its writers did not benefit from the "French connection": they seldom write with an eye on Paris publishers and the French audience. The country is practically compelled to self-reliance in publishing and can therefore boast a large number of local publishing houses. Its authors display great "authenticity" in many ways. A prominent example is Mbwila Mpaang Ngal (b. 1933): in the essayistic novels *Giambattista Viko; ou, Le viol du discours africain* (1975; Giambattista Vico; or, the rape of the African discourse) and *L'errance* (1979; wandering) he condemns Westernized writers who degrade traditional beliefs and customs into exotic attractions for European readers, and he tries to devise some sort of adaptation of the novel as a genre to specific features of the oral narrative tradition.

BIBLIOGRAPHY: Jadot, J.-M., *Les écrivains africains du Congo belge et du Ruanda Urundi* (1959); Mbelo ya Mpiku, "Introduction à la littérature kikongo," *RAL*, 3, 2 (1972), 117–61; Bujitto, K., *Pour mieux comprendre la littérature au Zaïre* (1975); Ntamunoza, M. M., "Quelques aspects de la poésie zaïroise moderne," *WAJML*, 2 (1976), 75–86; Kadima-Nzuji, M., "Approche de la littérature de langue française au Zaïre," *Afrique contemporaine*, 91 (1977), 13–18; Kadima-Nzuji, M., "Avant-propos pour une lecture plurielle de la poésie zaïroise," *PA*, 104 (1977), 86–93; Ngandu Nkashama, P., "Problématique de la littérature zaïroise," *PFr*, 17 (1978), 79–88; Gérard, A. S., *African Language Literatures* (1981), pp. 291–93; special Zaire issue, *Notre librairie*, No. 63 (1982)

ALBERT S. GÉRARD

ZAMBIAN LITERATURE

Zambia gained independence in 1964, when (as Northern Rhodesia) it broke off from the ill-conceived federation with Southern Rhodesia and Nyasaland to become a sovereign state. Its two largest groups are the Lozi and the Bemba, but Zambia has an extensive history of publication in many other local languages, in addition to English.

During the 1950s vigorous efforts by the Northern Rhodesia and Nyasaland Publications Bureau, with the assistance of major British publishers, gave the opportunity for several African writers to achieve publication in the vernaculars, although most of the titles are school readers of under a hundred pages that scarcely establish the basis for a national literature. Noteworthy writers of this period are Stephen Mpashi (b. 1920), who wrote in Bemba numerous novelettes and short stories and a distinguished novel, *Uwakwensho bushiku* (1955; he who leads you through the night), and M. M. Sakubita (b. 1930), a Lozi whose best-known work is *Liswanelo za luna kwa li lu siile* (1954; how not to treat animals), a long story. Books in the minority languages include M. C. Mainza's (b. c. 1930) tale *Kabuca uleta tunji* (1956; every day brings something new) in Tonga and Stephen Luwisha's (b. c. 1930) *Mukulilacoolwe* (1962; you have survived by luck) in Lenje. L. K. H. Goma (dates n.a.) writes in Tumbuka.

In 1965 English was made the language of instruction in schools. This emphasis led to the beginning of a contemporary Zambian literature, whose development was encouraged by NECZAM (the National Educational Company of Zambia), founded in 1967 to replace the old colonial Publications Bureau. It has published works in ten vernacular languages as well as in English.

Fwanyanga Mulikita (b. 1928) turned from Lozi to English to write the short stories later published in the collection *A Point of No Return* (1968), which present anecdotes of local life. His most ambitious work is a powerful poetic drama written in English, *Shaka Zulu* (1967), which celebrates the achievement of the great Zulu warrior in an epic chronicle. *The Tongue of the Dumb* (1971) by Dominic Mulaisho (b. 1933), on the familiar theme of the clash between old and new beliefs in a village, may be considered the first formal English-language novel from Zambia. The most widely read work, although it is more political than literary, is *Zambia Shall Be Free* (1962), the opinions of Kenneth Kaunda (b. 1924), who has been president since 1964.

The founding of the literary magazines *New Writing from Zambia* in 1964 and *Jewel of Africa* in 1968—the latter sponsored by the South African writer Ezekiel Mphahlele (q.v.)—gave further opportunities to younger authors.

Although no Zambian writer has yet achieved international stature, a number of recent novels published under the imprint of NECZAM indicate that literature is beginning to take a direction similar to that of other African countries. These novels focus on the urban scene, although city life is regarded with mixed emotions, as is suggested by the title of Grieve Sibale's (b. 1952) *Between Two Worlds* (1979). It tells of a man tempted by the prospects of wealth in the city, who meets with failure and returns in despair to his village, only to discover that he has lost his cherished and loving wife.

Storm Benjayamoyo (b. 1956) writes in *Sofiya* (1979) of divided cities, telling of "those who live in the shanty townships and those who live in the highrise flats and bungalows...of men in cars and men on foot." He shares the anger of other Africans who have written of the extravagant ways of the new elite. Political unrest is reflected in William Simukwasa's (b. 1948) novel *Coup* (1979), which is set in an unnamed black republic.

Zambia has particularly vigorous performing arts. The University of Zambia sponsors the Chikwakwa Theater, which shuns the formal stage and plays in the open air in remote villages. Masauto Phiri (b. c. 1945), in *Nightfall* (1970) and *Kuta* (1972), takes his themes from Ngoni history, which he depicts in dance dramas incorporating traditional music and dance. Godfrey Kasoma's (b. c. 1950) best-known work is *Black Mamba* (1973), an unpublished trilogy of radio plays depicting the rise to power of President Kaunda.

There are as yet no poets of distinction, but the poetry published in *New Writing from Zambia* may indicate the beginnings of a more notable production.

Zambia offers an unusually wide opportunity for local publication. It still remains to be seen how writers will respond to the advantages, as well as restrictions, this situation provides.

BIBLIOGRAPHY: Kunene, D. P., "African Vernacular Writing," *African Social Research,* 9 (1970), 639–59; Simpson, D., "Our Silent Voices," *Zambia Magazine,* No. 83 (1976), 16–19; Simoko, D., "Zambian Literature," *Zambia Magazine,* No. 84 (1976), 14–15; Roscoe, A. A., *Uhuru's Fire* (1977), pp. 269–70; Obuke, O. O., "Characterization in Zambian

Literature," *Busara,* 8, 2 (1976), 68–80; Kasoma, K., "Trends in African Theatre, with Special Emphasis to the Zambian Experience," *New Classic,* 5 (1978), 72–78; Gérard, A. S., *African Language Literature* (1981), pp. 226–32

JOHN POVEY

ZIMBABWEAN LITERATURE

In English

The literature in English that has come from Zimbabwe (formerly Rhodesia, earlier Southern Rhodesia) has until very recently consisted of two strongly committed streams—one celebrating, the other attacking the order of things established by European conquest. The first stream takes its rise in the personal memoirs, almost adventure stories of that conquest, like *Sunshine and Storm in Rhodesia* (1896) by Frederick Selous (1851–1917) and Robert Baden-Powell's (1857–1941) *The Matabele Campaign* (1897). It flows through the imperialist romances of Gertrude Page (1873–1922) and the strange novel *Rina* (1949) by Charles Bullock (1880–1952), in which racism appears as an austere chivalry, to the home-produced propaganda of the years of the Ian Smith regime.

The countercurrent begins early with the poetry and stories of Arthur Shearly Cripps (1969–1952), a missionary much taken by traditional Shona life, which he saw threatened by European influence. Doris Lessing presents a withering picture of white society in Salisbury before, during, and after World War II in four autobiographical novels—*Martha Quest* (1952), *A Proper Marriage* (1954), *A Ripple from the Storm* (1958), and *Landlocked* (1965)—although Africans play virtually no part. Her shorter fiction with a Rhodesian background is collected in *African Stories* (1964).

The critique of settlerdom began to be taken up by black writers. Stanlake Samkange (b. 1922) made use of white memoirs of the early period for *On Trial for My Country* (1966), in which the origins of Rhodesia are explored through a vision in which both Cecil Rhodes and the Matabele king Lobengula are put on trial in the afterworld. *The Mourned One* (1975) and *The Year of the Uprising* (1978) also make use of documents and historical memoirs. Ndabaningi Sithole (b. 1920) has written three novels: *Obed Mutesa* (1970) and *The Polygamist* (1972), both close to biography, and *Roots of a Revolution* (1977), close to a straight history of the political struggle for black-majority rule. Wilson Katiyo (b. 1947) has written two volumes that read like fictionalized autobiography: *A Son of the Soil* (1976) and *Going to Heaven* (1979).

During the 1970s there grew up side by side with these a new generation of black writers freed from the temptation or the need to use their work as a weapon in the struggle. Although effective black-majority government did not come until 1980, from the middle of the decade it was evident that the old white Rhodesian system could not be maintained unchanged. Somber realism had already overtaken protest in the stories of *Coming of the Dry Season* (1972) by Charles Mungoshi (b. 1948) and in his novel *Waiting for the Rain* (1975). S. Nyamfukudza (b. 1951) in *The Non-Believer's Journey* (1980) tells of people whose dedication to the cause is humanly unheroic and how they are caught up in the civil war. Dambudzo Marechera (b. 1955) dazzled critics and won the Guardian Fiction Prize in England with his book of stories *The House of Hunger* (1978). The same command of postmodernist techniques has won less approval for his novel *Black Sunlight* (1980), where the treatment of violence verges at times on self-indulgent fantasizing.

Much verse has always been published in the country, in poetry magazines and annual anthologies. In recent years black poets have contributed more and more. No really outstanding poetic talent is yet discernible, but the Mambo Press at Gwelo has published two good anthologies of African work, *Zimbabwean Poetry in English* (1978) and *And Now the Poets Speak* (1981).

BIBLIOGRAPHY: Chennells, A. J., "The Treatment of the Rhodesian War in Recent Rhodesian Novels," *Zambezia,* 5 (1977), 177–202; Pichanick, J., Chennells, A. J., and Rix, L. B., comps., *Rhodesian Literature in English: A Bibliography (1890–1974/75)* (1977); Muchemwa, K. Z., ed., Introduction to *Zimbabwean Poetry in English* (1978), pp. xii–xxv; Graham, R., "Poetry in Rhodesia," *Zambezia,* 6 (1978), 187–215; Kahari, G. P., *The Search for Zimbabwean Identity: An Introduction to the Black Zimbabwean Novel* (1980); McLoughlin, T. O., "Black Writing in English from Zimbabwe," in Killam, G. D., ed., *The Writing of East and Central Africa* (1983), pp. 100–119

JOHN REED

In Ndebele

Long before the Ndebele language was given a written form, European scholars were collecting and analyzing the oral literature. This traditional literary art served as a model for Ndebele writers, especially the early ones, in creating a modern fiction.

The first Ndebele novel was *AmaNdebele kaMzilikazi* (1956; the Ndebele of Mzilikazi) by Ndabaningi Sithole (b. 1920). He used a historical situation but made no pretenses about his political objectives; it was not surprising that the Ian Smith regime banned the novel in the 1960s. The historical novel *Umthwakazi* (1957; the owner of the state), by Peter S. Mahlangu (b. 1923), is on the surface an account of the Ndebeles, tracing their struggles from precolonial times up until their defeat by white settlers under Cecil Rhodes in the uprising of 1896–97. His true aim is to show the greatness of his people.

The period 1958–62 saw the emergence of works resembling European novels. The narration and characterization, however, were greatly influenced by traditional folktales. These novels are marked by a concern for social values in changing times. Isaac N. Mpofu (b. 1932), in *Akusoka lingenasici* (1958; no one is perfect) and *Wangithembisa lami* (1960; you also promised me), exposes human vanity and shows how modernization has brought out personality flaws.

Social themes were taken up by other writers, who yearned for the bygone days and condemned the new social order. This particular theme was pioneered by David Ndoda (b. 1925) in *Vusezindala* (1958; in days gone by), which was followed by Elkana M. Ndlovu's (b. 1913) *Inhlamvu zaseNgodlweni* (1959; the offspring of Ngodlweni). Ndoda's characterization was based on folktales, while Ndlovu's was inspired by modern Western models.

Although women played a leading role in narrating oral folktales, written creative work by women was slow to develop. A breakthrough came with Lassie Ndondo's (b. c. 1930) novel *Qaphela ingane* (1962; take care of the boy); the chief concern of the book is the proper upbringing of children. A similar theme had been used by Amos Mzilethi (b. 1914) in his *Uyokhula umfana* (1961; the boy grows up). The major weakness of such novels, and of most Ndebele fiction to date, is their didacticism; the reason for this is that publishers wanted novels with clear messages geared to young students, who formed the bulk of the readership.

The early 1970s saw an upsurge in novel writing. The themes were still social, dwelling on such issues as industrialization and its attendant problems, unemployment, squalor, and prostitution. Older writers tend to offer their criticism straightforwardly, for example, Sithembile O. Mlilo (b. 1924) in *Lifile* (1975; it has passed away) and *Bantu beHadlana* (1977; people of Hadlana). Younger writers, influenced by European literature, often find more subtle forms for these themes; examples are Ndabezinhle Sigogo's (b. 1932) *Akula zulu emhlabeni* (1971; there is no heaven on earth) and Barbara Makhalisa's (b. 1949) *Umendo* (1977; marriage).

Poetry and drama have lagged behind fiction. Several anthologies have been published, but no outstanding poet has emerged. The subjects have ranged from love, death, and nature to social and political problems. The styles and techniques have been based sometimes on English poetry, sometimes on traditional praise poetry, and sometimes on a combination of the two.

Only two plays have been written so far. *Indlalifa ngubani?* (1976; who is the heir?) by Ndabezinhle Sigogo is concerned with social problems related to traditional life, while *Umhlaba lo* (1977; what a world) by Barbara Makhalisa relates the plight of young women in the modern city. Both plays are constructed along the lines of realistic European drama, with Sigogo making use of traditional local humor.

BIBLIOGRAPHY: Krog, W., ed., *African Literature in Rhodesia* (1966), pp. 211–36; Gérard, A. S., *African Language Literatures* (1981), pp. 232–41

T. M. NDLOVU

In Shona

"Shona" is an artificial term used by scholars of African languages to refer to an agglomeration of mutually intelligible dialects found within and outside Zimbabwe. It was given various written forms by groups of missionaries active throughout Southern Rhodesia at the end of the 19th c. Missionary efforts to develop a written medium accelerated after the Southern Rhodesia Missionary Conference passed a resolution in 1928 asking the government to invite Professor Clement Doke to make a study of the languages. His *Report on the Unification of the Shona Dialects* (1931) initiated the "new" orthography, replacing the "old" which had been used in publishing the New Testament in 1919.

The Southern Rhodesia African Literature Bureau, established in 1953, sponsored the publication of imaginative works in the vernacular, and in 1956 Oxford University Press in Cape Town, South Africa, published *Feso (Feso,* 1974), an epic novel by Solomon M. Mutswairo (b. 1924). By 1982 ninety-four Shona novels had been published, using the standard orthography. They can be divided into two broad categories: those dealing with the precolonial period, and those set in the period after the arrival of the whites.

The precolonial novel—with fantastic and marvelous elements—is based on traditional Shona myths, legends, and folktales. An example is Patrick Chakaipa's (b. 1932) *Karikoga Gumiremiseve* (1958; Karikoga Gumiremiseve). The colonial novels, such as Aaron Moyo's (b. 1950) *Ziva kwawakabva* (1977; know where you came from), are concerned with the disintegration of traditional family life because of industrialization and Christianity. The colonial novel is often satirical and moralistic. For example, Patrick Chakaipa's *Garandichauya* (1963; wait, I will come) depicts the patience of a woman whose husband leaves her to go to the western city of Gatooma (Katoma); eventually he returns, blind, to his wife in the country. Typically, the novel contrasts industrial life unfavorably with the traditional way of life.

Herbert Chitepo's (1923–1975) *Soko risina musoro* (1958; a tale without a head), the first published Shona book in verse, is a long poem of epic proportions, whose hero searches for spiritual meaning in the midst of chaos. Eight anthologies of modern and traditional verse followed. The first devoted to traditional clan poetry was compiled by Aaron Hodza (b. 1924) and George Fortune (b. 1915): *Shona Praise Poetry* (1979), in Shona with English translations.

Modern verse, blending traditional and Western techniques, is, like modern fiction, highly moralistic. The themes include the erosion of traditional values and mores, their replacement by Western values, and the dominance of the capitalist economy over rustic life. Political themes, often disguised through metaphor and symbol, have also appeared in Shona poetry. The leading poets are Mordikai Hamutyinei (b. 1934), Joseph Kumbirai (b. 1922), Solomon Mutswairo (b. 1924), and Ignatius Zvarevashe (b. 1943).

The first Shona play, modeled on Western drama in form but not in content, was Paul Chidyausiku's (b. 1927) *Ndakambokuyambira* (1968; I warned you before). Based on a traditional theme, the play pokes fun at women for their inability to keep family secrets. About ten other Shona plays have appeared since 1968, but they were written not for the stage but for presentation in village arenas.

The new political climate established when black-majority rule was instituted on April 18, 1980, will in time undoubtedly bring a new tone to Shona literature.

BIBLIOGRAPHY: Krog, W., ed., *African Literature in Rhodesia* (1966); Kahari, G. P., "Missionary Influences in Shona Literature," in Bourdillon, M. F. C., ed., *Christianity South of the Zambezi*, Vol. II (1977), pp.

87–101; Hodza, A., and Fortune, G., *Shona Praise Poetry* (1979), pp. 1–116; Gérard, A. S., *African Language Literatures* (1981), pp. 232–41

GEORGE P. KAHARI

Index to Author Articles

Abrahams, Peter, 186–88
Achebe, Chinua, 126–29
Armah, Ayi Kwei, 68–69
Awoonor, Kofi, 70–72
Beti, Mongo, 28–30
Brutus, Dennis, 188–89
Camara Laye, 77–79
Campbell, Roy, 189–91
Clark, John Pepper, 129–30
Dadié, Bernard Binlin, 82–84
Dib, Mohammed, 7–8
Diop, Birago, 152–53
Ekwensi, Cyprian, 131–33
Farah, Nuruddin, 164–65
Feraoun, Mouloud, 9–10
Fugard, Athol, 191–93
Gordimer, Nadine, 194–96
al-Hakīm, Tawfīq, 47–49
Husayn, Tāhā, 49–51
Idrīs, Yūsuf, 51–53
Kateb Yacine, 10–12
La Guma, Alex, 196–97

Mahfūz, Najīb, 54–56
Mammeri, Mouloud, 12–14
Millin, Sarah Gertrude, 197–99
Mofolo, Thomas, 92–94
Mphahlele, Ezekiel (Es'kia), 199–201
Ngugi wa Thiong'o, 88–90
Okara, Gabriel, 133–34
Okigbo, Christopher, 134–36
Oyono, Ferdinand, 30–32
Paton, Alan, 201–3
p'Bitek, Okot, 226–29
Peters, Lenrie, 63–64
Plomer, William, 203–5
Robert, Shaaban, 219–20
Schreiner, Olive, 206–8
Sembène, Ousmane, 153–56
Senghor, Léopold Sédar, 156–58
Smith, Pauline, 208–9
Soyinka, Wole, 136–39
Tutuola, Amos, 139–41
Vieira, José Luandino, 19–20